Gift of the Estate of
Robert (1938-2013)
and Gay Zieger (1938-2013)
October 2013

CONFESSIONS
OF A UNION BUSTER

Confessions
of a Union Buster

Martin Jay Levitt
with Terry Conrow

Crown Publishers, Inc.
New York

Published by Crown Publishers, Inc., 201 East 50th Street, New York, New York 10022. Member of the Crown Publishing Group. Random House, Inc. New York, Toronto, London, Sydney, Auckland.

CROWN is a trademark of Crown Publishers, Inc.

Manufactured in the United States of America

Library of Congress Cataloging-in-Publication Data
Levitt, Martin Jay.
    Confessions of a union buster / by Martin Jay
Levitt, with Terry Conrow. — 1st ed.
        p.   cm.
    Includes index.
    1. Union busting—United States.   2. Trade-unions—United
States—Organizing.   3. Corporations—United States—
Corrupt practices.
I. Conrow, Terry.   II. Title.
HD6490.072U6493   1993
331.88'092—dc20
[B]
93-14736
CIP

ISBN 0-517-58330-5

10   9   8   7   6   5   4   3   2   1

First Edition

To Walter, Evelyn, and Harvey Levitt

Contents

Acknowledgments ix

Foreword xi

Prologue 1

Cravat Coal 7

Genesis 33

Seduction 45

Paradise 69

World Airways 81

The Storm 113

Pathos 153

Copeland Oaks 163

Bloodletting 201

Gates Mills 227

Poison 239

Descent 261

Apocalypse 275

Epilogue 287

Index 293

Acknowledgments

A very special thank-you to my wife, Alice, and my sons, Jason and Justin, for who and what you are. I love you.

—Martin Levitt

It is impossible to thank, or even to remember, all of the people who have helped me write this story. May this page stand as a very belated and sorely inadequate thanks to all those supporters who gave selflessly of their time, opened themselves and shared their passion so that this work would be as complete, as truthful, and as compelling as possible. Those to whom I owe a debt of gratitude include employees and former employees of the companies mentioned here; members and former members of a dozen international unions; university professors and other experts in labor and industrial relations; labor attorneys; and the library staff of the Institute of Industrial Relations at the University of California, Berkeley. I further wish to thank my agents at International Creative Management and my editors at Crown Publishing for their knowledgeable guidance as well as their dogged insistence on quality, accuracy, and fairness. I am indebted to my family, who shouldered the emotional and financial struggle of this book project with grace; in particular I thank my husband, Art Toczynski, who never wavered in his enthusiasm for my work and for this book. Finally I thank Marty Levitt for having the chutzpah to write this book in the first place, the inspiration to choose me as his collaborator, and the determination to stick with it.

—Terry Conrow

Foreword

I hadn't felt nervous during the sunny, one-hour flight from Reno to San Diego. But as I sat there at the speakers' table at the head of the cavernous Hyatt Islandia conference room, my throat suddenly felt dry. Beads of cold sweat crawled down my forehead and underarms. Before me, crammed into the hall around the endless rows of folding tables, sat four hundred union men, strong, thick-armed, sunburned workmen who had gathered for the 1988 Western Conference of the Brotherhood of Carpenters.

I tried to mask my panic with small talk and smiles, but while I waited for my name to be called my heart beat uncontrollably and my palms were clammy. Then, from somewhere off in the distance, it seemed, I heard my name announced; within my head the speaker's voice was muffled by my booming heartbeat and the sound of my own heavy breathing. I don't remember standing up or walking to the microphone, but suddenly there I was, clutching the podium.

The auditorium fell silent. A roomful of eyes met mine, bearing secrets I could not read, or dared not. I dipped my head so that my lips almost touched the microphone, and without my willing it, a throaty sigh escaped into the sound system and ricocheted off the ceiling and walls.

I had no choice but to begin: "I come from a very dirty business. . . ."

As I spoke I watched the carpenters' faces, hoping they would tell me something. Their eyes were still but not empty. Just what filled them I did not know: Was it hate? Was it anger? Was it disbelief? The men watched me intently throughout the eternal twenty minutes during which I revealed to them the villainy and treachery of my former field. I heard my voice as if it came from elsewhere, from somewhere above me, echoing throughout the vast ballroom.

Suddenly it was over.

The crowd remained silent for a brief moment, as if to give my voice a chance to make its last reverberations. Then the room erupted. Men jumped to their feet and beat their hands together with such vigor that I could feel the vibrations through the soles of my shoes. The force of the thundering applause pushed tears into my eyes, and as I scanned the crowd I saw dozens of carpenters wipe thick fingers over their own wet eyes.

It was not joy, but an overwhelming feeling of relief that filled the men who heard me that day: relief to know that the war they had suspected was being waged on them had been a real one all along and not just a creation of a union's paranoid imagination, as so many corporate bosses had told them.

Grateful for the sense of righteousness my speech restored in them, the men kicked away from their folding chairs and made their way to the podium, where, one after another, they embraced me with strong, welcoming arms.

CONFESSIONS
OF A UNION BUSTER

Prologue

Union busting is a field populated by bullies and built on deceit. A campaign against a union is an assault on individuals and a war on the truth. As such, it is a war without honor. The only way to bust a union is to lie, distort, manipulate, threaten, and always, always attack. The law does not hamper the process. Rather, it serves to suggest maneuvers and define strategies. Each "union prevention" campaign, as the wars are called, turns on a combined strategy of disinformation and personal assaults.

When a chief executive hires a labor relations consultant to battle a union, he gives the consultant run of the company and closes his eyes. The consultant, backed by attorneys, installs himself in the corporate offices and goes to work creating a climate of terror that inevitably is blamed on the union.

Some corporate executives I encountered liked to think of their anti-union consultants as generals. But really the consultants are terrorists. Like political terrorists, the consultants' attacks are intensely personal. Terrorists do not make factories and air strips their victims; they choose instead crippled old men and school-children. Likewise, as the consultants go about the business of destroying unions, they invade people's lives, demolish their friendships, crush their will, and shatter their families.

I entered the union-busting business in 1969 at age twenty-five. It wasn't an informed career choice, but a move motivated by ambition. I answered a blind ad in *The Wall Street Journal* for a management consultant with knowledge of the National Labor Relations Act. I had never read a labor law, but I knew how to sell myself, so I sent off a résumé to the post office box. At the time I answered the mystery ad, I had been running a successful executive recruitment firm for two years that did almost $100,000 in business annually, so I was pretty cocky. I had no biases for or against labor unions and no career goals save the desire to make money.

I was called to an interview with John Sheridan, a former union organizer from Chicago. His labor relations consulting firm, John Sheridan Associates, specialized in running campaigns to thwart union efforts to organize workers. I knew little about the work but was flattered to be considered for the job, so I put on my best show. Sheridan liked me from the start. My golden tongue won me a job with a starting billing rate of $250 a day.

Once I got a taste of the excitement, the power, the money, and the glamour in union busting, I was hooked. Right or wrong became irrelevant. It would be twenty years before I saw the field for what it is.

There are many forms of union busting. Some labor consultants and attorneys take on unions that already represent a work force, squeezing negotiators at the bargaining table, forcing workers out on strike, harassing union officers. My career took another path. I refined the Sheridan specialty called "counterorganizing drives," battling non-union employees as they struggled to win union representation. The enemy was the collective spirit. I got hold of that spirit while it was still a seedling; I poisoned it, choked it, bludgeoned it if I had to, anything to be sure it would never blossom into a united work force, the dreaded foe of any corporate tyrant.

For my campaigns I identified two key targets: the rank-and-file workers and their immediate supervisors. The supervisors served as my front line. I took them hostage on the first day and sent them to anti-union boot camp. I knew that people who didn't feel threatened wouldn't fight. So through hours of seminars, rallies, and one-on-one encounters, I taught the supervisors to despise and fear the union. I persuaded them that a union-organizing drive was a personal attack on them, a referendum on their leadership skills, and an attempt to humiliate them. I was friendly, even jovial at times, but always unforgiving as I compelled each supervisor to feel he was somehow to blame for the union push and consequently obliged to defeat it. Like any hostages, most supervisors could not resist for long. They soon came to see the fight through the eyes of their captor and went to work wringing union sympathies out of their workers.

Although I took on the supervisors face to face, my war on the union activists was covert.

To stop a union proponent—a "pusher," in the anti-union lexicon—the buster will go anywhere, not just to the lunch room, but into the bedroom if necessary. The buster not only is a terrorist; he is also a spy. My team and I routinely pried into workers' police records, personnel files, credit histories, medical records, and family lives in search of a weakness that we could use to discredit union activists.

Once in a while, a worker is impeccable. So some consultants resort to lies. To fell the sturdiest union supporters in the 1970s, I frequently launched rumors that the targeted worker was gay or was cheating on his wife. It was a very effective technique, particularly in blue-collar towns. If even the nasty stories failed to muzzle an effective union proponent, the busters might get the worker fired.

Such was the case of Jeannette Allen, an assembly-line worker at the Stant Company manufacturing plant outside Little Rock, Arkansas.

The Stant factory was torn by the conflict between a vigorous United Auto Workers organizing effort and a dogged counterdrive by corporate officers and their consultants. One night, as graveyard-shift workers pressed and cut hot metal into the shape of radiator caps, the plant foreman's phone rang. The foreman answered and heard the voice of a black woman announce that there was a bomb in the factory. He then let the crew go on working for nearly an hour before evacuating the plant.

The police got a warning call from the same person that night. When they searched the factory they found nothing, but they had captured the caller's voice on tape. Two plant managers identified the caller as Allen. I believed it wasn't she. (When I heard the tape, I was sitting with Jeannette Allen herself. It did not sound like the same person.) A black woman whose intelligence and integrity had earned her the admiration and loyalty of her co-workers, Allen also happened to be an outspoken proponent of the UAW campaign. Company bosses, it seemed, considered her the driving force behind worker support for the union, particularly among blacks, who made up one-third of the work force. They feared her. As soon as Allen was implicated in the bomb threat, she was fired. Meanwhile, her co-workers wondered what kind of union could corrupt such a stalwart character.

The UAW lost the election.

In 1975 I left the employ of consulting firms and set out on my own. Over the next eight years I ran a series of one-man union-busting enterprises I called by such disingenuous names as Employee Synthesis Program and Human Resources Institute, and I struck it rich. But by 1983 I had become hopelessly alcoholic; the addiction had badly complicated my life, and solo work was taking its toll on me. I landed a counterorganizing job at an Ohio coal company five hundred workers strong, and I decided I needed backup. I called on some former colleagues from a Sheridan spin-off called Modern Management Methods and invited them to join me as I feasted off the carcass of the United Mine Workers. They did, gleefully, and my reaffiliation with MMM continued until the death of my shameful career.

Then the change started. Watching the crude and abusive behavior of my old associates during those years, I was forced to acknowledge the vile nature of my field. Slowly I began to realize that my more polished techniques were just a distilled version of the same villainy. Not only were working people crushed by the cruelty of the union busters, but the companies themselves were raped, as consultants and attorneys conspired to wring as much money as they could out of their clients. The executives paid whatever they were asked, the consultants having convinced them that a union-organizing effort amounted to the worst crisis of their business lives. In the end I understood that a union-busting campaign left a company financially devastated and hopelessly divided and almost invariably created an even more intolerable work environment than before, as managers systematically retaliated against union supporters for the high costs of the campaign. I felt repulsed by what I saw and sickened that I was, in fact, a prominent member of the club. I renounced the field.

My awakening came in late 1987. I was making $200,000 a year and living on a five-acre wooded estate in an exclusive community. I traveled, dined, and lodged in first class, drove only the finest luxury cars. By then I had directed more than two hundred anti-union campaigns—and lost only five—and had trained thousands of craven managers to go and do likewise at their own companies. I was at the top of my field, one of the best and one of the richest. No, I was not driven from the field by need. I was driven by horror and remorse.

As labor laws have proliferated, the arena of employee relations and contract negotiations has become infinitely more complicated; more and more professionals have built their careers on advising employers how to manage their work force and cope with the maze of federal and state worker laws. Some such professionals clearly are needed, and a few even do an honest job. But within the field of labor relations the big money is in union busting. When I entered the field, only a handful of law firms and consulting companies specialized in combating worker organizations. Today there are more than seven thousand attorneys and consultants across the nation who make their living busting unions, and they work almost every day. At a billing rate of $1,000 to $1,500 a day per consultant and $300 to $700 an hour for attorneys, the war on organized labor is a $1 billion–plus industry.

Many consultants have given up union busting and quietly gone about building more honorable careers for themselves, sort of like former Nazis moving to America and setting up flower shops. Not I. At the time I made my conversion, I was struggling to overcome alcoholism. In my pursuit of recovery I also sought redemption, so I came to believe it was my moral duty to confront what I had done and somehow to make amends to my tens of thousands of victims. At that moment I vowed I would do whatever I could to stop the others in my trade from carrying out their hateful mission. I would not run and hide.

I placed a call to the AFL-CIO office in Washington, D.C., and spoke to Virginia Diamond, then a labor federation attorney who tracked the activities of more than five hundred union-busting firms across the nation in a publication called the *RUB Sheet* (for "report on union busters"). I told Diamond that she had one less union buster to worry about. That conversation led indirectly to my new vocation, as a consultant to unions on how to bust the busters.

Not long after my change of heart became the talk of labor circles, the United Auto Workers called me to testify as an expert witness in Jeannette Allen's wrongful termination suit against Stant Company. I immediately recognized the bomb threat ploy as a typical union buster's dirty trick, and I said so in court. I believed the voice on the police tape was not Allen's; after all, the company never prosecuted her, they just got her out of the way. I was convinced some of Stant's consultants had hatched the bomb scare scheme when their anti-union campaign was on the verge of collapse.

It was a contemptible plan. But it was a perfect one by the only measure that matters in the war on labor: it worked.

Cravat Coal

The sticky Ohio summer heat had given way to autumn's chill. A miner I'll call Hal Lockett fixed his hunting rifle in its rack on the back of his dust-covered Dodge pickup, gave the bald rear tires a kick, and climbed into the cab. His eyes were as cold as the coal he had been digging since dawn every morning practically since he was a baby—cold as the coal Lockett's daddy mined and his granddaddy before him. But Lockett's heart was burning. Two months had gone by since a handful of well-dressed strangers had walked into the converted roadside motel that housed the offices of Cravat Coal Company, bearing poison and promises. In those two months Lockett had stopped believing. Men who had worked together like brothers for years—some were brothers, for chrissakes—had started taking blows at each other's heads and saying nasty things about each other's wives. Some had stopped talking altogether. Lockett still wasn't sure who those strangers were. He knew they'd showed up just a few weeks after the guy from United Mine Workers had come around asking people to sign little yellow cards and saying the union would help the miners keep their jobs and make sure they could afford to see a doctor. Sure, Lockett knew all about that. That's what his daddy had told him, too. But somehow the whole thing had just gotten crazy. His foreman, usually a nice guy, had taken to badgering the men, threatening them, questioning them, and telling them didn't they know they'd lose everything if they let that goddamned union in. The workers were so divided, some couldn't stand next to each other in the pit without starting a fight.

Lockett kept his eyes straight ahead as he drove the winding road from the mine to a converted farmhouse at the edge of the gritty town of Cadiz, whose sole and incongruous fame rested in having been the birthplace of Clark Gable. Lockett drove the pickup practically into the side of the ramshackle building, one of the six Cravat field offices, slammed on the brakes, and shut off the motor. Inside, half a dozen secretaries tapped away at their mundane tasks. Lockett walked slowly to the back of the truck, lifted his rifle from its rack, and released the safety. He pushed open the door of the farmhouse and stomped inside. Then a one-man war broke out. Unintelligible curses streamed from Lockett's mouth as his free hand grabbed paperweights, staplers, and file folders from nearby desks and hurled them across the room. He gave his weapon a quick cock and squeezed the trigger. One shot rang out. Then another. Then another. Lockett tore through the building, pumping bullets out the windows and into the ceiling. A secretary screamed and dove under her desk. Then a man's voice was heard: "What the hell? Stop him!" Lockett blasted away, sobbing and raging all the time.

By the time the Cadiz police arrived, Lockett's face was stained with tears and mud. His eyes had lost their focus. No one was hurt, but a handful of townspeople and Cravat office workers had gathered for the spectacle. They knew the rifleman as a veteran miner out at one of Cravat's most remote pits. Everyone knew the union business had been getting to him, poor guy. He had enough trouble, with his marriage on the rocks and all. People had been talking about it for weeks. The police loaded a subdued Lockett into the car and drove off to the station. This was no good.

I first met Cravat Coal on paper. One hot August day in 1983, I sent the paralegal student who worked as my assistant to the National Labor Relations Board office in downtown Cleveland to poke through the filings. That was the method I had developed to generate work during slow times. It turned out to be a brilliant tactic, for often I discovered a union-organizing drive before company executives had any suspicions. The timeliness of my call made it impossible to ignore, and the chief executives' panic allowed me to suggest that, having caught the trouble early, we could launch our offensive while the union was still struggling to develop a strategy. That, in fact, was the case with Cravat. My student-assistant had discovered a union representation petition that had been filed just a day before by the United Mine Workers District 6, based in Wheeling, in neighboring West Virginia. The UMWA aimed to organize the 485 miners at what was then the nation's largest independent coal-mining company.

I gave Cravat a call. The call reached Mike Puskarich, the eldest of the four Yugoslavian-American brothers who, with their sons, ran Cravat Coal and a handful of related businesses.

"Mr. Puskarich, I'm Marty Levitt, president of Human Resources Institute of Cleveland. I thought you should know that your company has become the victim of a union-organizing campaign by United Mine Workers. Were you aware of that?"

He wasn't. But it didn't take Puskarich long to let me know where he stood: He wasn't going to have any fuckin' union, that was for goddamned sure. They had tried this shit before, he told me. Well, they were not going to get away with it.

That, of course, was the entrée I needed. I kept my language polished but my message tough as I pressed Puskarich. "If you're intent on beating the union, we should get together as soon as possible," I told him.

Puskarich wasn't sure. He didn't go in for outside consultants, liked to handle problems himself. He had an in-house attorney who could stifle any union shenanigans. I told Puskarich he might not be aware of how deadly a United Mine Workers organizing drive could be. If he lost the union election, there'd be no turning back, no recovering the days when he was boss of his own company. I recommended he talk to a labor lawyer I had worked with for several years, a brilliant attorney by the name of Earl Leiken. Puskarich said he'd meet with me the next day.

The drive down to Cadiz was a trip into another decade. The town of four thousand souls stood nestled in the scarred hills of the flattened Appalachians in eastern Ohio. There was only one highway through Cadiz, and the peculiar Cravat Coal building stood off that road like a camp symbol that the town was somehow lost in space and time. The long, two-story brick structure retained the sterile and prim look it must have had as a motel. The conversion to corporate offices seemed halfhearted, for secretaries and clerks could be seen roaming the outdoor hallways carrying papers and coffee from one executive to another, like motel maids.

When I found myself before General Manager Mike Puskarich, I understood that this anti-union campaign would be like no other. Puskarich was a hulk of a man, a 250-pound beast with bushy eyebrows, massive forearms, and huge, rough hands. I likened him in my mind to the late hard-line Soviet Leonid Brezhnev, then at the helm of the Communist party. Puskarich's long-sleeved starched white shirt and gilded cuff links looked out of place; his thick fingers were adorned with gold-and-diamond rings. Puskarich's language was crude, his temper explosive; as I sat across from him and explained my strategy, I could see that he was not a man of subtleties. Instinctively I knew the Puskariches would be a liability in an anti-union fight built on subtle distortions and manipulations. I knew I would have to rein in the Yugoslavians' tempers lest they give the union promoters more fuel for the organizing campaign.

As I explained my strategy, I watched Puskarich fidget. He was not used to this kind of talk. "The entire campaign," I told him, "will be run through your foremen. I'll be their mentor, their coach. I'll teach them what to say and make sure they say it. But I'll stay in the background. This will be a case of overcommunication. I will make the foremen feel they have postdoctorate degrees in labor relations before this is through. They'll fill their employees with so many nasty little facts about unions, they'll all wish they'd never let this get started."

Puskarich wasn't sure. He had never thought of foremen as management. The only management was the Puskarich clan. The foremen were just a bunch of stupid miners, grunts like all the rest and not to be trusted. How could he count on them to take on the union for him? Hell, they'd probably called the union themselves. "You'll have to do it," he commanded.

I objected. Think about it, I said. How could I come in, an outsider, and convince the workers not to trust another outsider? My anti-union message would turn on portraying the union as a power-hungry interloper, and nobody was going to buy it coming from the company's hired gun. No, the words and the warnings would have to come from people they worked with every day down in the pits, from the people they counted on for that good review and that weekly paycheck.

"Here's how it is," I told Puskarich, fixing a steady gaze on his angry eyes. "You'll come to see this union drive as a blessing in disguise. Once our campaign gets rolling, supervisors will learn to be the leaders they should have been all along. They'll learn to make their people happy and to love what they do. The men won't just be working for a paycheck anymore, and you'll never face another union problem again."

Puskarich couldn't be persuaded by such a high-road argument, I knew, but I decided to throw it in to make the Cravat attorney happy. I wanted him on my side. I warned Puskarich that I would do some unusual things throughout the campaign; some activities he might find offensive, others corny. He brushed aside the warning. His only doubt had to do with embracing his foremen as allies.

"We'll convince the foremen that when the National Labor Relations Board holds the representation election, the workers will not be voting for or against the union, but for or against the management, including all of them," I told the Yugoslav. "To lose the election would be a humiliation, an indictment of their management abilities. Once they see it my way, the foremen will gladly join the war on the UMWA."

Puskarich started to growl, but his attorney silenced him: "Listen to the man. We need him."

The boss lifted a diamond-studded hand to his fleshy face, twisted his mouth, and asked my fee. It was $1,000 a day per consultant—I planned to use several—plus a $10,000 retainer. Puskarich complained, "I've never known anybody worth a thousand a day." Then he barked at his secretary, Dottie, to make me out a check for $10,000. He offered his hand and commanded, "You're in charge."

During that first meeting, there were lots of logistics to map out. I insisted on holding the kick-off meeting in just two days; I didn't want the union to gain momentum while we chewed on our pencils. Cadiz was an uncomfortable four-and-a-half-hour drive from Cleveland, so naturally I was to stay in town during the week. Puskarich put me up in the best there was, a Sheraton hotel in a neighboring town. But even better was his weekend shuttle service. Every Friday evening throughout the seventeen-week campaign, he had the company plane fly me to the Cuyahoga County airport near my home in Gates Mills in suburban Cleveland, just a half hour away by air. Every Monday morning the plane picked me up and delivered me to Cadiz, where a company car awaited my arrival.

From the moment I read the UMWA petition for Cravat, I knew we faced a bitter fight. The key to my so-called union-prevention campaigns had always been to paint the labor organization as a greedy outsider and to convince supervisors and foremen that their jobs depended on its destruction. Meanwhile I worked to recast upper management with a human face—now silly, now generous, but always very human—so workers would come to believe there was no need for a union. In the UMWA I had a particularly formidable foe; not that the miners union was more honorable or more sophisticated or even more aggressive than any other. But to miners, the UMWA was more than a union. It was family. Some of the workers at Cravat were the first in three generations not to belong to the UMWA, and they were not happy about it. The only other major mining concern in Cadiz was R&F Coal Company down the road from the Cravat headquarters, another non-union outfit owned by the mammoth Shell Oil Company. In effect, the union had been locked out of the town. Yet among miners, to speak against the union was a sacrilege. Federal law blesses a union-organizing drive if 30 percent of the workers sign authorization cards inviting the union in. At Cravat, 80 percent of the miners had signed. How was I going to get people to fight a union they had been brought up to think of as the Mother Church?

I was convinced I shouldn't tackle Cravat on my own, so I called for help from four former colleagues at a Chicago-based labor consulting firm called Modern Management Methods, or Three M. By 1983 the union-busting field was bursting, and it was easy to find eager ass kickers in need of work. Joining me at the Cravat bloodletting were Tom Crosbie, an executive vice-president at Three M and my onetime mentor; Ed Juodenas, a large, imposing figure and a fifteen-year veteran of the ignoble trade; Dennis Fisher, a meticulous, softspoken methods man; and Kevin Smyth, an intense, portly man with a look of malevolence in his eyes. The firepower added by those union-buster heavyweights was phenomenal. Yet the aggressiveness of Cravat's union activists turned the Cravat war into one of the bloodiest of my career. By the time the defeat of the union was history, six Cravat foremen had been fired; one rank-and-file miner had gone crazy; at least one miner's marriage was in trouble because of unsavory rumors floated by the buster forces; and countless Cravat families and friendships were shattered as the entire population of southeastern Ohio chose sides.

The intensity of loyalty to the UMWA dictated that we use every tool available to divide the miners. One-on-one interviews with foremen would be the heart of the counterunion drive, as usual, but attorney Leiken, my fellow experts, and I knew we could begin our sabotage even before the first meeting. We needed just one tool, the National Labor Relations Act of 1935.

It so happens that the NLR Act, the bible of collective bargaining, can be a union buster's best friend. In its complexity the nation's fundamental labor law presents endless possibilities for delays, roadblocks, and maneuvers that can undermine a union's efforts and frustrate would-be members. In a bit of classic union-buster irony, we divided the Cravat workers by forcing them together. Cravat ran a handful of businesses in addition to its twenty-five Ohio mines: three trucking firms, a fuels company, a couple of quarries, a farm, and a Kentucky coal-mining concern called Blue Grass Mining. Only the Ohio miners had been approached by the UMWA, and we were betting that workers in other divisions could be turned against the union, particularly if we got to them first.

Our first legal move, then, was to petition the National Labor Relations Board in Cleveland to expand the UMWA voting unit to include all Cravat workers. Leiken was an opaque, colorless personality, but when it came to forming legal arguments, he was a genius. The UMWA, although it used a seasoned attorney, was caught unprepared for the kind of sophisticated maneuver of which Leiken was capable. The attorneys sat through a day-long hearing before an NLRB officer, which was held in the city clerk's office in St. Clairsville, a town about fifteen miles south of Cadiz and only slightly larger. Witnesses for both sides spent much of the time sitting on benches outside the city building, eating pizza and waiting to be called. The lawyers then submitted their briefs to the NLRB regional director and awaited a decision. The beauty of such legal tactics is that they are effective in damaging the union effort no matter which side prevails. Our petition to expand the Cravat voting unit was filed two weeks into the campaign, and the case took at least three weeks to resolve. That kind of delay steals momentum from a union-organizing drive, which is greatly dependent on the emotional energy of its leaders and the sense of urgency among workers. By dragging a union through the plodding legal system, we showed workers that the labor organization was sluggish and inefficient, certainly not the quick fix they might have hoped it would be.

When the sixty Cravat supervisors assembled for the inaugural meeting that sweltering day in mid-August, they could not have imagined the bloodletting yet to come. The foremen arrived under orders, having been commanded to appear at the meeting in a letter from Mike Puskarich, in which he condemned the union drive as a "crisis."

The Cravat headquarters didn't have a room large enough to fit its entire management—the Puskariches had never seen a reason to bring them all together—so the kick-off meeting was held in the basement of an aging but elegant white-steepled Presbyterian church on the outskirts of Cadiz. I got the first whiff of my prey as I drove into the church parking lot in my black Lincoln Town Car that first day. The lot was lined with aging American-made pickup trucks, each sporting a hunting rifle. Rugged men filled the church basement. They didn't know then how much time they would spend crowded around folding tables in the dingy cement hall. Twice each week, for four months, as I prepared to distribute a damning new union "fact sheet" among them, I would be calling the foremen together to make sure they understood and could promote its message.

As the men entered on that first day, most grabbed a polystyrene cup from the table in the back of the room, but not everyone filled his with the coffee cheerfully provided by Cravat executive secretaries. Rather, the cups would serve as spittoons for clumps of brown tobacco spat at regular intervals throughout the three-hour revival. A blank pad of paper and a pen sat on the table next to the cups, and next to it was a hand-lettered sign that read Please Sign Here. That was a prop, and one I had grown very proud of, for I had never seen it fail to make its point. I watched as, one by one, the men stooped to jot down their names. After signing, some sauntered to the edge of the hall and leaned against the gray wall to study the commotion before them. Others approached a circle of buddies, slapped one or two of them on the back, and exchanged tense laughter. A few seemed oblivious of the others, walking right up and claiming a folding chair, then swinging it around to straddle it like a horse. They stared at the hulking Puskarich brothers and the odd band of suited men who flanked them at the bride's table. These were mountain men. Young and old, all wore the faded flannel shirts, the hunting caps, and heavy leather boots of their trade. Their forearms and backs were massive, their hands rough, their faces ruddy and chiseled, their words few. Their mistrust ran deep.

Mike Puskarich spoke first. He got right to the point. "You all know the union's after us. Well, we're gonna stop them, and here's the man who's going to help us do it. This here is our hired gun, Marty Levitt. I want all of you to listen to him. He's in charge."

I stood and launched my campaign. Except for one disclaimer at the end of the morning, I didn't alter my kick-off show for the miners. They had to hear it all, no matter how esoteric, no matter how offensive. I had to convince those mountain men of at least the injustice, if not the villainy, of the union system they had been taught to revere.

"This is no union campaign," I announced to the silent gathering. "This is a war." I liked to entertain as I taught, so I packaged my message in melodrama and comedy. From beginning to end I paced up and down the aisles, gesturing dramatically, looking straight in the miners' eyes, making them take part. I never let the energy subside. "Guess who the union's fighting? Everybody. They're fighting you. This is going to be your victory or your defeat."

I didn't have their hearts, I knew. But all eyes were on me. Not a sound was heard, save the rhythmic *kersplatt* of tobacco wads as they hit the rigid bottoms of the cups. "If your workers vote in the UMWA, you will have failed. A pro-union vote is proof of your inability to lead. If you let it happen, both your workers and your company will suffer—permanently." My aim was to coerce the foremen into thinking of themselves as holy warriors. Of course, the Crusades imagery worked best if the foremen truly came to believe that the union was evil and that to sabotage it was akin to doing God's work. So the miners were in need of a little reeducation.

Putting on a mock air of ignorance, I challenged, "What is a union?" I scanned the faces, blistered by the sun. Already many eyes had softened. A few volunteered definitions: workers fighting for their rights; an organization that could negotiate a contract on behalf of the workers.

Wrong, I told them.

A union was a business just like we were. And what did any business need to survive? Money. Now, it so happened that the United Mine Workers had suffered great losses over the preceding decade. The U.S. mining industry was in deep retrenchment. The sulfur-laden coal like that mined in southeastern Ohio had been blamed for acid rain. Minerals companies had closed, merged, relocated, and otherwise restructured, shedding union contracts and union members in the process. In the preceding ten years the

UMWA had lost 60 percent of its members. Partly because of declining employment and partly due to admitted financial mismanagement, the union had operated in the black only once in the preceding twelve years. The net worth of the organization had dropped in half over that time.

I turned to Mike Puskarich, who apparently was learning something new himself that day. "Mike, what would happen to Cravat Coal if you lost sixty percent of your customers?" Fortunately, his posturing didn't get in the way, and I cut him off as quickly as I could.

A business gets money from its customers, I continued, and uses the money to pay workers, buy more equipment, expand the business. By federal law a union can get money from only one place— the membership. Everyone knows that unions charge dues: that's how they pay that organizer and that attorney back in West Virginia. But dues are only part of union money madness, I declared. Striking a tone of sympathy, I asked, "How many of you were aware that unions can levy fines on their membership? If a worker does something interpreted as 'anti-union'—it can be as trivial as talking against the shop steward—that worker can be sent to a union trial and made to pay a fine." When membership dwindles, as it had in the UMWA, the union starts to run out of money, I told my listeners. Sooner or later the union has to go on the warpath to colonize new groups of workers. That's what we had here—not an organizing drive, but an invasion.

"This union is desperate," I declared. "They're going to do whatever it takes to restore some of their lost revenue. That's why this is a war."

I went on, pacing energetically. I was preparing to deliver one of my favorite anti-union analogies, and I always got melodramatic when the time came. "Do you have any idea what supervising at Cravat will be like under a union?" I asked the group.

I scanned the faces and focused on a young, blond, gentle-looking man: "You married?" I asked.

"Yes, sir," the man replied, his twang revealing a life in the Appalachians.

I moved in closer. "You love your wife?"

"Yes, sir."

"You sleep with your wife?"

The man blushed. "Uh, yes, sir."

"Well," I continued, "how would you like it if your mother-in-law slept between you and your wife every night?"

The crowd broke out in laughter, and a voice from the back of the room hooted, "Not bad. You should see his mother-in-law." Well, maybe you're lucky, I told the boy, but most of us wouldn't want our mother-in-law in bed with us. That's what it will be like for you if we let the union in; everything you do or say to your employees will have to be cleared through the mother-in-law, the union steward.

"And who will the union steward be?" I asked. "Well, let me tell you; he'll be the laziest worker you have, the one with the biggest mouth. Union stewards don't work for nothing, you know. They get all kinds of union perks, time off for union business, super-seniority, special privileges, bonuses." That steward, I told my recruits, would be the foreman's nightmare and the nightmare of every hardworking miner on the crew.

So what could the foremen do about the union threat? It was time for a lesson in law. I walked to the back of the basement room and picked up the legal pad on which the miners had signed their names. I handed the tablet to the miner sitting nearest me and announced that everyone should make sure he had signed the paper. While the tablet was being passed up and down the aisles, I distributed copies of a federal government guide to the National Labor Relations Act. The fact that the booklet was a government publication was not serendipitous. It is crucial for the union buster to establish that what he is doing is sanctioned, even promoted to a certain extent, by the U.S. government. The labor law guide spelled out what an employer could and could not legally do to thwart a union-organizing attempt. The booklet would teach the miners the limits of the law, and I would tell them how to bend and even break those limits.

I started by outlining the four forbidden actions in an anti-union campaign. They were the fundamentals, not because I was so concerned about upholding the law, but because I wanted my trainees to learn to commit the acts without appearing to do anything illegal:

"A representative of management cannot threaten employees," I warned, "but we're going to show you how you can deliver threats without doing anything unlawful. A manager cannot interrogate employees. We'll teach you how to interrogate without asking any questions. You cannot spy on employees, but you can sure keep an eye on them, and you cannot make promises. The ban on promises is tricky. You'll see that while management is barred from promising anything, the union goes about wooing your workers by making generous promises that it can't keep."

I walked up to two miners. "Hey, you," I said in a playful tone to one, knocking him gently on the arm. "At the end of the meeting this guy here's going to give you one hundred dollars. I promise." The two laughed. "Well, what do you think?" I asked the rest of the group. "Would the law allow me to make a careless promise like that?"

The miners waved their hands and booed to show they knew better. Of course not. Ah-ha. Tricked you. Suspicious looks turned inquisitive when I declared that I had just given an example of the kind of promise unions make all the time, and that they are perfectly legal. "The law forbids the party with the power to deliver from making promises," I explained. Since the company, not the union, has the power to raise wages and benefits, authorize more vacation, guarantee job security, or improve safety conditions, the company is barred from promising any such rewards during a union-organizing effort. The union, on the other hand, can promise whatever it wants, because all it is really doing is promising to ask management for something. All the union representatives are going to do is go to the company and ask for the goods it has already promised the workers.

I referred to the discussion of collective bargaining in the government booklet I had handed out. I asked a miner to read one key sentence. While the chosen young man was still struggling to pronounce the first word, I realized he was illiterate and quickly moved on to someone else. The second man read: "Neither party is required to agree to anything or to make any concessions." There you have it, I told the group. When a union wins the right to collective bargaining, it wins only the right to ask. The workers may get more. But it is also possible to wind up with the same or get less than they already have.

"Do you suppose your workers knew that when they signed those union authorization cards?" I asked the men. "I bet most of them never even read the card."

It so happened that the United Mine Workers authorization card, like that of many unions, doubled as an application for union membership. I proposed that most of the workers who signed did not realize they were applying for membership and might be angry to find out that the union had hoodwinked them into it. The workers had, in essence, signed a blank check. I picked up the yellow pad signed by all the foremen and held it up for all to see. "Did all of you sign this paper voluntarily?" I asked the crowd as I moved slowly through the room. Heads nodded. "Well, let me tell you what you signed." I began reading a lengthy mock membership authorization statement, which included the following declaration:

> We the following individuals do, of our own free will, affix our signatures to a blank sheet of paper to formally bind us to this authorization. Effective this date, we unanimously agree to pay the Marty Management Union an initiation fee of $1,000 and subsequent monthly dues of $200. We also agree to pay any special assessments or fines, which, from time to time, will be levied. We swear our oath of allegiance and fealty, over and above all other considerations, to this union and its constitution and ritual.

The idea of the gimmick was to get the word out that the workers had been buffaloed into signing the authorization cards. It was our hope that some workers would call the union to ask for their card back. They would be told that the cards were union property and would not be returned. All we needed were a few skeptics to plant the suspicion among workers that they were being railroaded by the union. The skepticism also would serve to sow the first seeds of divisiveness.

What could the company do to fight for its freedom? I asked my audience. Then I answered for them. I told the foremen the legal limits were clear: to get our message out, they could make statements of fact, or of opinion, as long as the statements did not constitute a threat. They were not to worry about what to say. We, the experts, would take control and supply them with everything they needed for the campaign. We would supply the facts, in the form of twice weekly letters signed by the general manager to be distributed by foremen to the workers. We would supply the opinion, through group meetings at which the letters would be discussed. We would supply the methodology, teaching the foremen at group meetings and at individual sessions how to approach their crewmen and track each worker's union sentiment. All we asked from foremen was the emotional commitment to beating the union. From that day until the election, nothing was more important than the anti-union campaign.

Up to that point everything in the kick-off meeting was standard operating procedure with a homespun appeal. One thing was different, however. As the meeting drew to a close, I looked out over the roomful of weary faces and offered a disclaimer. Above the objections of my colleagues, I decided to confess to the men that I understood what the United Mine Workers meant to some of them. I said I knew some would find it impossible to rally to the cause of defeating a union that had helped put bread on the family table for generations. I invited supervisors to come to my office after the meeting and discuss any problems they had with the anti-union campaign. That afternoon, as I was going over strategies, six men appeared at the door. They asked me not to force them to fight the UMWA; it would be too hard on their families. I did not let the foremen out of the campaign. They would be expected to deliver letters to their workers like everybody else and to track their men's loyalty to the company. But I had to be realistic. I knew that those men's allegiance to the UMWA would make them a threat to the anti-union effort. So I told them I did not demand the same level of commitment I expected from the other foremen. My advice to Puskarich was to work around those men and let it go. But he never forgave their treachery. Within three months after the union had lost the election, Puskarich had fired all six.

Throughout the campaign, a small, bare conference room at the converted motel served as our mission control. The room was equipped with a table, a few chairs, and a phone, nothing more. That is where, week after week, my fellow union busters and I met with foremen, questioned them about their anti-union efforts in the Cravat pits and tipples, taught them how to "work" each of our bulletins, and interrogated them about the activities of any employee we considered an effective union activist and therefore dangerous. Crosbie, Juodenas, Fisher, and I stayed in Cadiz composing letters, planning strategies, running meetings, and keeping the pressure on the Ohio foremen.

A few weeks into the program, I convinced my colleagues in Cadiz that things would go better if we all dressed in jeans and sweatshirts rather than in the business suits they preferred. Being an entertainment-oriented consultant, I always liked to dress for my audience. The way I saw it, the only way to be successful with the Cravat miners, truckers, and machinists was to look like one of them. My colleagues disagreed. Most labor relations consultants, but particularly those at Three M, like to look expensive. They figure it is easier for a client to swallow a billing rate of several thousand dollars a day if the consultants are dressed for success. Nonetheless, since my Three M companions were working at my behest, they bowed to my wishes, and by the third week all of us were dressing as if we lived in the dusty mountain town. We sent Kevin Smyth to the Kentucky mines, where he gladly dressed in blue jeans and single-handedly annihilated the union.

Once the campaign was on its way, the Puskariches stepped aside and gave us run of the company. They left the executive secretaries at our disposal and ordered all other headquarters employees to do whatever we commanded. Throughout the counter-drive we had the managers doing research and the clerical workers—whom the Puskariches liked to call their "office princesses"—typing and distributing letters, supplying us with coffee, and otherwise catering to our wishes. For our individual meetings with supervisors to be fruitful, it was necessary for us to find out everything we could not only about the foreman, but about his workers. So one of our first demands was to the personnel director. At our request she drew up a detailed diagram of company employees, listing all workers in each division under the name of their foreman. The chart included the worker's date of hire, his pay, whether or not he was married, and other details from the personnel files. Armed with that information, we immediately held the advantage over our prey. When a foreman walked into the meeting room, sometimes after driving a hundred miles from the pit where he worked, he was confronted with two cool, well-rehearsed hit men waiting to work him over. He knew very little about us, yet we continually managed to surprise him with the information we had about him and his men. We kept charts on every employee, identifying each with one of five marks: a plus sign in a circle if he was staunchly anti-union; a plain plus sign if he leaned toward management; a minus sign in a circle for a strong union supporter; a simple minus sign if he was pro-union; a question mark for unknowns. Each time we interviewed the worker's foreman, we updated the grade. We also kept notes on whatever anecdotal tidbits our informant proffered, from statements the worker had made about the company or union to details of his finances and sex life.

Each session lasted thirty minutes to an hour. Part of the time was spent on small talk and gossip, a planned informality that was meant to make the foremen feel that we were their friends and confidants. In fact, in my first meeting with each foreman, I assured him that whatever he said was confined to that room; no one else would ever see the notes I was keeping or hear the secrets he revealed. That, of course, was a bold and cruel lie. Whenever a foreman divulged a potentially useful bit of intelligence about one of his troublesome pro-union workers, the word was passed to the Puskariches, let out on the grapevine as a damaging rumor, or filed away for use in a future strategy.

Yet the assurances got many men talking. After a few meetings with each foreman, I knew who was sleeping with whom; I was privy to the details of personal conversations among employees; and I knew many of the workers' vices, fears, and passions. One foreman was so taken by the confessional mood of the sessions that he admitted to having killed a man in a barroom fight. Even I in my cynicism was astounded to hear a man confess murder to a stranger. Yet I understood. The foreman, the front-line supervisor, has the worst job in any business—watched and hounded by upper management, mistrusted by his workers. He is alone in the middle, with no one to turn to. The supervisor's isolation and vulnerability make him the ideal tool for union-busting campaigns. The union buster shows up, and suddenly what the lowly foreman says and does really matters. I constantly reminded the Cravat foremen that I was now their main man and warned them that a union victory could mean an end to their job and possibly an end to the company. I insisted that they were responsible for both the job security of their workers and the well-being of the company at large.

Despite their weakness for the intimacy of the interrogation sessions, and their fears about the future, the Cravat foremen turned out to be one of the toughest group of supervisors I ever encountered. They resented the interview sessions from the beginning and were determined to obstruct them.

On the other side, the union's campaign was choreographed by a handful of District 6 staffers led by former miner Jim White. The group labored under the watchful eye of a higher local union official, UMWA executive board member Tony Bumbico. But White, Bumbico, and the rest of the men from the union office were not often seen at Cravat. They were not allowed; as soon as the organizing effort was uncovered, we advisers had the company tack up No Trespassing signs at every plant, pit, and tipple. That kept the union people away and forced them to do their organizing after hours. White and his men did their job; they spent evenings and weekends visiting workers' homes or meeting with them in saloons. Meanwhile they trained nearly forty men to work the organizing from the inside.

The organizing committee is the heart and the soul of a union campaign, for they are the people. At Cravat, committee members came from throughout Puskarichland; they were miners, mechanics, machinists, and drivers. There was hardly a Cravat employee without a friend—and quite often a relative—on the committee. The committee called itself Cravat Miners for the UMWA. I called them "pushers" in a not-so-subtle allusion to street crime. They were pugnacious, they were outspoken, they were unafraid. The guys didn't hide: they included their names on the committee letterhead, and some even allowed their photographs and direct quotations to be used in a brochure enumerating the many ways in which Cravat workers were mistreated. The inside organizers did their best to keep the pro-union energy high, talking continually to workers on the job, visiting them after work, meeting them on weekends. They passed out nearly as many letters as I did, each one bearing the motto We Deserve the Best.

The foremen, for the most part, sympathized with the organizing effort of their subordinates and were stubborn in their loyalty both to the union and to their men. They submitted to the structure of the counterdrive because they had no choice, and many played a skilled game of passive resistance. The foremen varied their avoidance techniques, playing dumb, lying, making up stories both about what they were saying to workers about the union and how each employee was responding. When a foreman was such a serious problem that we could make no impression on him, we referred to him as "useless" and began to work around him, assigning other, more "loyal" foremen to get to his workers.

We endeavored not to let a foreman get to that point, however. I was unforgiving of their diversion maneuvers, but it was not my style to badger, at least not at the beginning. I was fonder of trapping an incorrigible foreman in his own deceit:

"So how's Charlie doing these days?" I asked one foreman on his regular visit one morning about a month into the campaign, referring to one of the union sympathizers on his crew. "Have you made any headway with him? What's he saying about the union?"

"Oh, Charlie's come around," the foreman lied, waving his hand as if to dismiss the thought that the worker had ever been a problem. "He's not union anymore. I'm sure of that."

"How do you know? What doesn't he like about the union?"

"Oh, he says he doesn't want to pay all those union dues. He says it's too much money, just like the general manager's letter said."

I knew the foreman could not be trusted. He had never given me a straight answer. So, to throw him off balance I gave him an assignment. I handed him a letter detailing the UMWA's finances, including District 6 salaries and other expenditures. I told him to take the letter to Charlie and talk it over with him. I wanted to know just what Charlie thought about how the union spent their members' money, I said. Then the crucial order: The foreman was to be back in my office at two P.M. Such assignments and deadlines were part of my standard arsenal. An unwilling or unsuccessful foreman would find himself forced to confront the same pro-union workers over and over again day after day and report the conversations to me. He could keep on lying, sure, but the pressure usually got to him, and inevitably the supervisor would pass the pressure along to the wayward worker.

At the end of each week the advisory team met with the Puskariches to chart our progress, tally up the growing number of potential anti-union votes, and talk about the more troublesome supervisors.

In the end, most of the foremen did break down. They began asking their workers to vote against the union, but only when fear had overcome them—the fear of losing their job or of seeing their men or their families suffer even more than they already had. I knew foremen to approach workers and say, "Hey, I know you need this union, but please don't vote for it. If the union wins, that's the end of me. You and me are like brothers, and I just couldn't go on."

While my fellow advisers and I were busy making life hell for the foremen, attorney Leiken was working his magic with labor law. Five weeks into the campaign, the NLRB regional director upheld our contention that the union voting unit should be broadened to include the truckers, the farmhands, the quarry workers, and the Kentucky miners. That was good news, and a key to our ultimate victory. The expansion added about 150 souls to the roster of eligible voters, which meant more work for union organizers.

We had already started working those groups in preparation for the decision. The union, on the other hand, had to scramble to find the additional workers after hours and to recruit and train employees who would run their campaign at each new site. There was more to the victory than that, however. The petition and hearing process had been so encumbered and so lengthy that in pronouncing its ruling, the NLRB director also extended the usual time line for union elections. Theoretically a union election must be held within thirty days from the date the regional director calls for a vote. In the Cravat case the NLRB saw fit to triple the time, setting the election date for December 16. That gave us all the more time to discredit the union and plenty of time for any wounds we inflicted to fester.

Once a union voting unit is established and the election date is set, federal labor law requires the employer to provide the union with the names and home addresses of all eligible employees. That law, which grew out of a 1966 U.S. Supreme Court decision, was intended to give unions easier access to the employees they are attempting to organize. But a good union buster knows how to pervert the intent. When I prepared the list (called the Excelsior list, for the company Excelsior Underwear, Inc., involved in the landmark court ruling), I did so meticulously: I provided the minimum information legally required while withholding enough details to frustrate union officers in their hunt for employees. I never included first names, for example, only the first initial. I listed the employee's house number and street, as required, but always was sure to leave out apartment numbers and street designations such as Street, Avenue, Drive, or Place. I never included zip codes. Such a skeletal list guaranteed that some employees would not be found and that the union would take an inordinately long time finding others. To top off the sabotage, I sent a letter to every employee on the list before releasing their names to the union. In the letter, which was signed by company management, I informed employees that we had given out personal information on them to the union as required by law and assured them that we would never have given out such information otherwise. The letter went on to warn the workers to expect harassing phone calls and visits from union officials at their homes. Management apologized, of course, for the trouble the union drive was causing the good workers. I prepared Cravat's Excelsior list and warning letter according to the formula. Working in tandem with the expansion of the voting unit, the ploy was particularly effective. The union-organizing process was contaminated from the beginning.

We continued to hold mandatory meetings in the Presbyterian church basement; two mornings a week before reporting to their jobs, the foremen filed into the hall to hear a progress report on the counterunion drive, received another stack of bulletins, and learned how the latest information should be presented. The first letter that I had made the foremen hand out had been a sort of introduction to the power mongering and divisiveness of unions. "Dear Fellow Employee," the letter earnestly began, as did all that followed, and it introduced the union as a self-serving outsider. In the letter we warned workers that they would be lied to and used by organizers to further the union cause. In all the letters every word was carefully planned; terms describing the union always carried derogatory and threatening connotations. We always called union leaders "bosses," for example, to repel the image of the union as a true worker organization. Meanwhile management was painted as humble, caring, righteous. Subsequent letters detailed the union's policies on dues, fees, fines, and assessments, divulged union rules and disciplinary techniques, warned that a strike would ruin the company and jeopardize jobs, and otherwise argued that the union would poison Cravat.

The other experts and I coached the foremen not to put workers on the defensive when they were following up on a letter. We warned them against approaching a worker with a question like "Did you read the latest letter?" A one-word answer would put an end to the conversation. Worse, such a question from a superior could invite a hostile response and heighten the passion of the union war. Instead we directed the foremen to point out something interesting in the letter and to make a benign comment such as "Hey, I didn't know unions could fine their members and take people to trial, did you?" or "I had no idea the United Mine Workers spent so much money."

It was not enough, of course, to cast doubt on the motives or effectiveness of the union. At a company like Cravat, where upper management was the cause and the target of the union drive, even a feeble union organization would garner support. As long as the managers in question continued their abusive and arbitrary conduct, the union would appeal to the workers. So the second imperative of the campaign was to humanize the executives in the eyes of workers. That was a particular challenge with the Puskariches. Workers held a deep-seated hatred for the family, who seemed to think that the way they treated employees was their business and nobody else's. I convinced the Puskariches that they faced sure unionization if they continued to rule by intimidation. So, for the sake of defeating the union, Mike Puskarich and two of his brothers, Pete and Nick, were willing to play the part of the repentant bosses. The hulking owners visited the pits and other work sites and exchanged jokes, robust laughter, and gossip with the men—in effect, tried to show they really understood their workers. The Puskariches got carried away by the showmanship of the effort and within a few weeks actually seemed to enjoy their new role. It started to look as though they really were changing. In my early union-busting days I had been convinced that an anti-union drive could bring about such changes of heart, that the threat of a union could shock an arrogant management into recognizing its failings and transforming the company. By the time of Cravat, however, I had fourteen years and nearly two hundred union busts behind me, and I had learned that was rarely the case. The Puskariches were just doing what had to be done. After the union election they became even more tyrannical than before.

While the Cravat owners were parading themselves as kind and fatherly, their sons and sons-in-law set out to befriend the miners and prove that the workers could trust the younger generation. That was a strategy I used often in fighting a union at a family-owned business. When the old-guard family members were disliked, I liked to show that changes were coming. Our humanizing effort, then, featured the new generation, displaying its members as more sympathetic than their fathers and fathers-in-law.

The younger Puskariches had a dual mission: to win the hearts of the miners and to take over the anti-union propaganda work for foremen who had proven useless. In the final weeks of the campaign I named a sort of supervisor SWAT team headed by Mike Puskarich's twenty-three-year-old son, Little Mike. The fifteen supervisors in the team, including other Puskarich family members, took charge of visiting the crews of uncooperative foremen and making sure their workers got the same heavy doses of anti-union talk and subtle threats as everybody else.

At Cravat I was lucky in that some of the younger Puskarich clan were indeed good miners and well liked by their comrades in the pits. Little Mike in particular was a hardworking and articulate young man, truly one of the boys. He soon became the symbol of the Cravat fight, the sign that better times were ahead. When Mike took charge of the SWAT team, crisscrossing Cravat territory to reinforce the anti-union message among the troops, our chances of winning doubled.

We continued to monitor worker allegiance through the supervisor interviews and deep into the campaign formed a Vote No Committee of pro-company employees charged with rewarding workers deemed to be "loyal" to management. Those workers found themselves showered with extra time off, special favors, and other bonuses. Meanwhile the pro-union workers came to work each day to face ever-tighter scrutiny from their bosses and were forced to battle scurrilous rumors. By that time we had established an efficient communications network capable of spreading news of perks and peril throughout the company in a day.

As the campaign progressed, the towns that dotted southeastern Ohio were ripped apart. Families and friends were divided by their union sympathies. Water towers, street signs, and billboards were spray-painted with Vote No and Vote Yes. Cravat property was vandalized. Spontaneous fistfights broke out in town and at the pits. We welcomed it all; every act was fuel for our anti-union campaign. We blamed all violence and vandalism on the union, and we endlessly admonished our foremen to point out to their crews that the union had driven a wedge of hate into a once unified work force.

The Cravat war had been raging for two months when a miner drove his pickup to a company field office and began firing bullets throughout the building. Only a few workers were witness to the rampage, but I got a phone call about the incident almost as soon as it ended, at my office in the converted motel. I immediately called for a meeting with Mike Puskarich.

The boss's reaction was as predictable as it was uncompromising: he wanted the man fired, and he wanted to prosecute. My associates agreed; they figured we could blame the rampage on the union and use the event to demonstrate the violence and savagery inspired by the UMWA. But I had another strategy.

"Look," I told them, "this man has problems. Everybody knows it. If Cravat fires him and drags him through court, the company will be seen as the villain, picking on a poor crazy guy. We don't want that. We should come forward as the benevolent, compassionate employer, show we care."

At my suggestion, Cravat had the man sent to a psychiatric clinic instead of to jail, and we spread the word that he would be offered his job back as soon as he recovered. We also made sure that any workers who heard about the incident knew that Cravat was paying the entire bill for the worker's treatment, even the portion not covered by medical insurance.

My band of experts and I mentioned the shooting incident at the next supervisors meeting. The message: The union drive had caused a great human tragedy, but the good employer was trying to do right by the man. "Here's an obvious indication of the divisiveness of the union," I told the men. "But we're taking care of him." I insisted that they tell their workers of Cravat's benevolence in the unfortunate case of Hal Lockett.

With the election about ten days away and emotions at their peak, the time came for "fun," union-busting style. I had stowed a dozen last-minute tricks up my sleeve over the years, and at Cravat I called upon my old favorites. One was the sports book: to foment a sportslike mania, I started a $1 election-week pool among the managers and foremen. Participants were to fill out an index card with their name and the number of No votes they thought we would garner. The person closest to guessing the final No vote would win $100. It was amazing to see how the pool took off and how accurate the supervisors could be with a $100 incentive. Even some of the most dogged union proponents gave away their hand and willingly predicted a resounding union defeat in order to improve their chances of collecting the prize. I used the pool as a way to get an eleventh-hour reading of workers' union sympathies while circumventing labor laws that prohibit management from conducting straw votes among employees during an organizing drive. By getting the supervisors to predict the way their workers would vote, I could test our own predictions. In pool after pool the supervisors were astonishingly accurate. Generally the median guess was only a few votes off the final tally.

As it turned out, Mike Puskarich won the Cravat pool; it was a victory that seemed to thrill him as much as winning the election. In fact, he had already pocketed his $100 prize when I shamed him into handing over the winnings to his office cleaning lady.

The miners couldn't participate in my gambling game, but there were other activities planned just for them. Corniness had become a trademark of my campaigns, although not one that was fully appreciated by my colleagues in the anti-union business. The essence of the campaign was to make it a daily event, and never was that more important than during the final days. I knew that many workers would decide how to vote in the last couple of weeks, so I wanted the words *Vote No* everywhere the men looked. Typically, the way I did that was through such election campaign paraphernalia as T-shirts, hats, buttons, and patches.

When I floated the idea at a strategy meeting with my fellow consultants, they objected. Juodenas was particularly strenuous in his opposition; he didn't use such gimmicks in campaigns, and he feared the T-shirt ploy would make the counterunion forces look ridiculous. My experience proved otherwise; the ubiquitous Vote No message—even if it was announced by a T-shirt—had a powerful psychological effect on the voters. Nonetheless, I agreed to launch the shirts on a trial basis : about ten days before the election. By then it was late November, and the mountain air was frosty, so rather than T-shirts I ordered five hundred thick cotton sweatshirts. In white lettering on the front and back of each navy blue jersey the words *Vote No* and a box bearing an X declared the anti-union cause. On the back we also printed the rallying cry "Win with Cravat." Along with the shirts I ordered Cravat Coal caps and Vote No patches.

I gave a shirt and hat to three foremen and sent them out to the largest work sites. Within a few hours they came back with orders for dozens more. It seemed everybody wanted them. At the next meeting I handed out the shirts and hats to all foremen, who took the goodies to their eager crews. Two executive secretaries, Dottie and Kitten, became so intoxicated with the carnival atmosphere of those final days that they sewed anti-union patches onto strategic, suggestive spots on their blouses and slacks.

I knew that many of the workers wearing the shirts, hats, and patches were not against the union. In fact, some of the most aggressive pro-union people ordered the shirts as cover for their sentiments. Many others wanted the shirts just because they were free. It didn't matter. The net effect was that the anti-union message enjoyed a high profile in the week before the election.

Behind the scenes, the campaign was anything but frivolous. Ed Juodenas made up oversize copies of the plus-and-minus charts we had been keeping on the workers and papered the walls of our conference room with the humongous loyalty report cards. It was a dramatic military touch that had us calling the conference room our "war room" from then on. Any worker still classified as a question mark was being reported on practically by the hour, and we kept our Magic Markers handy so we could log the continual updates on our battle charts.

With a few days left before the vote, Cravat got a call from an NLRB election agent. The NLRB had designated twenty-six polling places throughout the Ohio Appalachians and Kentucky, and some of the nine board agents were afraid to drive their government cars along the winding, icy roads of those isolated mountain territories. Their concerns left us an entrée to make a pass at the NLRB. We told the agents we would gladly drive them to the polling sites— many of which were out at the pits—in company four-wheel-drive wagons. When the union activists heard about our plan, they were outraged and demanded that a union election observer be allowed to ride alongside the polling agent. We, of course, refused, threatening to take back our offer if union people were ordered along. The NLRB denied the union demand. So on election morning, several polling agents boarded Cravat trucks and headed for the polling sites in the company of a Cravat driver. That was one more victory for us: in a union-busting campaign, the relentless accumulation of small victories leads to the final big win.

By the time the balloting was under way, I had no doubt that the election was ours. Mike Puskarich was equally sure and even hand-delivered his $71,000 final payment to me before the election results were in, an unusual move among union-buster clients. The fight cost Cravat a tidy $250,000, not counting attorney's fees. My portion of the take exceeded $60,000.

White, Bumbico, and the UMWA were equally certain of a union victory—so sure, in fact, that top UMWA officers showed up to watch the ballot counting. The UMWA happened to be holding its international convention in Pittsburgh at the time of the election, and Richard Trumka, the young, charismatic international president of the union, took a day trip to Cadiz to observe the election. In light of the latter-day losses of the UMWA, the Cravat vote was expected to mark a turning point for the union. My fellow consultants and I stayed away from the ballot counting, which took place at a machine shop in Cadiz. We sat, from 4 A.M. election morning until night, in the comfort and protection of the executive offices. Telephones rang constantly as Cravat managers called to give us continual updates. The tension didn't break all day.

By 10 P.M. it was over. The final count was in, a chapter in Cravat history ended. With 391 workers casting ballots, the union won only 93 votes. The remaining 298 were ours. The Puskariches, company loyalists, and we advisers spent the night in drunken celebration at the Holiday Inn in nearby Steubenville as the union mourned.

Bumbico was devastated by the loss. He told the *Wheeling Intelligencer* newspaper following the election that Cravat workers had lied to the UMWA about wanting a union. The next week Bumbico sent an angry and sneering letter to Cravat employees. In it he reproached the miners for their lack of resolve and rebuked those who had signed UMWA cards and then voted against the union. Bumbico accused the workers of having used the United Mine Workers to push for the improvements they wanted, without any intention of forming a union. And he predicted, rightly, that Cravat management would never change. In closing, Bumbico vowed to never take on Cravat Coal again: "You and your Company [can] have your second chance. But there is one thing we can tell you as a certainty: if things don't work out—*WE WILL NOT COME TO YOUR AID TWELVE (12) MONTHS FROM NOW....*"

Two years later, in the middle of a four-year term as a regional director for United Mine Workers, Bumbico left union work and took a position as human resources manager with Central Ohio Coal, a private coal company.

Genesis

The field called preventive labor relations got its start the moment labor organizations gained legal sanction, with the passage of the National Labor Relations Act in 1935. The law, popularly known as the Wagner Act, established the right of employees to organize in order to negotiate collectively with their employer over wages, hours, benefits, and working conditions and to otherwise fight for their combined interests. The primary labor component of Franklin D. Roosevelt's New Deal, the Wagner Act also outlawed many employer tactics then commonly used to break unions—most notoriously, spying on and intimidating union activists, provoking violence, and enticing workers into management-controlled "company unions" in order to stifle their call for independent labor organizations. The new law defined such activities, and many others, as unfair labor practices and created the National Labor Relations Board to oversee and enforce its provisions. Passage of the Wagner Act clearly was a victory for workers, but they hardly had time for celebration, for the law itself set off a vigorous countermovement among employers and their attorneys. With federal law recognizing workers' rights to self-organization and collective bargaining, many of the old union-busting tactics would have to be traded in for more subtle techniques. Among employers there grew a great demand for expertise in the tricks of what was called "union avoidance." All that was needed were a few good capitalists ready to tap that burgeoning market, and a whole new industry was born.

The first nationally known management consulting firm that specialized in helping companies evade unions was Labor Relations Associates of Chicago, Inc. Labor Relations Associates was formed in 1939, just two years after the U.S. Supreme Court upheld the

Wagner Act and ordered its full implementation. The firm was founded by a veteran personnel man named Nathan Shefferman, a member of the original National Labor Relations Board in 1934, who a year later became director of employee relations at Sears, Roebuck & Co. Today perhaps few people recognize the name Shefferman. But when Shefferman's company folded in 1959 after twenty years in business, his name and that of his firm had become forever linked with the more shameful elements of organized labor. That year, Shefferman was charged with conspiring to help Teamsters president Dave Beck avoid paying income taxes.

Although the charge against Shefferman was dropped, Beck was prosecuted and convicted; Shefferman's longtime association with Beck, and thus with the dark side of organized labor, would not be forgotten. Beck was convicted of three union-related financial crimes: income tax evasion, grand larceny, and filing false union income tax returns. The only conviction to stick, however, was for filing tax returns; the other two were dropped and pardoned, respectively. Beck served thirty months of a five-year sentence.

Throughout the 1930s Sears was engaged in continuous battle to block unions from the retail industry. The Chicago-based chain carried out a particularly vicious, ongoing war with the Teamsters union, which was attempting to organize drivers and other workers at several companies that supplied merchandise and distribution services to Sears. Sears executives were uncompromising; with the help of Shefferman they had managed successfully to ward off the unions on both fronts in the pre–Wagner Act years. But union organizing, active throughout the 1930s, turned relentless after passage of the Wagner Act, and the countermeasures needed to defeat the unions became infinitely more complex. For those reasons, by 1939 Shefferman's anti-union duties so dominated his work at Sears that he set up a separate company to handle the union-evasion business. With seed money from Sears in the form of a $10,000 retainer, Labor Relations Associates was born.

Enter a family named Lederer. Handling the legal logistics of forming Labor Relations Associates was a Chicago law firm called Lederer, Livingston, Kahn & Adsit, primary counsel to Sears. The Lederer on the masthead, Charles Lederer, had served as one of Sears's lead attorneys almost since the formation of the company in 1906. When his son, Philip, got his law degree, the father brought the younger man aboard. For nineteen years Phil Lederer practiced law with his father. He started out helping Dad with his duties as Sears's general counsel, but later on the younger Lederer got himself some training in labor relations and won an appointment as chief labor attorney for the Sears corporation. And where did Phil train? At the offices of Nathan Shefferman and Labor Relations Associates, of course. As Phil explains it, he dropped out of the law for a bit during World War II to bone up on employee relations and thus possibly win a commission to the navy as a personnel expert. The commission never came through; instead Phil spent the war years working as a consultant for Labor Relations Associates—taking the place of other consultants who were called to military service—and learning the back-room tricks of the burgeoning preventive labor relations trade. Although he was functioning as an on-site consultant at the time, not an attorney, Phil was called upon by several management attorneys to argue cases on their behalf before the National War Labor Board, created by Franklin Roosevelt to arbitrate labor disputes during the war in return for a no-strike pledge from labor. By VE Day Phil Lederer had developed a solid grasp of both labor law and anti-union personnel theory.

After the Second World War, Phil Lederer went back to a busy law practice. Throughout the next decade and a half he worked in close harmony with Labor Relations Associates, where business was flourishing in a climate of renewed anti-unionism. The war ended, corporate America had unleashed an angry anti-labor propaganda drive. At the time, Shefferman was building a daunting business on a foundation of false premises, the same silent assertions that continue to serve as the dogma of anti-union consultants, lawyers, and business managers. Perhaps the most incredible—and most widely believed—is the myth that companies are at a disadvantage to unions organizationally, legally, and financially during a union-organizing drive. In the postwar furor, business leaders characterized unions as fat, greedy, corrupt, and decidedly un-American. They demanded that Congress amend the Wagner Act, complaining that the law gave unions an insurmountable advantage over management. Executives charged that by protecting unions, but not management, from improper practices during organizing drives and elections, the Wagner Act allowed unions to be coercive, to threaten, and to intimidate workers at will. They just wanted to level the playing field. In 1947 Congress bowed to management's wishes. After a prolonged and stormy debate, conservative Congressmen won passage of a sweeping labor reform law, overriding the veto by President Harry S Truman, who condemned the law as designed primarily to weaken unions. Commonly referred to as the Taft-Hartley Act, the 1947 law attacks unions on almost every front. To this day union leaders consider the Taft-Hartley Act a primary cause of labor's failure to organize the majority of American workers. Among the law's most significant provisions are the establishment of unfair labor practices that can be charged against unions; a listing of specific "employer rights" available to management during union-organizing efforts, including a broad freedom of expression; an outright ban on the closed shop, in which union membership is a precondition of employment; and an open invitation to states to pass even more restrictive legislation. One provision, since removed from the law, required union officers to file affidavits proclaiming that they had no affiliation to the Communist party. Taft-Hartley was devastating to labor. It led to a proliferation of state legislation disingenuously called "right to work" laws, which prohibit mandatory union dues; perpetuated the red baiting that already haunted the labor movement; and loaded management's union-busting arsenal with complicated restrictions on fundamental union activities. Executives and their labor consultants knew that with the Taft-Hartley amendments in place, employers would enjoy great freedom in combating worker organizations. Management always had the upper hand, of course; they had never lost it. But thanks to Taft-Hartley, the bosses could once again wage their war with near impunity.

Labor law grew more complex almost by the day in the 1940s and 1950s, and good attorneys were at a premium. Phil Lederer, it would seem, was in the right place at just the right time. During the postwar years, Lederer worked as Sears chief labor counsel, not only taking charge of all labor matters at the mother company, but handling as well the labor relations and civil rights cases for Allstate Insurance Co., a Sears subsidiary. A little more than a decade later, Lederer's insurance connection would provide the spark that ignited a firm named John Sheridan Associates, my first union-busting employer. But before that, labor was to suffer yet another legislative catastrophe.

Almost from its inception American organized labor has had to combat a grave public image problem. Violence against employers and union members alike, reports of Communist infiltration into the labor movement, and evidence of union ties to organized crime plagued labor leaders and provided their enemies with strategic weapons for destroying their cause. The Wagner Act had helped tame the violence by the late 1930s, and labor leaders worked feverishly during the 1940s to purge their ranks of avowed Communists. But within some of the nation's largest and most powerful unions, racketeering persisted, and labor's mob connection grew more entrenched. By 1957 organized labor seemed so rife with corruption that the Senate appointed a special subcommittee to investigate allegations of criminal activities. The committee, headed by Senator John McClellan of Arkansas, boasted such lofty membership as John F. Kennedy, then a young senator from Massachusetts, and had as its chief counsel a youthful Robert F. Kennedy. The televised hearings stunned Americans with its revelations of rigged union elections, collusion of union leaders and employers, embezzlement, and theft. One of the chief targets of the Senate investigations was the Teamsters union, and the committee found evidence of corruption at nearly every level, up to the international president, Dave Beck. Beck had been elected president of the Teamsters in 1952 on a promise to clean up the union. But five years later witnesses testified before the McClellan Anti-Racketeering Committee that Beck was diverting large amounts of union funds for his own purposes, misappropriations that included payments to Labor Relations Associates. Largely as a result of the hearings, Beck was convicted of tax evasion and grand larceny; his successor, the notorious Jimmy Hoffa, was convicted and jailed for jury tampering and mail fraud; and the Teamsters union was expelled from the AFL-CIO.

Although the McClellan Committee concentrated on the misdeeds of organized labor, the senators also took a peek behind management's doors. What they found was no less disturbing. For two and a half weeks the committee heard testimony about improper management practices; for several days they focused on the dealings of one man, Nathan Shefferman. By the mid-1950s Shefferman's firm, Labor Relations Associates, boasted three hundred clients from coast to coast and was probably the largest employee relations consulting business in the nation. Witness testimony, combined with information gathered during an investigation led by congressional aide Pierre Salinger, showed Labor Relations Associates to be a very lucrative and clearly unethical enterprise: Shefferman's battalion of consultants traveled the country, using whatever tactics they could get away with to keep the employees of client companies from joining unions. According to hearings transcripts, those means included conniving with local labor officials; manipulating union elections through bribery and coercion; threatening to revoke workers' benefits should they organize; installing union officers sympathetic to management; offering to reward employees who worked against the union; and spying on and harassing workers— all clearly illegal under federal labor law. Named in the testimony as one of Shefferman's consultants was one Herbert Melnick.

When the McClellan Committee hearings ended in 1959, the American public was left with a dreary portrait of U.S. business and labor. As McClellan himself said at the close of the testimony concerning Shefferman: "The activities disclosed before this committee reflect a great discredit on some business firms in this country." The committee vigorously condemned the shenanigans of many labor unions, but they took U.S. management to task as well. Said McClellan, "[I]t was the services which management desired which created the need for Nathan Shefferman. It was management who paid the bills for the activities of Nathan Shefferman, and it was management which knowingly utilized the services of Nathan Shefferman with no compunctions or regrets until the revelations in recent months. They were aware of what they were doing and how their money was being utilized."

Following the hearings, Beck was sent to prison; meanwhile Congress went to work on a law to regulate the internal practices of unions and thus stem the tide of corruption.

In 1961, two years after Labor Relations Associates dissolved in shame, Shefferman published a book entitled *The Man in the Middle*, a 292-page justification of his four decades in anti-union employee relations work. In the book Shefferman whines a great deal about his treatment before the McClellan Committee and defends his work ad nauseam. His key defense lay in his claim that union avoidance constituted "a tiny percentage" of his labor relations work. By way of illustration, he cites a laundry list of other personnel services he provided, as reported by one client to the McClellan Committee. The list included the administration of opinion surveys, supervisor training, incentive pay procedures, wage surveys, employee complaints, personnel records, application procedures, job evaluations, and legal services. The other services were rendered, to be sure. But the truth is, if union busting was part of the work, then the entire package was tainted. Everything else had to be performed in concert with the overall goal of keeping top management in complete control. Every other piece of a company's employee relations work had a part in that drama. To borrow a line from Shefferman's own book: "So we find that even the hidden thread is basic to the fabric of labor-management relations."

In Shefferman's labor relations work can be found the seeds of all subsequent union-busting techniques, as well as the language employed to shroud the deeds. He is the true godfather of modern union busting. Shefferman laid the bedrock of the industry. He designed scores of strategies for countering unions, techniques that formed the core of his work—and later mine—and that continue to dominate labor relations. But Shefferman's contribution was much greater than his repertoire of tactics. We have Shefferman to thank, perhaps more than anyone else, for the development of a magnificently insidious doublespeak that persists in labor-management theory to this day. The language of employee relations as articulated by Shefferman and the thousands he influenced masks a fundamental distrust of workers and a view of management as defenders of the crown, with words and schemes that seem to promote the opposite. It is easy to fall for the words; the ideas are beautiful. In his 1961 book Shefferman wags a finger at paternalistic bosses; calls for managers to recognize workers' individuality; promotes continual two-way communication between management and workers; and challenges bosses to respect their employees' dignity.

So what's the problem? The problem is unions. Mix the fear of unions into management's employee relations potion and the result is poison—a poison so potent that it contaminates even the most seemingly altruistic plan. Every program, every new workplace strategy, is twisted, inverted, perverted into a tactic for undermining the collective spirit of workers.

Here is an example from the Shefferman school of subterfuge: Under the real or even theoretical threat of a union, Shefferman advised management to institute a device called an employee roundtable. Purportedly designed to give workers a way to air their grievances and influence company policy, in reality the roundtable becomes management's tap into the worker grapevine and its repressive thumb on the informal worker power structure. The regular group meetings provided management with a system for planting information, as well as for identifying and controlling the leaders among employees. Shefferman lays out the blueprint for such roundtables in his book. Calling them "rotating employee committees," he presents the sessions as open forums, absent any supervisors, opportunities for workers to gripe without fear of reprisal. But the fact is, such committees serve management's interests more directly than the needs of the workers. The operative word here is "rotating." Shefferman, no fool, advised management to steer clear of programs that could foster in workers a group identity. He boasts in his book, for example, that he took the contrary view in admonishing Sears executives against the formation of a company union during the 1920s, when many firms were using employee associations as a shield against true labor organizations. Shefferman says he argued that the company-union strategy could backfire by teaching employees how to work in concert and thus making them more susceptible to an independent union.

In his book Shefferman doesn't spell out the reason for the rotating participation in the employee committees. But his students—who later became my teachers—learned it well and passed it along: by continually changing the makeup of the employee committee, management could keep abreast of complaints and rumors circulating in the various departments without creating a bond among the participants or inadvertently developing leaders. The goal was to foster cooperation between employees and management, not among the employees themselves. In tandem with the gripe sessions, Shefferman prescribed a very intricate supervisor training course. Each front-line supervisor, whom he refers to as the submanagement, would be taught to identify and analyze the power relationships among his subordinates, in order to focus his coercive energy on the workers with the greatest influence and thus more efficiently control the attitudes and behavior of the whole group.

Although I scarcely recognized the name Shefferman when I entered the union-busting business, ten, twenty, even thirty years later I was promoting a very similar system to my clients as a long-term union-repellent strategy.

While Dave Beck was preparing to go to prison, President Dwight Eisenhower signed into law the Landrum-Griffin Act. The nation's little cadre of labor consultants cheered. Landrum-Griffin, officially the Labor-Management Reporting and Disclosure Act of

1959, contains five major sections, including a Bill of Rights for union members designed to make unions more democratic and open, particularly with regard to union funds. What gave labor consultants glee were the financial provisions, which required unions to file a copy of their constitution and rules with the secretary of labor and to file yearly financial reports, and compelled union officers and employees to report any financial transactions involving themselves or their family members that might constitute a conflict of interest. Wow. Union busters couldn't have asked for a bigger break. For the first time, detailed, timely information on the inner workings and finances of unions and labor leaders would be available to consultants and attorneys for the price of a photocopy. Thank you, Congress.

The Landrum-Griffin regulations were not aimed solely at unions, however. The McClellan Committee were clearly disturbed by the tactics used by employers and their consultants in their fight against unions, and Congress addressed the scandal in Landrum-Griffin. In order to place companies' anti-union efforts under public scrutiny, the law requires companies to report to the secretary of labor certain expenditures related to their anti-union activities, including the hiring of labor relations consultants. And the consultants must report the terms and conditions of their contract with the company and reveal the amount of money received. Had it not been for a couple of well-placed loopholes, those disclosure provisions could have snuffed out the anti-union consulting industry in its infancy. A master of illusion, the union buster pulls off his tricks amid the confusion of smoke and mirrors; his magic disappears under the blazing lights of center stage.

But the loopholes in Landrum-Griffin are shameful—enormous, gaping errors in the law that have left room for a sleazy billion-dollar industry to plod through without even sucking in its bloated middle. The law states that management consultants only have to file financial disclosures if they engage in certain kinds of activities, essentially attempting to persuade employees not to join a union or supplying the employer with information regarding the activities of employees or a union in connection with a labor relations matter. Of course, that is precisely what anti-union consultants do, have always done. Yet I never filed with Landrum-Griffin in my life, and few union busters do. Here's why not: According to the law, in order to be considered engaging in "persuader" activities, the consultant must speak directly to the employees in the voting unit. As long as he deals directly only with supervisors and management, he can easily slide out from under the scrutiny of the Department of Labor, which collects the Landrum-Griffin reports.

A handful of labor consultants do file; since they do not mask their efforts to convince workers to vote against the union and therefore are legally classified as "persuaders," not to file would set off an alarm over at the IRS. But they know well that the Labor Department has no reliable method for checking the accuracy of the reports. The consultants' role as spy is similarly protected by Landrum-Griffin loopholes. All kinds of information gathering is allowed to go on with no disclosure consequences if the information is to be used solely for a specific legal proceeding. Of course, we consultants wouldn't limit the fruits of our espionage to use in a single court case, but it is easy enough to make it appear that way. With the help of our trusted attorneys, our anti-union activities were carried out in backstage secrecy; meanwhile we gleefully showcased every detail of union finances that could be twisted into implications of impropriety or incompetence. Helping all this along is Landrum-Griffin's ambiguous treatment of attorneys. It is not clear under the law whether labor lawyers should be bound by the same reporting requirements as anti-union consultants, even when they perform similar duties, as they often do. Attorneys therefore can get away with direct interference in the union-organizing process without being forced to disclose their deeds or the corresponding fees. It is common in large labor law firms today to send out the junior associates to do the kind of work I once did for companies. Sheltered by the broad umbrella of attorney-client privilege, the young lawyers run bold anti-union wars and dance all over Landrum-Griffin.

Two former consultants from Labor Relations Associates, John Sheridan and Herbert Melnick, were shrewd enough to know that the best defense against Landrum-Griffin was to be found within the law itself. Using the language of the law as a blueprint, the two designed a daring new approach to union busting and recast the entire industry. The seed for the plan had been planted by Shefferman himself: during four decades of personnel work, Shefferman had pegged front-line supervisors as the most effective lobbyists for management, and he had teamed up with labor attorneys to fight unions. It was just one small step from there to a system of anti-union campaigning built on the legal specialness of those two groups.

While the labor world was still reeling from Landrum-Griffin, Sheridan and Melnick swam ashore from the sinking Labor Relations Associates ship and teamed up to start a consulting business of their own. They rented an office in downtown Chicago and went to work trying to sell their new concept. Rather than peddle their services directly to companies, Sheridan and Melnick called on attorneys and pitched their work as a complement to the duties of labor lawyers. The duo argued that together, attorneys and consultants could orchestrate a double-barreled attack on union drives and thus outmuscle and outwit the unions while staying out of reach of Landrum-Griffin. The arrangement also would provide a constant source of work for both the attorneys and the consultants, with each side continually referring work to the other. It was a brilliant plan. Few law firms appreciated the opportunity at first, but Sheridan landed the one that counted—Lederer, Fox & Grove, Phil Lederer's firm.

It so happened there was a great deal of organizing activity in the insurance industry at the time, and Phil Lederer had plenty of insurance clients who wanted help battling the unions. Lederer knew Melnick from his days with Labor Relations Associates, had brought him in on an anti-union job at Allstate, and he liked the spunk and style of Jack Sheridan. The tripartite combination was a winner. Lederer describes the alliance succinctly: "I would bring two of them in to do the consulting work, while I did the legal work. I did not try to run the campaigns against the unions. I pretty much stuck to the law."

Thanks to Lederer's experience, not to mention his rich and loyal client base, Sheridan's business prospered. It wasn't long before there was more work than the two could handle. And so the Sheridan expansion began. In 1969 John Sheridan Associates took on a rookie union buster named Marty Levitt.

Seduction

When I interviewed for my first job as an anti-union consultant, I knew nothing of the field's ignominious history. In fact, I knew nothing of labor relations at all. I had seen an enticing job announcement in *The Wall Street Journal* and badly needed a change in my life. I figured my personal salesmanship would come through for me as it invariably had since high school, when my glib tongue won me acceptance both with the street-tough greasers and the likely-to-succeed intellectuals. I wasn't feeling so sharp in 1969, however. There I was, twenty-five years old and already emotionally ravaged by my divorce of a month before. I was sitting in the psychiatric ward of Ridgecliff Hospital, where my frightened parents had taken me after watching me sink deeper and deeper into depression. One sunny morning I entertained myself in my hospital room by scanning the Job Mart section of *The Wall Street Journal,* just as I had done at home every Tuesday and Wednesday morning for the previous two years. With the help of the *Journal*'s job announcements, I had managed to build a daunting clientele for my burgeoning executive recruitment business, through which I found key employees for my clients by luring executives away from competitors. With a client list that included the likes of Goodyear Aerospace and Diamond Shamrock, then known as Diamond Alkali, I was billing out $100,000 a year. My personal income of $25,000 a year was awfully good money then. I was troubled, though, eager to get out of Cleveland, and desperate to do something that would take my mind off my disastrous marriage.

Then I saw the ad.

It was a large, bold announcement positioned in a box to set it apart from the others. Some unnamed company sought an "employee relations consultant" with management experience and knowledge of labor law. Clearly I should have stopped there, since not only did I know not a word of labor law, but I had no thoughts about employee issues. I had been brought up in an unusually apolitical Jewish family. In Cleveland during that era, the formidable Ohio Teamsters and the organization's Jewish leadership made the papers almost daily. Labor strife was common, and many Cleveland Jews considered being pro-union almost a part of the religion. My parents were of another bent, however. My mother, beautiful and elegant, never worked a day in her life and always kept a maid despite my father's unremarkable middle-class income. From her I learned that making money and living well—or looking as if I did—should always be my top priority. My father taught me the thrill of self-reliance. A relentless if only marginally successful entrepreneur, he encouraged me to live off my wits—specifically, to develop a quick tongue in order to attain whatever it was I wanted. Dad's own fast talking hadn't brought him riches, but it had sustained him as a dogged self-made man and kept him living comfortably alongside Cleveland's gangster class. Dad hopped from one venture to another, walking a moving line between business and scam. When I was still small, he quit his job as manager of a small department store in order to distribute comic books and nudie magazines in partnership with Rube Sturman, who would later distribute hard-core pornography. During the 1960s and 1970s, Dad ran a legitimate bookstore in downtown Cleveland but subsidized the receipts with a back-room business in racetrack bookmaking.

While I was growing up I had no conscious contact with labor issues or union men, yet my life paralleled the lives of many who would come to lead the checkered Ohio labor movement. Long before I embarked on my career as a union buster, my hometown was supplying the labor world with some of its most notorious personalities, men whose names would establish an indelible link in the minds of most Americans between organized labor and organized crime. Behind the walls of aging storefronts in the Italian enclave of Cleveland, a crumbling working-class neighborhood called Murray Hill, Teamsters bosses were conspiring with Mafia godfathers and loan sharks to ensure the continuing power and wealth both of organized labor and La Famiglia. The Jewish enclaves of Cleveland where I went to school, played, and learned to hustle during the 1950s and 1960s produced some of the most notorious names in Teamsters history: the late Jackie Presser, international president and Mob darling turned FBI informant; his father, labor racketeer Bill Presser; and Harold Friedman, Bill Presser's partner and the revered commander of the Ohio Conference of Teamsters for more than a decade. Meanwhile, in Little Italy, or the Hill, as the Italian neighborhood was known, a dual generation of Teamsters chiefs and Italian mobsters flourished.

It so happens that the path of my youth crossed right in front of some of those powerful men, including prizefighters-turned-Teamsters leaders Louis "Babe" Triscaro, Al Micatrotto, and Tony Hughes, as well as some of the biggest names in the Cleveland Mob leadership.

Yet I remained unaware: when I was seventeen and the Teamsters called a strike against Cleveland newspapers, my father, being an enterprising businessman, saw the strike as a way to make money. He began bringing in out-of-town papers for twenty-five cents each and selling them for one dollar. One Sunday I accompanied my dad's older brother and business partner, Manny, to the nearby Greyhound bus station, where we picked up the newspaper shipments. As Uncle Manny was unloading the bundles, four burly, angry-looking men surrounded him and started pushing at him. I backed away, disoriented and frightened. I didn't know what was going on; I didn't know who the Teamsters were or what strikes meant. All I knew was Uncle Manny was in trouble. I ran the half block to my father's bookstore, grabbed his gun, and hurried back to the bus station. For a few moments, until the police came and broke up the scuffle, I held a gun on four Teamsters enforcers who worked for Babe Triscaro.

Two years later I met the Mob. Nineteen years old and by then a practiced hustler, I strutted into a Murray Hill finance firm, MDM Investment Co., one afternoon and asked a cadre of muscular Italians in T-shirts and suspenders to bankroll my first business venture—the singing career of my high school sweetheart, who was briefly my wife. So moved were the tough, apple-chomping racketeers by the sultry voice of Iris Rubenstein as she belted the Italian ballad "Mama" that they instantly made a plan to send her to Los Angeles under the able tutelage of Mark Anthony, the Murray Hill–bred business manager to Bob Hope. In the end the Italians invested at least $25,000 to make Iris a star. But after two years of coddling and coaching their awkward vocal filly, they gave up. As a performer, Iris was pathetic—rigid and hopelessly dull.

She had a Barbra Streisand voice with an Olive Oyl presentation; she could never make it. The Italians decided their investment would not pay off. They wanted out. Oddly, and quite happily for me, my disreputable bankers decided they could recoup some money from the soured Iris deal by investing in Marty Levitt: they would set me up in business and reap half the profits. With another $25,000 the boys of MDM formed a firm for me in the only line of work that my occasional summer jobs at employment agencies had prepared me for—executive recruiting.

I read the *Journal* ad over and over. It promised all the right things: travel, a chance to hobnob with top business people, great money. Despite my obvious lack of qualifications, one item convinced me I had a shot: the firm sought someone with good "communication skills." Communication—now, there was something I knew about. As soon as I left the hospital, I dashed off a résumé, complete with a laundry list of my recruitment firm's clients. Two weeks later I was called to an interview at John Sheridan Associates in Chicago.

John Sheridan, Jack to his employees and intimates, was a demigod among labor consultants. Revered and reviled by his disciples, Sheridan was author and master of much of the doublespeak that is the foundation of the anti-union consulting business.

A bright and articulate man with a degree in English from Loyola University, Sheridan had been an effective union organizer with the International Brotherhood of Electrical Workers in Chicago in the 1950s. After only a few years in union work, armed with an insider's knowledge of the mechanics of organizing, Sheridan switched sides, joining Shefferman's Labor Relations Associates. By the time I applied for a job in 1969, the firm had grown to about a dozen full-time consultants.

I was thrilled to be invited to the Sheridan interview. Still not sure what I had gotten myself into, I donned my finest suit and set off for my date with the mysterious firm at 221 North La Salle, in downtown Chicago.

I didn't know who Sheridan was, but his demeanor told me I should. Dressed in his signature turtleneck and sports coat, he strode around his office during the interview, gesturing eloquently and exuding an air of importance. Rather than ask about me, Sheridan spent the first hour of the interview acquainting me with his work, his company, and his accomplishments and warning me about a band of treacherous competitors who were to be considered by all Sheridan employees as a vile enemy. At times he deferred to his associate Jim Bannon, who dutifully elaborated upon everything the master said. During much of his flamboyant speech, Sheridan relaxed behind his mahogany desk, reclining on his luxurious stuffed chair, his feet propped decidedly on the desktop. As he spoke he threw open his jacket, sucked on a slender Antonio y Cleopatra cigar—another personal trademark—and gazed upward. Bannon, meanwhile, looking prim and proper in the conservative business suit that Sheridan required of all his underlings, perched on the corner of the desktop. Sheridan was an impressive figure, to be sure. He stood six feet four inches tall and possessed a strong build. A dark-eyed, dark-haired Irish American, he was a solidly handsome man of just under forty.

So just what does John Sheridan Associates do? I wanted to know. "We do the Lord's work," was Sheridan's answer. I was electrified as Sheridan and Bannon described their business, and I found myself seduced into coveting the job. "We force management to clean up its act," Bannon announced. "Our job is to thwart union-organizing drives. You see, a union-organization effort only results from one thing: bad management. If the employees are pushing to organize a union, the management only has itself to blame." To that synopsis Sheridan added a cynical refrain that has served as a mantra of sorts to union busters for a generation: "We're not anti-union. We're pro-company and pro-employee." Bannon ticked off a list of the five key corporate failings that drive workers to seek union help: lack of recognition, weak management, poor communication, substandard working conditions, and noncompetitive wages and benefits. If a company takes care of those problems itself, Bannon said, it can achieve a happy work force and never have to fear a union invasion. So what John Sheridan Associates do is first take care of the immediate threat, the crisis, by quelling the union-organizing drive. With the union trouble put to rest, the consultants then teach management how to run the company so that employees will not feel they need a union. "In our work, we use the threat of the union to force management to change its ways, to supervise more effectively, communicate better with the workers. We humble management, make them see how they've called the union trouble upon themselves. When our work is done, the company remains union free because no union is needed. Management does its job right, the workers are happy, and the company is profitable."

Sheridan handed me a copy of the company's first brochure. It bore a Latin motto: *Hominem pagina nostra sapit.* Translation: Our work is people. Sheridan then went on to describe his firm as a "class act." Everything was to be done first rate. Each campaign was to be custom-designed. The consultants on the job were always to look professional, travel first class, stay and dine at the best places in the area. Corporate executives, after all, would not have faith in a company that cut corners, that settled for less than the best. Sheridan said he always billed clients "portal to portal"— that is, the client company paid every single expenditure of the consultants for the duration of the campaign. That was on top of the $500 daily billing rate per consultant.

I was wowed. I couldn't have dreamed up a more fantastic job description. I thought, "What could be better? I could make great money and appear to be helping people at the same time." That afternoon in Chicago I could not have predicted that the field Sheridan and Bannon were describing with such reverence was one in whose service I would come routinely to dupe frightened managers, rob corporate coffers, betray confidences, and break the law and in the process turn myself into a desperate alcoholic.

As the interview progressed, Sheridan and Bannon came to know me as sharp and sure. I demonstrated how quickly I could learn their idiom, and they figured I would soon embrace their modus operandi. Sheridan was glad I seemed so promising. He had chosen just a handful of people to interview out of nearly one thousand enthusiastic applicants. His interest in me despite my blatant lack of experience was piqued by a jewel contained in my application: my mouth-watering list of corporate clients. Sheridan Associates was having a little client trouble at the time, the consequences of defections by some of the erstwhile darlings of the firm. Sheridan was hoping I would help him tap into a new and lucrative client base.

A few weeks before, Herb Melnick decided to set out on his own after nearly ten years in partnership with Sheridan. Once Melnick announced his departure, Sheridan quickly called a staff meeting to inform the troops that the partnership was dissolved. He magnanimously told the associates they were free to go with Melnick if they preferred, never imagining that they would choose the thick, plodding Herb over him. In fact, many did. Sheridan was stunned by what happened over the next few days; he watched more than half his staff gleefully jump ship. In the mutiny Sheridan lost some of his most brilliant stars, the very core of the company: Tony McKeown, whom Sheridan considered his own creation and who was, in fact, a sort of Frankenstein's monster of union busting; Ray Mickus, a technical wizard with a Humpty-Dumpty look; and Tom Crosbie, dark, diabolical, a supreme manipulator. Weeks later Sheridan's lips still trembled as he pronounced their names. These were evil, evil people, I was to understand. The revolt didn't stop with a simple secession, either; after leaving, the enemy maneuvered to destroy the mother ship. At McKeown's suggestion the roguish band pirated Sheridan's client list and mailed a fraudulent letter to each company. In the letter the defectors announced that John Sheridan Associates had been dissolved and invited clients to call on the new firm of Melnick, McKeown and Mickus, a company that would achieve fame under the name of Modern Management Methods Inc., and the moniker Three M.

As Sheridan recounted the tale of treachery, I could see him shake. I watched him, listening intently, numbed by the intensity of his anger. His eloquence gave way to mania; his face reddened, he breathed heavily, paced, and at times exploded, spitting invectives. A month after the stinging revolt, Sheridan placed the ad in *The Wall Street Journal,* seeking to replenish his ranks.

Working for Sheridan over the next three years, I came to understand the irony and portentousness of the 1969 insurrection. Truth be told, the attitude that allowed the three M's and Crosbie to betray Sheridan so boldly and so thoroughly they had learned from the master himself. And it would not be the last time Sheridan would be double-crossed by his own crew. Over the years, one associate after another would defect, no longer able to tolerate Sheridan's overpowering ego, which offended their own, and lured by the chance to make better money than Sheridan would allow. Out on their own, the former Sheridanites inevitably re-created themselves in Sheridan's image and ultimately suffered the same fate as their mentor, abandoned and pillaged by their own. One after another they left him. One after another they became him.

Sheridan was impressed with me in the interview, and he told me so. He wasn't prepared to make a job offer, though, until I had met with his number two man, Nick Sangalis. As a rookie consultant I would be answering directly to Sangalis, so Sheridan wanted to be sure Nick saw my potential as he did. I went back home to Cleveland not knowing if I would, in fact, get the job. A few days later I got a call from Sangalis. He flew me to Washington, D.C., where we met in the airport red carpet room for another interview. During the interview, Nick confessed that he and Sheridan had run a routine background check on me—the kind I would later conduct on supervisors and union proponents—and had found the one criminal skeleton in my closet: a conviction of receiving stolen property. When I was a junior at Ohio University, I had shared an apartment with three other young men, one of whom was quite a talented thief. Throughout the year, as my young hoodlum friend plied his trade, my pals and I had become the willing recipients of stolen tables, chairs, stereos, and other costly furnishings. In the end, all the roommates were found guilty of receiving stolen property, not the highest recommendation for a job in business. I was embarrassed by Nick's discovery, but he said not to worry; he and Sheridan would not hold my boyhood failings against me. They just wanted me to be aware that they knew about it. Years later I would realize that the two were actually quite delighted with my apparent willingness to ignore the law.

Nick was a portly, gap-toothed Greek in his early forties, who carried Greek worry beads in order to remain in touch with his heritage. He possessed an easy, jovial manner embodied in his wide grin. But the smile and the belly laughs masked the deadly seriousness with which he worked. It was Nick, after all, who taught me how to snuff out any spark of defiance in a supervisor. He taught me the value of the well-timed, accurately placed threat. When Nick ran a counterorganizing drive, he made sure supervisors went home wondering if they would have a job in the morning; and he was very effective. Before teaming up with Sheridan, Nick had worked many years as the chief negotiator for Geno Palucci, owner and chief executive of Geno's, the frozen pizza giant. He enjoyed a reputation as a shark.

When Nick called me a few days later to tell me I had the job, he told me John Sheridan wanted to hire me not despite my ignorance of his field, but in part because of it. I went to Sheridan with no union biases; my brief encounter with the Cleveland Teamsters as a boy had left only a small impression on me and had given me no insight. Frankly, Sheridan considered my union virginity an advantage. To him, my particular blend of ignorance and bravado made me the perfect candidate for the job; it would be easy for him to mold me in his image.

"He likes the fact that you have no one else's bad habits," Nick confided with a smirk. When Nick ratified my hiring, he commented to Sheridan that the kid from Cleveland was "the best damned bullshit artist I've ever met."

A con artist was just what Sheridan needed, for he ran a great scam. His business was not so much busting unions as it was billing clients. As soon as I was enlisted into the company, even before I had learned the business, Sheridan began charging $250 a day for my services. Throughout months of training during which I mostly sat and watched the other consultants as they blustered, entertained, and interrogated, Sheridan's clients paid a stiff price for my presence on the job. On my first day Sheridan instructed me to lie about my experience; should it ever come up, I was to say I had been in the business two years. And so the fraud began.

Sheridan made sure all of his consultants billed out for five full days, regardless of whether there was enough work to justify the charges. His general staffing rule was one consultant per one hundred employees for each campaign. But if one job concluded before another became available, he sent us flying off to help our brethren at a campaign in progress, whether we were needed or not. Often I arrived at a campaign and just sat or did "gofer" chores for the consultants. At $250 a day Sheridan figured he could pack a junior associate like me in anywhere; but he did the same with his $350-a-day senior associates. The executives we worked with generally were in a state of panic about the union drive, and Sheridan taught us to exploit their fear for maximum profit. Because of their hatred and fear of the union—and their belief that we were their only hope—our clients were at our mercy. They rarely dared to mention any suspected deception.

It wasn't long before I was playing the game as well as the rest of them, stretching a few hours' work into a leisurely full day or, more boldly, leaving the job early to spend the afternoon downing drinks at the hotel. After a few weeks on most campaigns the job was pretty easy; we generally knew which supervisors were on our side and which ones would have to be pressured, and we already would have assembled a pro-company squad of managers to pick up the work of the weak links. With the internal machinery in motion, we could laugh away much of each day for the remainder of the campaign. As for Sheridan, he rarely worked the campaigns himself. Quite often, however, he would make a cameo appearance, tour the plant, meet with the CEO, go to lunch. Executives seemed to like to see the top gun at the show. Whenever Sheridan did appear, he was sure to charge the client $500, his price for a full day's work.

And then some.

Consider one Sheridan client, Alpine Designs, a Cheyenne, Wyoming, manufacturer of down-filled sportswear. Alpine sold its jackets, coats, and vests to high-priced sporting goods chains and department stores and kept a close eye on quality control. Even a minor sewing error would banish the garment to the seconds bins, where it awaited sale to less pricey outlets. During the counterorganizing campaign, company executives dug into the bins to give me and my associate one coat each. This was the kind of perk that we consultants came to expect, but in Sheridan's hands the concept of the perk was stretched to the extreme. During the Alpine campaign, Jack flew to Cheyenne for his customary one-day visit. He spent his typical $500 day, then, at the plant manager's invitation, pulled a dozen or so coats from the seconds bins as gifts for friends, clients, and family. At company after company, Sheridan's partners and employees followed his lead. We collected sterling pen sets from the Parker Pen plant in Janesville, Wisconsin—Herb Melnick got himself some two hundred sets and had them all engraved for free. At the Prince Gardner factory in Missouri we amassed leather wallets and key cases. I didn't have to buy holiday gifts for years.

Sheridan paid me a starting salary of $24,000 a year. That was a healthy income in 1969, but even more thrilling was the host of benefits showered upon me as a Sheridan consultant. On my first day I was handed a fistful of credit cards to use at will while on campaigns; the bills were to be sent to client companies no matter how extravagant. It was a routine sermon of Sheridan's that corporate executives would not respect our work unless we were expensive and conspicuously classy. Whenever he drew up a contract for a union fight, Sheridan advised executives that it would be essential for his consultants to be "comfortable" while working a campaign, so that we could concentrate on the problems at hand. He insisted, therefore, that we always eat, drink, live, dress, and travel in style, courtesy of the host company.

The key to Sheridan Associates lay in the firm's first commandment: Never win too big or too fast. A quick campaign only meant that the client got off cheap, Sheridan reminded us again and again. A big win was worse. Enthusiastic young consultants like myself liked to trounce the union, thus proving our prowess and, we figured, our worth to the company. But Sheridan frowned on landslides. To him, a lopsided election only meant the loss of a client. NLRB statistics showed that if a union won at least 30 percent of the vote, half the time it would return for a second organizing attempt, usually within a year. That could mean yet another counterorganizing job for Sheridan. To Jack, then, the closer the vote count the better. If the company barely squeaked by the union, he lectured, corporate execs would be convinced that the consultants had been necessary and would pay their bill gratefully. What's more, they would be likely to purchase a few months' worth of Sheridan's postelection management training package and call on Sheridan in the case of a renewed union attack. On the other hand, a big victory could start the company men wondering if they could have just as easily won the fight themselves. Maybe the union never had a chance, they would think, in which case Sheridan's bill for $60,000 would be pretty hard to swallow. "Don't kick the union's ass," was Sheridan's refrain. To do our job right, then, we had to beat the union and make it look hard.

Personally I always liked the big wins. They felt great, for one thing, and during my solo career I found that dramatic victories helped bring in the work. To Sheridan, however, a shutout only made our work look too easy.

During my time with Sheridan I was stationed in Cleveland, unhappily, since I had first applied for the job in hopes of escaping Ohio. The location of my home port mattered little, as it turned out, however. Sheridan was religious about never allowing consultants to work their hometown; the anti-union operations he assigned me were scattered across the country, and I traveled from Sunday through Friday. As the junior associate I inevitably drew the short straw, so I usually ended up in the most remote outposts: from St. Joseph's Infirmary in Louisville, Kentucky, to the Marvin Window plant in Warroad, Minnesota, to the Fraser Paper mill in Madawaska, Maine, to the Vollworth Sausage factory in Hancock-Houghton, Michigan, I traveled the country first observing, later assisting, and finally directing anti-union campaigns. As I skipped from campaign to campaign learning the method, Sheridan admonished me: "Absorb every technique from all the people you work with. But create your own style." The travel excited me, and often I stayed on assignment during the weekends, living for weeks at a time in a roadside motel in some forgotten village. Newly single and restless, and still smarting from my divorce, I found it more entertaining to be on my own, even if it was in some frozen town in northern Minnesota, than to be home with Mom and Dad and the memory of Iris.

After a few months of campaign hopping, Nick Sangalis decided it was time for the newest associate to take the lead on an anti-union drive. He sent me to Marquette, Michigan, on the state's upper peninsula, to battle the retail clerks union at the Angeli's Super Value grocery store.

The Super Value belonged to the powerful Angeli family, who owned several other businesses in Marquette as well as two other Super Values elsewhere in Michigan. Union proponents hoped to organize the one hundred or so checkers, butchers, box boys, and stock clerks at the Marquette store in order to insulate workers from the Angelis, whose family feud and economic hold on the town had made the employees fear for their jobs. In that campaign, more than in any before it, I learned to operate the basic machinery of union busting. The campaign included classic delay maneuvers before the NLRB; threats to have the store manager fired unless he cooperated in our anti-union drive; and wire taps on the motel telephone of the union organizer.

During the campaign I stayed at the only motel in town, which stood two doors down from the Super Value. I held the supervisor interviews in my motel room, there being nowhere else to go in Marquette. Since most of the supervisors were young women, I took great pleasure in the motel room encounters; once, the meeting turned into a spontaneous tryst as I ended up in bed with one of my captives. At the time I did not consider that the young woman could be regarded as a victim, particularly since it had been she who initiated the sexual liaison. Later I came to comprehend that the power we wielded as agents of the boss tainted all our relationships with workers—made all our encounters with employees manipulative at least and often abusive. I learned to use that power well.

I had a ball in Marquette—even learned to drive a snowmobile—but the Super Value job was anything but frivolous. One who learned the deadly seriousness of the campaign was Gary Peretto, the affable store manager who happened to support the union efforts of his co-workers. After watching Gary and asking other supervisors about him for several weeks, I realized he was doing more than sympathizing; he was cheering the union effort. At the root of his union support, it seemed, was an ongoing rivalry between Mike and Richard Angeli and their older brother, Libero. Gary sided with Libero, the company president, who kept his eyes hidden behind black sunglasses and played the role of the family godfather. In the other corner were Mike, the fat and comfortable director of a local bank, and brother Richard. Gary had been protecting pro-union employees with the blessings of Libero.

The complicity of the store manager with the union activists created an obstacle I did not know how to overcome. So I asked for help from Nick Sangalis, who was keeping an eye on me throughout the campaign. Nick didn't hesitate. "Get him over here," he commanded. "You're going to learn how to shape these people up."

When Gary arrived at the motel room, we spent a couple of minutes on small talk, then took our places, with Gary and me sitting on chairs facing Nick, who sat on the edge of the bed. Nick abruptly abandoned his congenial tone.

"Gary, I hear you're fucking us," he said with an icy stare. Immediately Gary's smile disappeared; his eyes darkened. Nick went on in a modulated voice: "You're not doing your job, Gary. You know what happens if you don't do your job, don't you? It would sure be a shame if you lost your job at Super Value. You'd be pretty hard-pressed to find another one. Where are you going to go?" The performance demonstrated the clear advantage union busters have, particularly in smaller towns and in regions dependent on one industry. The threat on Gary's job was simple, straightforward, and, by the way, perfectly legal under labor law, since it was directed toward a management employee.

One Super Value maneuver that *was* clearly illegal was the wire tap we arranged on the telephone of the retail clerks organizer. The nearest retail clerks local was based in Green Bay, Wisconsin, so organizers were forced to camp out at motels the same way we did. There were only half a dozen motels in and around Marquette, and the chief union organizer and I found ourselves sleeping only a few doors away from each other whenever he was in town. Nick saw the rare opportunity, and he mentioned to Mike Angeli that it would be fabulous if we could eavesdrop on union organizers as they planned their activities. Say no more: Mike arranged for the motel PBX operator to ring my room whenever the organizer placed or received a phone call and to plug his line into mine if I was available. There I sat in my room with a reel-to-reel tape recorder and a suction-cup microphone fixed on the telephone receiver, privy to the private conversations of my opponent. As often as not, I ended up listening as he talked to his wife.

In the second week of the campaign I was trained on the most basic tool of union busting: Nick called to say it was time for me to write my first "Dear Fellow Employee" letter. I was terrified. I had read the other consultants' letters many times but had no idea how to write one. I sat in my motel room puzzling over the task, reading the sample letters I carried in my briefcase. But I was frozen with fear and couldn't come up with a single sentence. In a panic, I telephoned the lead attorney on the case, the renowned management-labor lawyer Phil Lederer. Lederer liked me and was glad to help. He gave me an impromptu lesson in propaganda, thus furnishing me with the framework for the letters and fliers I would compose throughout my career. He recited a few simple rules: Keep the letter simple by addressing only one subject and limiting it to one page; make it readable with clever word play; emphasize strategic words and phrases with capital letters and underlines; never capitalize the name of the union; write the way you talk. Lederer then proceeded to compose the entire letter himself, reciting it extemporaneously over the phone. The dispatch was brilliant, packed full of alliterative jabs at the union crafted in exaggerated prose: "All this union wants to do is get a PIECE of your PAYCHECK," it warned. When Sangalis saw the letter he praised it as one of the best he had ever read. He also recognized it as Lederer's and commended me for having sought the attorney's help. Within management circles Lederer's artful use of both the language and the legal system was legendary.

Lederer relished melodrama. Aging, lanky, and bald as a cue ball with a hearing aid sticking out of each ear, he made a comical performer. To dramatize his displeasure at the opinion of an NLRB hearing officer at one hearing I attended, Lederer thrust his bony, naked head forward and, fixing an angry look on the hearing officer, switched off both hearing aids with an exaggerated gesture. Such theatrics worked well for Lederer, who understood not only the subtleties of labor law, but also the foibles of unions and of human nature as perhaps no one else in the business. Lederer's specialty was delay tactics, for he understood that management would almost always win a war of attrition.

Lederer's centerpiece technique, now a common strategy among management lawyers, was to challenge everything. He tried to take every challenge to a full hearing, then prolonged each hearing as much as he could. Finally he appealed every unfavorable decision. In one case Lederer hired a photographer to take thousands of pictures of a factory that was in the midst of an organizing drive, purportedly to show that the voting unit was not properly defined. He then submitted the photographs into evidence one by one, a deadly, tedious process that took days. Almost invariably Lederer refused to work out agreements with the union on such issues; called "stipulations" in legal lexicon, out-of-court agreements on matters of fact are meant to save court time and speed the legal process. But such legal congeniality would short-circuit the Lederer strategy. He knew that if he could make the union fight drag on long enough, workers would lose faith, lose interest, lose hope.

Since a law degree is not required to practice before the NLRB, Lederer often, and quite happily, found himself facing off with a union business agent rather than a fellow attorney. Clearly he held the advantage; there was no reason to agree to anything. Lederer also understood that NLRB hearing officers, who generally did not have extensive legal training themselves, often were ill prepared to control the sophisticated big-city labor lawyers hired by companies. He always knew where to hit, and he delivered his punches with flair. Whether in a letter, at a hearing, or at the bargaining table, the Lederer touch could disintegrate a union effort.

By introducing me to Phil Lederer, the Super Value case laid the foundation for my future achievements. Lederer, more than anyone else, was responsible for my labor education. The veteran attorney grew fond of me through the nine-month campaign, and I came to think of him as a beloved, if irascible, professor. During many long, cold evenings in Marquette, Phil and I met at the local steak house, where we ate beef from the Angelis' cattle ranch and drank red wine while he entertained me with stories from his rich past. Phil taught me the genesis and evolution of modern union-evasion methods, and he gave me a private tour of the snug alliance between labor attorneys and anti-union consultants.

I was exhilarated by my work at Sheridan. Sure, I knew we played hardball—that's what made it fun—but I had swallowed the Sheridan ruse. I accepted the argument that however hurtful our campaign tactics, in the end we were helping a company to better itself by compelling management to recognize and correct its deficiencies. That's what my brethren said, and I believed them. Why not? After all, we were family. Even more intoxicating to me than the work was the warmth and camaraderie I felt among the Sheridanites. Like any boys' club, we drank together, traded tales of conquest—on the job and in the bedroom—and talked in code. Sheridan fostered the secret-society aura of his organization, holding monthly two-day staff meetings in the glamour of swank executive clubs or in the gilded privacy of Bear Lodge, his one-hundred-acre wooded estate on the Lac du Flambeau Indian Reservation in Wisconsin. There we ate fine meals, talked business, went fishing, shot pool, and drank and drank and drank. Each year Sheridan staged even more elaborate events for regular and prospective clients. At those annual conventions, which Jack called JSA outings, we staff members worked as escorts, drivers, and valets to the executive guests. Sheridan, the master of manipulation, assured that the outings would be lively by booking speakers sure to anger and excite his distinguished guests.

I attended what was perhaps Sheridan's most inspired outing in 1972, when he invited Saul Alinsky, the late celebrated organizer of the Ladies' Garment Workers Union and champion of the downtrodden, to address 150 or so executives of the banking and insurance industries. Sheridan kept his guest's identity a secret until the day of the speech; when Alinsky was introduced, a rumble of protest rose from the three-piece-suit crowd. As the CEOs fidgeted and sputtered, Alinsky stormed in from the back of the hall. A wiry, wrinkled man with a shock of unkempt gray hair marched angrily down the center aisle, stopping every few feet to deliver a malevolent glare into the eyes of one executive after another. When he reached the podium, Alinsky affected a tone of reverence and thanked his illustrious audience for all the fine work they had done over the years as managers and owners of businesses.

"I want you to know how grateful I am to you for keeping us working for so long," Alinsky began with a wink. "You have been such assholes and such idiots that we have had great success." Alinsky then launched an attack on American management for the shameful way it continued to treat its workers. "Keep up the good work," he admonished. "In the end, it's not unions that organize employees, it's stupid, inept management."

From my first meeting with Sheridan I thought he was brilliant, but he proved it to me definitively with the Alinsky ploy. It was uncanny: he had managed to use a prominent labor radical to market his union-busting outfit.

When I entered the world of Sheridan men—and an occasional woman—I had more to learn than the philosophy and technique of the union-prevention ruse. There were social conventions as well, and those almost always involved alcohol. Drinking was a continuous exercise among Sheridan associates and indeed a requisite activity throughout union-busting culture. For me, however, it was a difficult skill to master. When I joined Sheridan I hated the taste of alcohol and could barely tolerate a drink. But my lack of prowess at the bar was unacceptable. There was no room for lightweights in the Sheridan clan. That was made clear one evening in a Huntsville, Alabama, steak house during my first campaign. As I joined in the hilarity with fellow consultants and the executives from Automatic Electric—a division of GTE—who were paying us to keep the union out of their Huntsville plant, I felt myself sinking into a stupor under the weight of the relentless drinking. Nick Sangalis took note of my condition and, not wanting to embarrass me or the firm, quickly dragged me out of the restaurant and loaded me onto the backseat of our rented car. He made it clear I would have to do something about my little problem. After that I worked on my drinking day by day. It was unpleasant at first, but it got easier with time. After a year I could down shots of Scotch all night just like the rest of them. Another year and I couldn't be without it.

Throughout my Sheridan years I admired my colleagues, even idolized them the way a boy reveres his older brothers and uncles. Most were very kind to me, initiating me patiently into the Sheridan clan and sharing their personal formulas for success in corporate back rooms. I cared so much for my companions that the day Jim Bannon stood up at a Bear Lodge meeting to tell us he was leaving, I actually cried. Bannon, with tears in his eyes and a quiver in his voice, explained that he had decided to go back to college to get a postgraduate degree. It was a painful decision, he said, because of the devotion he felt for John Sheridan and for his other friends in the firm. The announcement was followed by embraces, tears, and heartfelt toasts. Much later we were to learn that Bannon had not returned to school at all but had started his own union-busting firm, a company called Management Board, and had

taken some Sheridan clients with him. Although the Bannon episode hurt me, I felt honored to be a part of the exclusive Sheridan
society.

I would not always feel that way, for one night during my first
year a tiny seed of doubt was planted. It happened as I was enjoying a rare dinner engagement with the guru himself: Sheridan, who
rarely socialized individually with his employees, had asked me to
join him for dinner at Stouffers in Cleveland in order to meet John
Rogers, the top industrial relations man at Cleveland Trust Bank,
later called Ameritrust. Not long before, Sheridan had managed to
beat the Laborers International Union in a drive to organize tellers
and other operations people at the bank. The dinner was meant as
a celebration of sorts and a chance to introduce Rogers to a rising
star from his hometown. After a leisurely meal and the customary
several rounds of drinks, Sheridan excused himself to use the rest
room. Rogers seized the opportunity to praise Sheridan, who not
only had beaten the Laborers International Union, but had trained
Cleveland Trust officers to manage the bank in a way that would
keep the union out. "Jack does great work," Rogers confided, leaning across the table. "He taught me the most important word in
this business. You know what I mean?"

I was sure I did, and I answered, "You mean communication,
don't you?"

Rogers looked stunned. Then he chuckled. "Well, you got the
first letter right. No, Marty, the word is control," he scolded. "You
should know that."

After that night I began to see that the business was, indeed,
all about control. I realized that control was both the objective and
the method in union busting. I learned that it was essential for me
to gain complete control of a company the moment I walked in
the door if I was to forward my plan. And I began to understand
that the success of my plan meant, quite plainly, that management
would continue to wield absolute control over its workers—that
lust for control is, of course, what moved chief executives to agree
to hand over control to us; they swallowed their pride for a few
months; then, when we were through, they got us out of the building as fast as they could.

With my eyes opened just a slit by the dinner conversation with
Rogers, I began to see a multitude of ways in which Sheridan
abused not only his clients, but his associates. And I came to know
that his subordinates despised him for it. Sheridan's *hypocrisies*

shouldn't have surprised me, for I knew from the beginning that he was a provocative character. Bravado saturated his business dealings, sometimes even in relations with his own staff, and the staff resented it. They resented Sheridan's waltzing into their campaigns to collect his fat per diem fee while helping himself to the perks, telephones, and secretaries that they had come to think of as their own. They resented the salaries he paid, substantial as the money was, knowing that if they were out on their own, they could make as much on one or two big campaigns. But most of all, Sheridan's stable of consultants resented the fact that the sire kept the plums for himself. During the late 1960s and early 1970s, the most coveted labor consulting clients were banks. At that time, unions had banking executives in a panic. Many unions had their pension money in the National Bank of Washington, and they had succeeded in organizing tellers and other operations people there. Managers at banks throughout the East feared that their institutions would fall next, and they called on Sheridan to help. Such powerhouse institutions as Chemical Bank and Chase Manhattan Bank in New York brought in Sheridan to give speeches, seminars, and workshops on union prevention and to run training programs at bank branches. Naturally Sheridan did most of that work on his own; he never seemed to mind the company of bankers or the billings he kept for himself.

Yet when I got the itch to leave in 1972, it was not born of resentment. I was still in awe of Sheridan, as irritating as he may have been. But I was sick of Cleveland. I thought it was stale and horrid. Having traveled the continent for the previous three years, I was eager to leave Ohio behind, and as many midwesterners do, I saw California in my future. I put in a call to Sheridan from my parents' home, where I stayed when I was not on campaign duty. By now I was recognized as one of the hot dogs of the firm, and Sheridan himself had told me I was destined to be one of the best in the business. I figured he might indulge me just a bit and grant my wish to emigrate to the Golden State. I proposed starting a Sheridan branch in Los Angeles or San Francisco. Sheridan may have been pleased with me, but he was not pleased enough to squash the egos of the few longtime associates who had remained loyal. If a California office were opened, surely one of his more senior consultants would want the job. However, Sheridan had an alternative offer: perhaps I would be interested in moving to Chicago and working out of headquarters. For the moment I accepted.

Sheridan put a consultant named Alex Hornkohl, who had been hired at the same time as I, in charge of finding me a place in Chicago.

I jumped into my brand-new silver Lincoln Mark IV and headed up the turnpike for Chicago. Still, I just couldn't get California out of my mind. It was a freezing January day, that thick, gray kind of cold that always gets midwesterners dreaming about faraway places. I had been to Los Angeles with Iris years before and more recently had visited a college buddy in San Francisco. In my behind-the-wheel reverie I felt the warm sun, I saw ocean waves spill onto the sand, I gazed through the fog across a calm green bay at the Golden Gate Bridge. There just had to be a way to get out there.

When I arrived in Chicago, Alex Hornkohl greeted me with good news: he had found an apartment. It was in a high rise called Eugenie Towers, not far from Sheridan's office downtown. We could see it that afternoon. Great. Things might have turned out differently if Alex had not gone out for a while, leaving me alone in his apartment. In my solitude I began thinking again about California; I was determined to have my way. If Sheridan wouldn't send me out west, then perhaps someone else would. I grabbed the phone and asked the Chicago operator for the number of Melnick, McKeown and Mickus.

While I waited for Herb Melnick to take my call, I prepared myself to do some smooth talking. It was hardly necessary. Herb told me straight off that he had heard good things about me and invited me to his home that Saturday, where perhaps we could chat more comfortably. I always was touched when someone opened his home to me, so I had a good feeling about Herb from the start. I warmed up even more when I arrived at his sprawling ranch-style house in an upscale suburb. Beside the front door hung a mezuzah, a Hebrew inscription from the Torah displayed at many Jewish homes. The fact that Herb was Jewish suited me fine. I knew how to schmooze other Jews; drop in a Yiddish word here and there, throw in some color from my Jewish upbringing, and the two of us would be like family in no time.

The door was answered by Herb's wife, a friendly, matronly woman with a comforting look. She led me to the family room. There, I waited in the warmth of what seemed to me the ideal home, the domicile of a loving family. When Herb walked in, he completed the picture. Then in his middle forties, Herb looked as though he should have been in the dry-goods business. He was balding, paunchy, of average height and unassuming manner. In style, at least, he was as unlike John Sheridan as a person could be. We began our meeting with some easy chitchat, and I decided to dismiss up front the gangster image that Sheridan had painted for me.

"I've heard a lot about you, as you can imagine," I said with a chuckle. "You look like a nice enough person to me. From all I'd heard I expected to walk into Captain Hook's office."

Herb smiled. He reciprocated by revealing what he knew of me: "I've heard great things about you from Phil Lederer. He says you're quite a comer." Then, more directly, "What do you want from me?"

I confessed my lust for California and said Phil had told me Three M had recently opened a Los Angeles office. I wondered if I could be of help out there.

"Where would you like to work?" Herb wanted to know.

I picked San Francisco. "I'm a good salesman," I announced. "I know how to bring in work. I could help you open that market."

As our conversation progressed, and it seemed I might well be joining Three M, Herb decided I should meet his partner, Tony McKeown. He called McKeown at his home, and just a short while later in walked Tony, a tall, striking man with thick red hair and a rich Irish brogue.

I was in awe. In the company of Sheridan I had heard Tony described with many expletives, but the preferred epithet was "prick of pricks." Sheridan flew into a rage whenever he heard McKeown's name; he felt he had created Tony. Sheridan had also thought that he and Tony were close friends—the two had even lived together for a while—and he was deeply wounded by Mc-Keown's betrayal. I played Tony by telling him all I had heard about him; he seemed to relish it. He played me by pouring on the Emerald Isle warmth and gaiety, a routine I came to refer to as his "Irish jig." Tony was a lovable, despicable character. Smooth and seductive, he seemed to thrill at the knowledge that he was feared. He bore the reputation as the most lethal in the business. A fiery-tempered man, McKeown referred to just about everyone as a "motherfucker." Sheridan had met Tony in the early 1960s and lured him away from Ford Motor Company, where McKeown was working as a labor relations executive. As Sheridan saw it, he molded his disciple into the big-ticket consultant Tony ultimately became, taught him everything. Yet rather than gratitude, Tony showed contempt: at the time of the MMM split, Sheridan suspected, it had been Tony's idea to send the letter announcing that Sheridan Associates had been dissolved.

Still, I found Tony to be a most beguiling fellow, full of wit and charm. His one soft spot was his beloved Ireland. A native of Northern Ireland and defiantly Catholic, Tony waxed lyrical when speaking of his homeland and his family. He drank almost patriotically—Irish whiskey and Scotch—and regaled dinner parties with tales of the old country. Tony had married his boyhood sweetheart, Ann, and pampered her. As an example, when Ann was due to deliver their child, Tony rented a hospital suite for her and had her admitted in advance of labor so she would not be in any danger should her waters break while he was on the road. Tony seemed the archetypal Irish family man, loving and genuine. Eventually, however, he abandoned all that. By 1985 Tony's seemingly wholesome family life had rotted through; Ann had filed for divorce.

But on that first day, I was as dazzled by McKeown as I was touched by Melnick. I liked them, and they both seemed to like me. They were eager to pick another plum from the Sheridan tree, but I would have to earn one more stamp of approval before being inducted into MMM. Tom Crosbie, who grudgingly shared the executive vice-presidency of Three M with partner Ray Mickus, directed the firm's West Coast business from his home on the Los Angeles seacoast. In the way Sheridan had sent me to interview with Nick Sangalis three years earlier, Melnick and McKeown insisted I meet Crosbie, since he would be overseeing my work. The partners handed me some air checks, a type of air travel credit voucher widely used in business, and told me I should meet with Crosbie the following weekend.

Crosbie and his wife, Ellen, lived in a rambling home in Palos Verdes Estates, an elegant neighborhood overlooking the gorgeous Palos Verdes peninsula on the southwestern tip of Los Angeles. Tom's home was big and warm and wonderful, and so was Tom. A good-looking man about ten years older than I, Tom stood over six feet tall, boasted a head full of thick, black hair, and spoke in a rich, baritone voice. He laughed easily and opened his home to me so completely that I liked him immediately. We spent the weekend talking business and enjoying a particularly balmy L.A. January. By the time I was to catch my plane back to Chicago, I couldn't imagine a more fabulous place to live than California or a better man to work for than Tom Crosbie.

I left Tom knowing I had made a good impression and almost sure he and his partners would decide to hire me. I was just as sure that Jack Sheridan would send me to hell when he found out what I had done. Daydreams of California tussled with my dread of facing Sheridan, turning my car into a mental torture chamber during the drive home from O'Hare Airport. The moment I arrived at my parents' house I ran inside to call Crosbie. I had to know immediately. Good news, he said. Call Herb right away. Herb offered to put me in charge of a new San Francisco office and match my Sheridan salary. I had two weeks to get out to the West Coast. My dream had come true; the nightmare was about to begin.

The two weeks were generous, as Herb must have known. Sheridan was not going to let me work another day knowing I would be leaving. To Sheridan, to quit was to become a traitor. There would be no final days, no long good-byes. I sensed that, and not wanting to face Jack directly, I called Nick Sangalis instead. I couldn't bring myself to admit even to Nick that I would be joining the enemy. So I lied. I was moving to California, I said; just couldn't stand the Midwest anymore. No, I didn't know what I was going to do. Then I waited for Sheridan to find out. When he did, he was every bit as angry and as cold as I had feared. In his characteristic "you can't quit, you're fired" huff, Sheridan told me to go away and not come back. I was a disgrace.

I never saw Jack Sheridan again; seventeen years later he was still telling people I had been fired.

Paradise

My California days were anchored in Marin County, home of the redwood hot tub, the wealthiest county in the state, and cradle of 1970s hedonism. There I lived an enchanted existence amid the wooded hills just across the Golden Gate Bridge from San Francisco. When I first arrived on the coast, I was taken in by an old high school and college friend named Michael Krasny, and his wife, Leslie. The couple were kind to me during my stay; I relished the feel of my surrogate family. But after a couple of months it was clear I should have found a place of my own long before. I combed the classifieds of the *Marin Independent Journal* for days and finally circled an ad for a country home rental tucked in the semi-rural affluence of Fairfax. It sounded perfect. No phone number was listed, so it was up to me to hunt down the mystery house on Holly Road. I navigated my hulking Lincoln Mark IV along the narrow winding roads of the Marin hills until we happened upon Holly Road and arrived at a charming hillside chalet. The house seemed like something out of a storybook, at once wonderful and frightening. It stood alone, set back from the road amid the lush hillside flora. An elegant cabin it was, built of redwood shingles, but it seemed to be made more of glass: great windows stretched along each wall, inviting in the sunlight and exposing the tastefully decorated interior to the outside world.

I took it.

The serenity that enveloped Holly Road was something I had never known. Part of me loved the home, felt comforted by the solitude it afforded. But I was never one for much reflection, never particularly liked being alone. So the place also made me nervous.

As it happened, I never had the chance to grow accustomed to Holly Road's silence and splendor, for geographical irony had followed me out west. I may have lived in Eden, but I spent most of my time in that purgatory of the Midwest—Detroit. Just days after I had settled at Holly Road, Tom Crosbie called to tell me to pack up. I was going to Motown. There I was to serve as an on-site consultant at the privately owned Harper Grace Hospital downtown, where two thousand janitors, housekeepers, and cafeteria workers were struggling to unionize. For the next six months I flew red-eye flights to Detroit on Sundays and returned home Friday nights, which left me just a day and a half at a time to recover from jet lag and enjoy Holly Road and San Francisco. I worked Harper Grace under the direction of Sheridan defector Jim Bannon, who had merged his St. Louis consulting firm, the Management Board, with Three M just a few months earlier. Meanwhile Crosbie led another bunch of Three M consultants in an attack on an organizing drive involving the two thousand or so service workers at another private facility just a few blocks away, the Henry Ford Hospital, which was endowed by the Ford Motor Company.

The pace was exciting. But those twin campaigns were just a morsel for Three M, which would grow fat busting hospital union drives over the next eight years. During the 1970s, the ferocious anti-unionism of hospital administrators across the country would transform Three M from a primarily local consulting firm into a multimillion-dollar business with more than one hundred practitioners on three continents. The health care industry, more than any other, made Three M the union-busting giant it became.

I joined Three M just as a ground swell of union organizing hit the U.S. health care industry. During the 1960s administrators of hospitals and nursing homes across the country watched with horror as their housekeepers, cooks, and nurse's aides took to the streets by the thousands in virulent protest of the poverty and indignity imposed on them by their employers. Union fever ran particularly hot at nonprofit hospitals, which employed some 40 percent of all health care workers but where workers had not yet won the legal right to organize. Service employees at those facilities, mostly blacks and other minorities, were paid as little as $25 for a sixty-hour week in some regions. In anger and desperation, and despite the lack of legal protection, workers at nonprofits formed unions and demanded recognition. The inevitable refusal by management led to strikes and work stoppages, often prolonged, sometimes violent, and always frightening to the community. Meanwhile Congress came under siege by labor leaders and hospital workers, who insisted that the National Labor Relations Act be amended to extend collective bargaining rights to employees of the nonprofits.

Three unions were attempting to organize health care workers in the 1960s and 1970s. Of those the most vigorous—and most reviled by employers—was Local 1199 of the New York–based Retail, Wholesale and Department Store Employees Union, affectionately known as 1199. Later reorganized as the National Union of Hospital and Health Care Workers Union Local 1199, the union flourished under the charismatic direction of Leon Davis, a forceful and politically progressive labor leader. Organizing among nonprofits had begun as early as 1959, when thousands of service workers at New York public hospitals walked off their jobs and into the streets to demand union recognition. The strike grew violent, the citizenry was horrified, and the workers lost. But the war had not ended; another mass strike in 1962 was even more frightening. Organizing was slow; working in the employers' favor was a public terrified by the virtual closure of their hospitals and horrified by the violence in the streets. But 1199 was relentless. The union fight became increasingly aggressive and effective under Davis. Then an era of triumphs began. The state of New York passed a law that granted employees of nonprofits the right to union recognition. Similar events occurred across the country: New Jersey ended a rash of strikes with a judicial decision; California and several other states passed laws similar to that of New York; and in 1968, in my hometown of Cleveland, the city fathers voted to give hospital workers there the right to organize. By the early 1970s 1199 was known as one of the most ferocious labor unions in the country.

Local 1199 entered the 1970s emboldened by its triumphs and determined to abolish nonunion hospitals. With the help of in-house films depicting the devastating financial and emotional hardships suffered by the families of hospital workers and dramatizing union triumphs, the union managed to turn public opinion in its favor as it convinced more and more workers to fight the system. But by the time I was plotting tactics and querying supervisors in a back room at Harper Grace, Three M had turned the union propaganda pieces into forceful anti-union tools. The most celebrated film, *Like a Beautiful Child,* documented a one-hundred-day strike in 1969 by five hundred South Carolina hospital workers, mostly black women, who demanded the right to organize. In the film, weary workers lamented the horrid conditions of hospital service employees and sang the praises of 1199, which eventually won the organizing drive as well as substantial raises for the workers. Designed to arouse union sympathies and motivate organizers, the film was twisted into a unique anti-union motivational device for Three M kick-off meetings. We particularly liked a scene in which a very fat, very dark female face fills the screen, and the woman says in a thick southern drawl, "Jes' gimme eleven nahhhnty-nahhhn." That always drew snickers. We deftly used *Like a Beautiful Child* at hospitals and factories alike, to awaken within the mostly white supervisor corps a hatred of blacks, fear of violence, contempt for women, mistrust of the poor, and, of course, a loathing for the union that brought together all those despicable elements. We didn't say much when we showed the film. We didn't have to; with a few well-chosen remarks, we tapped the fears that resided in the hearts of our listeners. Robert Meuhlenkamp, director of organizing at 1199 throughout the 1970s, told me when I spoke to him almost twenty years later, that he considered Three M's use of the film hateful but also very typical of the union-busting industry: "Imagine . . . using this story of bravery, of workers struggling for recognition, to make people laugh at the Negroes. It only reveals what slime these people are."

With union organizing gaining momentum in the 1970s, health care executives were in a panic; and the folks in the union-prevention trade were ecstatic. Business exploded. Since at least 1970 Sheridan and Three M had recognized the profit potential in the health care industry, and they had been carting their anti-union road show to industry association meetings, conventions, and conferences around the country. The timely performances yielded many years' worth of business for the two firms and their cadre of labor lawyers. Hospital executives stampeded to workshops on union evasion; commanded supervisors to attend anti-union training courses; purchased union-prevention kits; and, in desperation, contracted for counterorganizing campaigns. They bought just about any union-busting product the consultants could concoct. If a comparable union-organizing boom were to occur in one industry today, the benefits to union-avoidance specialists would be spread among the more than ten thousand anti-union consultants and attorneys at work across the country. But in 1973 there was just a handful of us. The bulk of the union-fighting dollars were divided between Sheridan and MMM, and Three M made millions off hospitals alone.

In 1974, with the blessing of the American Hospital Association, which wanted to end the devastating chaos within its industry, President Nixon signed an NLRA amendment into law, giving employees at the nonprofits the right to collective bargaining. Then the union-busting dam burst open. Although 1199 and other unions had organized a great number of nonprofits before passage of the law, the amendment acted as a catalyst of fear on hospital administrators, particularly those in charge of small facilities where workers had felt they didn't have the strength in numbers to force union recognition, as did workers at huge big-city hospitals. Under the new law a union was but an election away. Local 1199 filed thousands of organizing petitions in the wake of the 1974 amendment. That, of course, meant thousands of jobs for anti-union consultants: "Union busters saw a ripe field, and they went after it," said 1199 organizer Meuhlenkamp.

Indeed, Sheridan and MMM were ready. The two firms had developed extensive client lists of hospitals, clinics, and nursing homes during the preamendment years, and Three M in particular had fattened its staff in order to cope with the seemingly endless demand. In 1978, a peak year for Three M, the firm claimed to have more than five hundred hospital clients. For Sheridan, hospitals were a sideline. Even as he drummed up hospital work, he continued to concentrate on the banking and insurance industries, where he had the advantage of a well-worn welcome mat. But Herb Melnick and company had no such cash cow; they went after the health care world with the vigor of conquistadors. And conquer they did. Former hospital union organizer Meuhlenkamp believes that Three M alone cost him hundreds of thousands of members during his organizing days. That counts not just the workers at hospitals where Three M squashed organizing attempts, but all those at neighboring facilities who witnessed the bloody union losses and decided not to risk one themselves. "If they watched all the workers at the only other hospital in town try to organize and saw all that happened to them, only to lose, they weren't going to attempt the same thing," Meuhlenkamp told me.

I hated commuting to smoky Detroit from radiant San Francisco. The dismal commute had its compensations, however. Like other corporate executives, the Detroit hospital directors were so obsessed with beating the union that they spared no expense to keep us in luxury while we plied our trade. While in Detroit we were treated as royalty, pampered and coddled around the clock. The hospital executives found us the finest accommodations in town, at the ultrachic Detroit Athletic Club. The club was a regal downtown hideaway for three generations of blue bloods. It reeked of corporate wealth and flaunted its affluence with its stately club room, elegant dining room, handsome handball courts, and an exquisite mahogany bar that served the finest liquor to silk-stockinged alcoholics. So exclusive was the blue-blooded heritage of the club that guests joked that the ashes of distinguished deceased members were kept in the fine porcelain urns that adorned the club room. All club guests were white, all the service workers blacks dressed in the traditional uniform of male servants to the upper class, tails and white gloves included. The club was the most pretentious place I had ever seen. I was amused. There was one glitch in our lodging plans, however. At the time, labor leaders and union busters shared a common heritage: most were either Irish or Jewish. To corporate America, however, the latter were still undesirable. Jews were not permitted in the Detroit Athletic Club. So, his own lineage notwithstanding, Herb Melnick instructed fellow Three M consultant David Schwartz and me to adopt fictitious identities during our stay in Detroit, so as not to embarrass our hosts. We appropriated WASPish surnames and, under that cover, enjoyed our venture into American aristocracy. As we mingled with the corporate elite, David and I were pleased that the distinguished guests disregarded certain physical characteristics of ours that, in other circumstances, they would have interpreted as decidedly Semitic.

For the six-month campaign at Harper Grace, Jim Bannon and his gang ordered several hospital rooms set up as interview stations and secured the main conference room for group meetings. I spent most of my time interviewing young women supervisors in the disquieting privacy of a hospital room, cranking out letters, and playing caddy for Bannon at his witty and melodramatic group presentations. Bannon insisted on calling supervisors to two or three meetings a week, ensuring that they would see the union drive as cumbersome and intrusive. When the troops were sufficiently cranky from the fight, he delivered a most convincing piece of counsel: You'd better win, because you sure don't want to have to go through this again.

As burdensome as the meetings may have been to his audience, for Jim Bannon they were invigorating, for he loved the stage. He kept all the key performances for himself and was always terrific. I learned a lot from him. Bannon wasn't handsome, really, but he was very appealing, particularly to women. He made the best of his pleasant looks, self-consciously dressing his slender figure in tailored three-piece suits and combing his fine brown hair into a boyish wave that swooped down over his forehead. Bannon sported an easy, clean smile and textured his conversation with witty small talk. By the time of the Harper Grace campaign he was in his mid-thirties, but his youthful charm was as fresh as ever. People liked Jim; he quickly won their trust. In job after job Jim's victims seemed always to want to please him, and he made efficient use of their loyalty.

Meuhlenkamp, the 1199 organizer, says union leaders were caught off guard by Three M in the early 1970s. It wasn't until about 1977 that organizers were familiar with the personalities and tactics of Three M and other anti-union consulting firms. But even armed with that knowledge, they often found themselves over-whelmed by their enemy. Meuhlenkamp explains why:

"Union busters wield great power through their program of terror and manipulation—people don't, can't possibly know what's going on and who's telling the truth. You have to appreciate that most of the people [at a workplace] are just regular people. They in their lives have no experience with violence, with being lied to, with manipulation, with being harassed in open, gross, insulting ways. The first time this program happens to regular people, they're terrified. Their fondest wish after a few months of this is that it would just go away and go back to being like it was. The union busters know this. None of this is intellectual at all. It works on the gut."

We worked on the guts of Harper Grace employees for six full months. I guess they had strong stomachs, though. We lost. Workers voted in the union.

At Henry Ford it went the other way. Executives triumphed, probably due as much to union infighting as to Three M sabotage. There, three unions had competed for the employees' loyalties, a situation rarely seen these days. In the early 1970s the AFL-CIO had not yet succeeded in convincing its member unions to embrace the principle of jurisdictional respect that reigns today, and unions fought one another with regularity. The four-choice ballot at Henry Ford—the choices being one of the three unions or none—made work very easy for Three M. The unions were tearing each other apart, and all the consultants really had to do was egg them on. Even with a solid majority of workers favoring organization, no single union could overcome the doubt planted by its competitors and cultivated by Crosbie and company. None managed to garner enough votes for a win. Despite an almost guaranteed victory, Three M was taking no chances. When a blizzard hit Detroit on election day, the company managers hurriedly called all the taxi companies in town and had them pick up anti-union employees and shuttle them to the polling place. The hospital also dispatched company-owned four-wheel-drive Fords to the more remote residences, to ensure that every "no" vote was cast.

During my fleeting weekends back at Holly Road, there wasn't time to do much more than inhale the beauty of Marin and mope about how horrible it was back in Detroit. Since I coveted every hour I spent in California, the one endeavor I made time for early on was a thorough research of San Francisco–Detroit flight schedules. I wanted to take the airline with the latest Sunday night departure from San Francisco—and so it was that the first-class cabin of American Airlines became my skyway home twice each week. And so it was, also, that I met the beauty who would become my partner in a very turbulent yet enduring marriage.

There I sat, chain smoking as usual and looking out the dinky jet plane window, already bored in anticipation of the five-hour flight that awaited me. I never read on the planes; I didn't like books enough to bring one, and I wasn't drawn to the glib airlines magazines. Instead I spent the hours drinking and smoking, day-dreaming, and occasionally joking with the other first-class travelers. I also liked to flirt with the stewardesses; they were so beautiful and always cheery. The playful banter made the time pass more quickly. But one Friday evening an air hostess appeared in the cabin whose presence made all my past flirtations seem silly and trite. She was gorgeous, slender and delicately curved, with thick golden hair that tumbled down her back past her waist. She moved gracefully, almost gliding throughout the cabin. Her voice was soothing, her smile soft and genuine, her laugh delightful. I couldn't take my eyes off her. I desperately wanted to get her attention, but as I considered various overtures I embarrassed even myself. So stunning a creature as this surely had heard every conceivable male hunting line and just as surely had dismissed them. The tag pinned above the left breast pocket of her trim navy blue uniform announced the name *Alice*. Moved by Alice's grace, I spent the next few hours of the flight writing what ended up being an eight-page ode to the beauty of a woman I hardly knew.

During the weeks that followed I couldn't get Alice off my mind. Her image filled my days, fed my dreams, and woke me every morning. I was drowning in love. I had to do something. But what? So I wrote a second letter, this one more passionate than the first; I dropped it off for Alice at the American Airlines ticket counter of San Francisco International. And I waited. When, after a few weeks Alice still hadn't answered, I figured my "airborn" love was a bust.

Then, late one night, many months later, long after midnight, the phone jolted me out of a deep sleep. It was Alice. In a quivering voice, she said she was calling from a hospital where she lay bruised and aching from an automobile accident. She was lonely, scared, and in pain. She had received my two letters—which contained my phone number—and my eloquent impetuousness had touched her. Now she needed me, and I went running.

The next morning I drove out to San Leandro, a semi-industrial middle-class suburb just south of Oakland where, it turned out, Alice lived with her parents. On my way to the hospital I stopped at a florist and bought a hundred-dollar bouquet of orchids. Alice was overwhelmed. Our courtship had begun.

The courtship of Marty and Alice, like the house on Holly Road, was of storybook quality. We were a carefree, jet-setting pair of lovers living out an extravagant fantasy romance. We dined, drank, danced, and made love all across America, always in the finest establishments and usually at someone else's expense. Alice had the advantage of a stewardess job that took her traveling around the country—and furnished her with hotel rooms in all the great American metropolises from Boston to Phoenix. I had learned very well how to bill clients for nearly everything I did, so, with a stack of credit cards and a pile of prepaid air tickets, I was able to engineer a lavish love affair. Giddy with the excitement of our young passion, Alice and I plotted our rendezvous points every week. I juggled my Three M schedule and arranged for flights with oddball connections so that I could catch up with her wherever she was on layover. I was working in Detroit and living in San Francisco, so the client companies were paying for my round-trip flight between the two cities every week anyway. If I substituted my homebound trip with another flight, say, to Phoenix, where Alice would be on stopover, who was going to complain? The client might save a few pennies on the shorter flight, and I would get in a couple days of love.

In no time Alice Campouris had become my reason for living. As excited as I was about my accomplishments with Three M, my real creative energy went into romancing a ravishing twenty-four-year-old and making myself worthy of her. The way I saw it, nothing was too good for her; I could never do enough. As time went on, even as our personal troubles mounted, Alice continued to be the driving force in my life. Throughout the years, as we battled viciously over money, sexual infidelities, and the alcoholism that plagued us both, I never doubted that I wanted Alice in my life. She was my reason for remaining a union buster long after I could no longer feel good about it. The money and power the work brought me allowed me the illusion that I could continually buy her affection. Later, she would become my reason for leaving.

Despite the thrill of my itinerant romance, the commute between California and the Midwest was wearing me out. Alice and I spent our most memorable times not in a hotel suite in Boston or New York, but in the cozy serenity of Holly Road. There, on the rare occasion when we were both in the Bay Area, we threw parties, slept late, cooked breakfast together, went for long walks, and drank wine in the hot tub. I rarely got the pleasure of more than a few days at a time in California; by now I was determined to drum up some local business so that I could. Aggravating that itch was a pang of guilt at having sold myself to Three M as a rainmaker yet not having captured even one new client. I was uneasy about that, and the uneasiness was eating away at me one weekday morning as I sat in my sunny Holly Road living room browsing through the *San Francisco Chronicle*. Obligatory reading for all transplants to the hilly city is the daily column of Herb Caen, San Francisco oldtimer, commentator on the city's political and social scene, and three-dot journalist par excellence. There, at the top of the column, was this item:

LAST OF the rugged individualists. Oakland's Louis A. Celaya, senior representative of the Office and Professional Employees Union Local 29, now has a letter suitable for framing. Few days ago, he wrote to Edward J. Daly, board chairman of World Airways, suggesting a meeting to discuss Local 29's efforts to organize World workers. Daly's reply, signed with a flourish: "Go f— yourself."

Who was this Edward J. Daly fellow? I had no idea. But one thing I knew for sure: I wanted to work for him.

World Airways

When I met Edward J. Daly in November 1973, he was not widely known. Eighteen months later, however, on April 3, 1975, Ed Daly grabbed international headlines when his Oakland-based charter airlines company, World Airways, completed a wildcat evacuation of fifty-eight orphans from Vietnam. Newspapers had been following the story for weeks, chronicling the exploits of a gruff ex-boxer from Chicago's south side—multimillionaire, international business tycoon, daredevil adventurer, and theatrical sentimentalist. The news hounds wanted to be there—and Daly wanted them there—when he pulled off his most spectacular display of philanthropy. They had followed Daly to Danang, where he was clawed bloody, wounded in the stomach and head, and nearly killed as he and his crew fought amid machine-gun fire and exploding grenades to rescue Vietnamese children from the blood-letting that followed the American pullout from Vietnam. They related how he slugged South Vietnamese soldiers who were pushing aside women and children trying to board the plane, and how he strained for two hours to hold closed the rear door of the damaged 727 during the flight to Saigon. The newspeople followed him on to Saigon, where from his suite at the Caravelle Hotel he tussled with the South Vietnamese government, the U.S. embassy, Secretary of State Henry Kissinger, and even President Ford over the political urgencies of the on-again, off-again plan to save the children. Daly reportedly launched that famed first flight in defiance of Saigon airport tower officials. Newspapers covered the story lustily. They carried wire photos of the pugnacious, thick-faced Daly, sporting his trademark green beret and safari suit and displaying a heavily bandaged right arm, at a Saigon news conference where he announced the rebel flight. When the jet landed at Oakland International Airport a day later, the newspeople were there. Accompanying lengthy and dramatic accounts of the mercy mission were black-and-white photographs of crying children and sweet young women, of somber-looking pilots, of crowds gathered around the hull of a World Airways jet waiting to greet the most defenseless victims of the war in Southeast Asia. The next day the *Oakland Tribune* quoted an angry Ed Daly rebuking President Ford and Henry Kissinger for having ignored warnings that a massacre of refugees in South Vietnam and Cambodia was imminent. "I didn't even get the courtesy of an answer to my cables," Daly protested to the *Tribune*. That was Ed Daly.

At the time of Daly's airlift, newspapers also carried another, decidedly more lighthearted World Airways story. In the restrained prose of business journalism, newspapers reported World's proposal to offer regular $89 flights between the East and West coasts. The drastic cut in coast-to-coast air fares, from the typical price of $194, was a bold move in those years, when fares and routes were tightly regulated. That, too, was Ed Daly. Over the previous decade World Airways had become a household word throughout the country as the largest charter airline in the world. By the early 1970s 21,000 travelers a year gladly boarded World's crowded DC-8s for a bargain-priced journey to Europe, Asia, and the Middle East. They willingly tolerated the discomfort—the jets had been reconfigured to fit additional seats—for the chance to fly across the world for a fraction of the regular ticket price. The newly proposed scheduled service was, for Daly, a characteristically bold move and a unique challenge to the major airlines. As it turned out, the service would not be approved for six more years, during which time Daly tussled with federal regulators over volumes of objections lodged by the major airlines and watched his business descend into insurmountable debt.

When he dared to dive into competition with the likes of TWA, United Airlines, and American Airlines, Daly was known in the industry as the irreverent chief of a most unusual airline company. Daly was an outsider—simultaneously respected and resented by many of the more conventional airline executives. He was impetuous, unpredictable, and utterly arrogant; now abundantly generous, now shamefully tight. The same paternalistic boss who personally paid medical bills for the children of needy employees was also a raving maniac who once demoted a stewardess on his private plane for forgetting to replenish the A.1. sauce. Daly was severely alcoholic; when he died of kidney failure in 1984 at the age of sixty-one, friends said he looked at least twenty years older. Working or dealing with Daly was a complicated affair, and he inspired intense and conflicting emotions in those around him. They revered him, they despised him. He would not be told what to do; the only rules he followed were those proclaimed by him, and even then he would consider himself exempt. Do as much as imply to Ed Daly that there was a rule or a convention that bound him, and he would find the most spectacular, most destructive, and often most humiliating way of breaking it. The rules he hated most were those imposed on him by labor unions.

When I read Daly's name in the Herb Caen column, I didn't know a thing about World Airways, new as I was to the Bay Area. But I found out that, to Oakland, anyway, the company was a big deal. It was the Oakland Airport's leases to World that, more than anything else, gave the upcoming airport a chance at the big leagues. In 1973 World ran four major operations: the commercial charter business, a $60-million-a-year enterprise that made World the largest charter airline on earth; military airlifts under contract to the Department of Defense; aircraft leasing, with clients the likes of Jordan's King Hussein and the Republic of Yemen; and aircraft maintenance. In 1973 World had signed a forty-year lease with the Port of Oakland, which administers the airport, for a mammoth $14 million jet maintenance complex built for World by the port and the federal government. The maintenance facility soon became one of the Bay Area's largest business centers, employing two thousand workers within a two-hundred-thousand-square-foot hangar on a sixty-acre site at the entrance to the airport's general aviation field. In addition, World filled a large hangar deep within the airport compound, which served as corporate offices, and leased a terminal gate for commercial charter flights, by far the largest component of World Airways business at the time. World was traded publicly, listed both on the New York and Pacific stock exchanges, but really the company belonged to Ed Daly. The one-time pugilist and ex-GI built World from the ashes of a two-year-old debt-ridden cargo airline that he bought in 1950 for $50,000—legend has it that he made the purchase with winnings from poker games aboard a troop ship during World War II. Until his death Daly owned 80 percent of the stock.

World was a high-profile airline, owing to its ultrahigh-profile chairman. The company always seemed to be cooking up some daring business feat, taking on impossible foes, and confronting insurmountable odds. And it seemed always to be winning. But that image was somewhat distorted. "World was an insignificant airline, really," says David Mendelsohn, former deputy to Chairman Daly. "[But] Ed was a firm believer and a great practitioner of creating the image he wanted to create. His way of giving [the company] life, weight, was for him to appear bigger than life. It was his way of getting the airlines in the paper. The media focused on him as chairman, as a personality, and gave him the PR he wanted."

Despite its grand public face, by the time I was introduced to the company World Airways was already in trouble. Twelve long years before the company shut down everything but its minuscule leasing business, laid off thousands of workers, and pulled out of Oakland, the seeds of financial disaster were spreading their roots. In 1973 World Airways made a profit of just over $1 million, peanuts, really, considering the company's revenues that year were almost ten times as much. The company lost nearly $11 million on its four core businesses, only partly because of the oil crisis that year and resulting rise in fuel costs. The only way World managed to show a profit for 1973 was from the sale of a California bank, First Western Bank & Trust, which World (read Daly) had purchased in 1968. As with the rest of America, the year 1968 had been a pivotal one for World Airways. It is no coincidence that 1968 and 1969 were peak financial years at World Airways: the United States was at the height of its military involvement in Vietnam, and World was bringing in more than $50 million a year—accounting for more than one-third its annual revenues—in military contracts for cargo and passenger airlift services between the United States and overseas bases. By 1970 World's military contracts dropped almost to half, and they didn't recover until near the end of the decade, interestingly, after the Iran hostage taking.

Hidden within World's 1973 financial report was the essence of Daly's entrepreneurial forte: deal making. The charter business, although it grew to be huge and was considered the backbone of the company, never did make money for World, Mendelsohn said. In fact, World rarely made money on its continuing operations. But Daly had a Midas touch when it came to deals; buying and selling were his gifts. Ever since 1955, when he bought a fire-gutted DC-4 for $75,000, renovated it, flew it for five years, and still made a $100,000 profit off its sale, it was clear that Daly was a born negotiator. "That's what Daly did best," Mendelsohn said. Woe to those who sat across the bargaining table from him.

It was no secret that Daly longed to take on the major commercial airlines, to show them, by God. His foray into scheduled air service was proof that his dream of being one of the big boys was as constant as it was sincere. In a slap at his weighty competitors, Daly's newspaper advertising campaign promoting the scheduled service pictured World Airways as the biblical David slinging stones at the airline industry's Goliath. Nonetheless, the cowboy executive never sacrificed his other businesses to that ultimate ambition, for the leasing, airlift, and charter businesses afforded Daly an entrée into global affairs. Through his international business, both military and commercial, Edward J. Daly was able to play a part on a larger world stage and participate in major global events. In addition to his role during the Vietnam War, through World Airways Daly insinuated himself into the Hadj, the annual pilgrimage of Moslems to Mecca, providing charter service to the holy city; invested in Jordanian hotel resorts; and helped set up airlines in Jordan, Yemen, Mali, and South Korea. Daly was constantly on the prowl for other international deals as well and was forever flying off to the South Pacific or the Far East or Africa to confer with some powerful foreign head of state. According to Daly lore, the World Airways chieftain would drink and haggle over price for hours with kings and presidents, then settle the dispute with an arm-wrestling competition. Daly always won. His first mate knew why: "He would cheat," Mendelsohn says with a wink.

Despite Daly's lust for bartering, the ultimate deal he might strike was almost beside the point. The around-the-world sojourns played a more meaningful and much more complex role in the life and psychology of an impossibly complex human being: Daly's internationalism made him big and important and powerful. Often he put his greatness to work on behalf of the very meek. Daly never managed to establish the Samoan airlines he longed for, for example, but his perpetual dialogue with the Samoan government led to a close relationship between him and the highest-ranking Catholic clergyman in the islands. A proud and resolute Irish Catholic, Daly ended up donating a great deal of money over the years to the church projects and even financed the education of six Samoan students at the University of California at Davis. As compulsive in his charity as he was in other arenas of his life and work, Daly's benevolence sometimes took the form of highly publicized acts of philanthropic bravado, as in the Vietnam airlift. Other times his generosity was silent and sweet. Daly was known to pass out $100 bills to the diminutive residents of Bay Area orphanages every Christmas. He wrote out countless checks to nuns for their pet charities and made continuous donations to the University of Santa Clara, a Jesuit college near San Jose, where he sat on the board of regents and board of trustees for two decades.

Although Daly's paternalism inspired loyalty and love in many, it also bred resentment. Paternalism works only as long as the recipients are willing to be treated like children and to maintain a posture of gratitude and humility. People might well go along with it, I suppose, as long as their needs are being met. But among World Airways office workers, that was just not so. Pay was low, benefits were almost nonexistent. The core of the problem, however, was Daly himself. His blustering and rash behavior, intensified by heavy drinking, made Edward J. Daly a very troublesome boss.

I started calling Daly's office as soon as I read about him in the Herb Caen column. I called for ten days solid. I talked to the receptionist, to the executive secretary, and to Daly's personal assistant. I insisted, I warned, I cajoled. Daly wouldn't bite. Later in my career I would come to pride myself on my ability to reach the chief executive, no matter how expert their secretarial screens. Others in my field would come to envy the way I schmoozed and bamboozled my way into executive suites, while they were stuck bickering with weary secretaries in the outer office. Daly was a different breed, however. The executive ego was nothing new to me, and I knew well how to kiss it, massage it, and threaten it to get what I wanted. But Daly was not just another schmuck executive, he was a king. Truly. A meeting with Daly was referred to as an "audience." When he wasn't globe-trotting, Daly kept himself locked in a lavish, ballroom-size suite furnished with antique inlaid tables, Chinese vases, Persian rugs, stone sculptures, and other treasures. There, accompanied by his Pinch Scotch and Russian vodka, which he poured into a large Baccarat crystal glass, Daly remained insulated from the prosaic with the help of three layers of offices and a contingent of vice-presidents, assistants, and secretaries. The ladies and gentlemen of the Daly court were expected to protect His Majesty from intrusions, fielding all pleas for charity, handling daily business matters, and doing away with pests like me. After the hundreds of sales calls I made over two decades, Daly remained the only chief executive who never came to the phone.

It took me two days just to get my phone calls to World routed into the executive offices. Finally my message of urgency made its way to David Mendelsohn, which was as far as it was going to go. When Mendelsohn called me back, he told me plainly, "You'll have to deal with me." Even he wasn't going to make it easy. His calendar was full. He would meet with me in two weeks.

Well, damned if I was going to let this fish get away, not with an idyllic home and a gorgeous new girlfriend waiting to make my California dream come true. I was working another campaign at the time—in Michigan, of course—and I saw World as my way out of that deadly air commute. I shot back at Mendelsohn, "You're wasting precious time, you know. Time is critical here. Every day you leave this thing unattended you're giving the union momentum and strength. There's no one who can better handle this than the man you're talking to right now. You're a damn fool if you let it get out of control. Will you be around tomorrow?"

Dave wasn't budging. He answered opaquely, "I'll be in the office, but I'm booked up all day."

I started thinking about Alice, about all we could do together if I were in town more, about all we could have if I proved my worth to Three M and won a fat raise. Hell, if I could sell myself to John Sheridan and Herb Melnick, I could sell myself to Ed Daly. But I had to get to him first. The next day I drove my pumpkin orange Volvo station wagon out to the Oakland Airport and found my way to hangar six, home of the World Airways corporate offices.

I knew I would not be readily received, and I was prepared to camp out at the World offices all day. I ate a big breakfast and brought along a full pack of Winston cigarettes—the only nonunion brand at the time—and my trusty nail clipper. I always kept my clipper in my pocket. I clicked away with it in the way Nick Sangalis used to clack worry beads, fiddling with it sometimes for hours to relieve tension and boredom.

At the receptionist's area outside the executive offices on the second floor, I told the young woman behind the desk that I was there to see Dave Mendelsohn. She warned me that since I had no appointment she didn't know when he could see me. I assured her I would wait as long as I had to and took a seat on a small sofa. There I sat, quietly reading magazines, smoking, and fidgeting with my nail clipper. Occasionally I smiled at the receptionist, but otherwise I kept to myself, seemingly undisturbed by the wait. After about an hour and a half the receptionist picked up the telephone receiver in response to a buzz, looked over at me, then whispered, "Yes, he is." A few minutes later, out stepped Mendelsohn.

Dave Mendelsohn wasn't really an airline executive. He was really a banker, and that's just what he seemed. He outfitted his six-foot frame in traditional blue or gray suits, carried himself upright, moved deliberately, and spoke sparingly, generally without a trace of emotion. He was a serious man and a brilliant accountant, whose cold circumspection provided a crucial counterbalance to the raging genius of his boss. As a senior vice-president at Bank of America, Mendelsohn had been Daly's banker for four years. When, at age forty, Mendelsohn was offered a promotion at B of A that was to take him away from Daly's accounts, the World monarch made him a counteroffer. The way Mendelsohn tells it, "Daly said, 'Come with me and write your own ticket.' Banks paid terribly then, so I accepted." Mendelsohn took over a tiny office not far from Ed's and toiled for the next three years to keep the lid on Daly and World's bottom line in the black. Mendelsohn shared the responsibility of Daly damage control with half a dozen other men who guarded the corporate inner sanctum. Their titles and official duties varied, but their job was essentially to pamper Daly and cater to his every wish, but somehow to keep him from destroying his company and himself.

It was an impossible task. Daly refused to delegate or in any way relinquish control, insisting on making all decisions himself. Yet if he wasn't off on a transcontinental jaunt, he was usually drunk and in no condition to be deciding how to spend money or whether or not to fire somebody. The titles bestowed on some of World's top officers reveal the autocratic nature of Daly's leadership. The title of vice-president and director went to Daly's wife, Violet June. After her, assistants abounded: there was Mendelsohn, vice-president and deputy to the president and chairman of the board; there was Charles Patterson, vice-president and assistant to the president and chairman of the board; there was James Cummins, vice-president and personal assistant to the president and chairman of the board. Below them came Michel Rousselin, chief administrative assistant to the president and chairman of the board. Even those with less complicated titles, like senior vice-president Brian Cooke, were called upon regularly to serve as Daly's attendants and messenger boys.

"Daly made everyone become his personal valet," says Michel Rousselin, who worked for Daly from 1970 to 1980. He told of a time when Daly had Cooke open a door for him, then compelled his senior vice-president to remain in the doorway for five minutes so that the door wouldn't slam shut. Daly expected such indulgences, Rousselin says. He craved attention, and image was all-important: "That's why he wanted flunkies like me standing around all the time."

Just months before I arrived, Daly's manic control had driven the president of the company to quit in disgust. Howell Estes, a dear old friend of Daly's, had been recruited just two years before, but it didn't take the newcomer long to understand that his presidency was a sham. Estes was no lightweight army buddy. He was a retired four-star air force general, tough, bright, and accustomed to being in charge. That was the trouble. There was no room in Daly's world even for a second-in-command. Estes had no authority; he was just another member of the emperor's court. After Estes quit, Daly appropriated the title of president, abandoning the more bureaucratic designation of chief executive officer.

Under Daly's crazed and explosive command, World's spending was chaotic and sometimes ill advised, and employees—including top executives such as Mendelsohn—were constantly being fired for no apparent reason, sometimes only to be rehired as soon as Daly sobered up. Yet many loved working for Ed Daly; he made life interesting. If he wasn't throwing a fit or a party in the office, he was stirring up gossip on some far corner of the earth. It was exciting even to be an accounting clerk for such a brash soul, to watch him storm through the building, to be picked by him for some small personal task, to whisper about his latest tirade, to hear the tales of his personal abandon. Also, as fiercely as Daly punished impertinence, he rewarded loyalty. He knew most employees by name; they could count on his help with their personal troubles. If Daly got wind that some hardworking employee had suffered a family tragedy, he might send flowers, but it would be accompanied by a check for $5,000. During the Christmas season, it was not unusual for Daly to fill his pockets with a few thousand dollars in cash and take a stroll through the office, doling out the money along the way.

What made Daly fascinating, however, also made him treacherous. The sudden and rash firings were no secret, and office employees knew they worked at Daly's whim. "He ran the company with fear," says Curt Steffen, World's vice-president of labor relations during the 1970s.

Of World's 3,000 employees in 1973, 2,500 were already union and therefore somewhat protected from the uncertainties of Daly life. The mechanics, drivers, pilots, and cabin crews who made up the bulk of the World work force were represented by a nearby Teamsters local. Only the white-collar employees were still not organized, and Daly was loath to let them fall. He resented having to deal with the Teamsters and spent a great deal of time and money over the years just to make the union's job tiresome and difficult. If the Teamsters wouldn't go away and leave him alone, then he would make them slug and grunt for every inch. For example, whenever a union member filed a grievance against the company, he challenged it on principle and steadfastly refused to settle the difference, Steffen says. Daly insisted that Steffen take each and every complaint through the full, months-long grievance process, all the way to the last step, arbitration. The company spent thousands of dollars along the way, and so did the union. Steffen said he personally fought more than one hundred grievances on behalf of World, and lost only two. Daly also spent hundreds of thousands of dollars during the mid-1970s to prevent the white-collar workers from unionizing; the Teamsters tried twice to bring the clerical workers under the union's wing. Daly tried to oust the Teamsters altogether during a string of labor strikes and work stoppages from 1975 to 1977. Although he never succeeded in ejecting the Teamsters, Daly did become quite adept over the years at weakening the union's grasp. Former employees tell how, by laying off workers from World Airways and having them hired by his foreign airlines, Daly was able to remove a number of pilots and flight attendants from the union contract. The fact that Daly kept Air Mali and Air Yemen employees out of the union riled the Teamsters and was a continual bone of contention during contract talks. But Daly was intransigent. He said simply but emphatically that those were separate companies, and they were non-union.

Daly's anti-unionism was virulent. Perhaps that is because "it was less a business philosophy than a personal battle," as Michel

Rousselin says. "No one [told] Daly what to do. He was a one-man band, and no one was to stand in his way." Lest the battle lines be unclear, Daly designed a workplace motto to inspire and guide his troops. As clerks and mechanics labored, they could look upward and receive their Daly counsel. On the wall above them hung the admonition: "Perfection, not correction." Indeed, there was one voice at World, and there was never any question whose it was.

My first meeting with Mendelsohn went well; he was intrigued by my spiel about utilizing the supervisors and clearly entertained by my zeal. He wasn't going to give in easily, however, knowing it would be up to him to build the case to Ed Daly: "What you say makes sense, but we already have good representation in these matters." Mendelsohn told me World had an industrial relations man, Steffen, whose full-time job was to deal with labor issues. On legal questions the company turned to Gibson, Dunn and Crutcher, the Los Angeles–based mega–law firm that has represented numerous celebrities, including Ronald Reagan during his presidency. My presence, it seemed, would be superfluous. Yet Mendelsohn was charmed enough by my youthful gutsiness that he agreed to talk it over with the attorneys. Before leaving his office, I was sure to get the lawyers' names. I knew I needed them on my side if I was going to get this job. I planned to give them a call myself.

With Gibson, Dunn and Crutcher, World was in very capable hands indeed. The airline's lead labor lawyer, Jerry Byrne, was an expert in the Railway Labor Act, the 1926 law that, together with its 1934 amendments, still defines worker-management relations in the railroad and airline industries. His partner, Steve Tallent, also was well schooled and intelligent. It would be a pleasure working with such a top-notch pair, if only I could get their blessing. I reached Byrne by phone at his Los Angeles office and launched my pitch, mixing my practiced tone of certainty with just the right amount of deference for Byrne's superior knowledge and his seniority: I wouldn't presume to tell him how best to do his job, oh no. I wanted only to offer the services of my company for the technical tasks.

"As a labor attorney you already know that the best way to get to the workers is through their supervisors," I teased. "Now, I'm certain you don't want to go in and do all that work with supervisors. Well, that's what we do. We run the campaign at the company level and let the attorneys concentrate on the law."

Byrne thought he had heard of Three M, but he was skeptical. Labor law could be tricky, and he didn't want to risk letting World fall into legal trouble because the consultants had been clumsy. It just didn't seem smart to hand over control. Now, the last thing I wanted was for an attorney to feel he was being shoved aside. So I promised Byrne, "We won't pass gas unless we clear it with you. Even though we're planning the campaign, you have the last word. If there's an emergency and we have to get a letter out right away, I'll call you and read it to you. There won't be any surprises." I always kept my word, too. Not only did it keep me just out of reach of the law, but it fed the attorneys' piggy banks, and they always remembered that. I needed attorneys to get work, and there was no faster way to get the lawyers in my corner than to make money for them. Every time I called an attorney to clear a letter, it was another fifty dollars on his meter. They loved it.

Byrne said he would be in Oakland in two days and agreed to meet with me then. In the meantime he talked to Mendelsohn and set up a conference at World headquarters. There, I was to meet one more member of the World inner circle—Brian Cooke, Daly's somber, even-tempered senior vice-president, who was to assume the presidency after the emperor's death. After letting me talk for a while, Byrne quizzed me on my knowledge of the Railway Labor Act. True to form, I hadn't even bothered to look at the railway act before going into my meeting. But Tom Crosbie had warned me that the question might come up and had supplied me with the official Three M bluff: "If they ask you, tell them you haven't worked under it, but that there are principals in the firm who are very expert at it," he told me. Three M liked to sell itself as a highly evolved company, with a methodology so developed and a staff so highly trained that the consultants could be considered "interchangeable parts." A client need never worry that we might not be able to handle a situation.

The Railway Labor Act would be no problem; I had been briefed enough on it to know that it is even more generous to employers than the National Labor Relations Act, because it does not specify what employers may and may not do to combat a union-organizing attempt. The National Mediation Board, which oversees union elections for railroads and airlines, does not involve itself in the organizing process to the extent that the NLRB does. There are few ground rules and no list of unfair labor practices for union election campaigns. If a union feels an employer has broken the law, its only recourse is to sue in federal court, which of course is very time consuming and costly and holds to higher standards of proof. That gives railroad and airline companies an even greater advantage over unions than other employers, who at least have to contend with the nuisance of responding to unfair labor practice complaints.

Crosbie had told me, however, that attorneys wouldn't want to hear how we would take advantage of the law. They would just want to know that we wouldn't cause them any headaches. So I delivered my lines as instructed: "I'm not the expert, but from what I know, we would still conduct the campaign as if it were under the National Labor Relations Act." So we would be law abiding. Byrne liked that.

The World executives and their attorneys endorsed my campaign strategy. It made sense: if we wanted the office workers to turn down the union, we had to convince them that Daly was willing, indeed eager, to change the way he ran the company. In order to do that, we had first to convince their supervisors, who felt more directly oppressed by Daly than their subordinates. But the kid-glove approach would be so out of character for Daly. How were they going to sell him on it? Mendelsohn, Cooke, and the attorneys said they needed to talk it over, then they'd ask for an audience. Would I please wait outside?

I returned to my perch in the reception area and resumed smoking and clipping. Time dragged on. I was uncharacteristically nervous, too nervous to read or chat or smile or do anything but wait. As the minutes ticked by I began to feel vaguely sick. My stomach was upset, and I was dizzy. The anticipation of this Daly character had gotten to me. Finally Mendelsohn emerged: "Mr. Daly will see you."

Oh, God.

Before Mendelsohn and I were allowed to enter Daly's chambers, Michel, Daly's personal assistant, checked my appearance. He then led us through his office to the solid wood door that stood as the final separation between Daly and the commonplace. Michel knocked lightly, then opened the door, holding it in the manner of a butler as we entered. When I saw what lay beyond the door, I almost rubbed my eyes. Before me stretched a great room, so filled with treasures that I felt I was entering a sacred museum. The suite was sixty feet long and at least thirty feet wide; everywhere there were handwoven rugs, Oriental screens, marble statues, and porcelain vases. Daly sat at the far end of the room, behind a heavy antique desk. The entire suite was darkened except for a pair of white lights positioned on the high ceiling directly above the desk, which illuminated Daly like a holy shrine.

Mendelsohn and I approached slowly, silently, with the reverence of worshipers entering a great cathedral—or perhaps the throne room of Oz. As I walked I half expected to hear a thundering voice intone: "I am Daly, the Great and Terrible. Who are you?" I knew instinctively that I should not be Marty the Small and Meek. Powerful men rarely respect submissiveness, even if they demand it. I would play Daly the way I had played other corporate chieftains—only much more so.

The great and terrible Ed Daly looked oddly out of place amid his ornate surroundings. A broad, rugged-looking man with a bulbous nose, he seemed more suited to the corner bar. But, of course, Daly didn't have to go to the corner. On the top of his desk, shimmering in the spotlights, stood a tall crystal glass filled with an amber liquid. The air around him was thick with the pungent smell of Pinch Scotch. Daly was half-drunk and feisty.

"So you're the fella who thinks he can help us get rid of this union bullshit," he boomed. "Why should I hire you?"

I was ready for the pissing contest. "I don't think you have any choice, Ed," I said coolly. "From what I've heard, this union's gonna kick your ass."

He knew it, too, and he launched into the most profane tirade against unions I ever heard, before or since. When he recovered, we got down to business. I explained how my program worked and forewarned him that he would be called upon to humble himself, just for a while, if the strategy was going to work. He would have to tell his troops that he knew he had made mistakes and convince them that he wanted to change. He hated the idea of playing the softie. He was a fighter; he wanted to make war, not love. Ed Daly was not about to do any sweet talking. Most of the bosses I worked with felt the same: here they were, all primed for rape, and I come around and start talking seduction. But then I explained how it worked, how we wouldn't hold back, we would just make department managers and supervisors do it for us. Then the cruel smiles appeared. That was even better. Let them rape each other.

Daly relished the maliciousness of the plan as much as the rest of them. He wasn't too happy with the nice-guy approach, but the strategy intrigued him. He was going for it. "I hear you're expensive," Daly said with a snort.

"You get what you pay for, Ed," I shot back. As a junior member of the firm, my fees were then $350 a day. I was going to be working with two more senior consultants, who charged $500 a day. I couldn't say how much the whole thing would cost; that depended on how long it took.

Daly didn't like uncertainties. He didn't mind spending money, and lots of it, to slaughter the union, but he wanted control over how much. "Do the whole thing for twenty thousand and you're hired," he pronounced.

I jumped for it. I had been with Three M only a few months, and surely didn't have the authority to sell a job at a discount. As it turned out, the voting didn't take place until July 1974, seven months later. The final bill would have been more than twice Daly's offer. But I was afraid to let Daly get away, so I made the deal. I was to catch hell for it later from Melnick.

On the job with me were Tom Crosbie, whom I had called constantly during my courtship with World, and Jim Bannon. We set up shop in Howell Estes's old office, which had remained vacant since the general's resignation, and also made use of the ornate corporate board room. Bannon and Crosbie both were based out of town, and they juggled the World campaign with others they were running simultaneously. As the West Coast partner, Crosbie also was responsible for coordinating a dozen other consultants. He hopscotched around the country Sheridan style, looking in on campaigns and collecting fat fees for his presence. For Crosbie, World Airways came in handy as yet another base of operations for Three M's itinerant business. When he was present he spent much of the time holed up in the president's office, phoning clients and associates, hunting down work, and helping out with other campaigns in progress. I was on the World job more consistently than the others and therefore handled the bulk of the one-on-ones and the letter writing and was the designated emissary to Daly's office. But the dynamics among the three of us were crucial to our drama. Each had a specific role to play, with a script written to suit his character. We played off one another masterfully.

Bannon was the numbers man. He could churn out anti-union statistics like no one else. From union leaders' salaries to the potential cost of a strike, Bannon could combine the numbers so that they told only the story we wanted workers to hear. Crosbie played bad cop. He was expert at it; he knew how to be mean and to make his meanness effective. From a white hot rage he could suddenly turn cold as ice, frightening reluctant supervisors into obedience. I got the part of good cop, my favorite. As Crosbie beat away at the managers, I romanced them. I was their refuge from his cruelty. They turned to me for protection, and I became their priest and their pimp. I heard their confession, counseled them, then sent them out to sell our lies to their friends.

We launched the World campaign with a flurry of activity, as we always did, cranking out two or three letters a week and calling in the supervisors for propaganda rallies each time. Daly didn't involve himself, except to sign the letters and hear a weekly progress report. Daly gleefully signed any letters that ridiculed the union. If the tone was even vaguely conciliatory, he was less willing and had to be cajoled. Occasionally Daly was too drunk even to read the letter. Then we would take the circular to Michel, who had become quite expert at forging Daly's signature. It was just as well that Daly stayed away from the campaign. It would be a lot easier to do a makeover on him if he remained out of view. At the group meetings we stuck to our roles: Bannon filled the crowd with facts, Crosbie intimidated, and I made love. "Remember the Golden Rule at World," I told my captives time and time again. "We're family." We divided the supervisors among us for the private meetings, then cross-checked each other continually. We had learned that although some supervisors would be able to deceive one of us, virtually no one would be adept enough to trick all three consistently.

Since we were dealing with office workers, most of the supervisors were women. Generally women were more easily intimidated than men and also more eager to believe in the possibility of change. But the World Airways ladies were a tough bunch. Anyone with a few years of Ed Daly behind her was sure to have developed a hard edge and a thick layer of skepticism. They were even more mistreated than their subordinates, and they dumped their complaints on me in the interviews: "We need something that can protect us from Ed Daly"; "Look what Daly did to Wanda—that could happen to any of us"; "He gives us a ton of responsibility and no authority"; "You never know what he's going to do when he's drunk."

Daly was a loose cannon, they knew. They told me how every few months he'd turn up in the large, open, office area and go on a rampage. Like a trigger-happy sniper, he would survey the office inhabitants, looking for a target. Anything could set him off: a cluttered desk, a little casual chatter, an unbecoming outfit or hairdo. He'd zero in on his prey and fire. Towering over the victim's desk, he would curse and pound his fists, shouting insults like "Get off your butt, you lazy slob. What are we paying you for?" or "What makes you think you can work here looking like that? Go comb your hair." Often he would drive the poor woman to tears.

Daly was not always so terrible, but he always kept the pressure on. Supervisors despised his meddling into the day-to-day affairs of their departments. He kept his fingers on all the controls yet still held them accountable for every detail. So tight was his hold that department heads could not even give their employees time off to go to the doctor or to a funeral without his written approval. The invisible thumb of Daly was pressing on them all the time, even when things were quiet. Many supervisors told me privately that they would organize a union for themselves if they could figure out how to do it; they would have loved to have a contract. They seemed quite unconcerned about the possible consequences of their private blasphemies. Like the rank-and-file employees, the management people had learned not to waste time wondering how Ed Daly would react. He'd do what he'd do, and not even he would know what it would be until the last second. There wasn't a thing anyone could do about it.

Perhaps no one knew that better than Michel. Michel's formal title was chief administrative assistant, but that oblique designation belied his intensely intimate relationship with Ed Daly. Michel was a genteel, dignified man, one who dressed impeccably in European suits and spoke with a refined French accent. He occupied the office just outside the chief executive's and thus was the final buffer between Daly and the irritations of the outside world. Daly compelled all his executives and assistants to serve as attendants and whipping boys; it was not uncommon for him to phone Mendelsohn or Brian Cooke or Michel at two in the morning to harangue them about a misdeed or demand some immediate service. But no one carried a more personal burden than Michel. Michel cared for Daly's drunken body, battled his angry spirit, and endured his humiliations more than any of the others. Michel poured the drinks, drove the limo, did the shopping, fetched the coffee, carried the luggage, and listened and listened and listened. From 1970 to 1980 Michel was the companion Daly loved, then reviled, then loved again. He was fired and rehired at least six times during those years.

Michel was not at all of one mind about unions. He felt the Teamsters behaved horridly, for one thing, and he didn't know what to make of their antics. But he did know Daly. "He was an animal, very primitive," Michel says. "Ed Daly was a genius: he could sit with a pack of lawyers and outwit them all. It was instinctive. But he was terrible with personal relations. He hurt people terribly, over and over again." He also was very stingy. Michel calls World wages "just adequate." Employees received minimal medical coverage and enjoyed no pension plan.

Clearly the job of convincing Daly's employees that they didn't need a union was going to be tough. Taming Daly would be impossible, we knew. We would have to try to keep him on a tether until the voting was done; he was going to be a big, big problem. From the beginning, we had another problem. It, too, had a name: Curt Steffen.

Curt, a veteran union organizer, former airline executive, had been working as World's labor relations hit man since the year before Three M arrived. Just weeks after Curt was hired in 1972, Daly had bumped the former personnel director out of his office and installed Curt, with the title of vice-president. From that moment until 1977, Curt worked as a one-man front line in Daly's never-ending battle with the unions, slugging it out with the Teamsters day after day. He did Daly's bidding in the tedious war over grievances and executed His Majesty's orders to fire or demote or punish employees as suited each particular transgression. Curt was tough, and he was loyal. A stocky, muscular man with a permanent scowl and a smoldering temper, he was perfect for the role of union antagonist. Curt had started his labor career much like Sheridan, as a staff member and eventually president of an IBEW local in Chicago. He went on to become an organizer and negotiator with the Airline Pilots Association and later landed a job as the vice-president for labor relations at Universal Airlines in Chicago. Then, somehow, word got to Daly that Curt Steffen was looking for a job. Daly knew of Curt and had been looking for a toughie to help him keep the unions humble; he made Curt an offer. There was no time to think. Daly had told him, "Get here on Monday." Curt took the job.

Thanks to Ed Daly, Curt was on the rise. He was the resident expert in labor matters at a daring airline and was forever talking in the president's ear, telling him how to handle this or running to get his approval for that. Over the past year Curt had come to consider World employee relations his personal fiefdom, and he guarded his domain jealously. Then along came Three M, and suddenly Curt Steffen was irrelevant. He was not invited into the anti-union campaign. In fact, he was shoved aside. Curt was expected, like everybody else, simply to show up at our meetings and do as he was told.

From the first day it was clear that Curt meant to cause us trouble. It enraged him the way we came in, took over his job, and started bossing people around. Here he was, up to his elbows in Daly's dirty work every day, and suddenly he wasn't good enough to shovel the real shit. Who were we, anyway? Three soft-skinned boys in fancy suits walk in and suddenly everybody has to sit up straight. Well, he sure as hell wasn't going to. He had been doing just fine without us. Daly cherished him, wasn't that so? It was Curt, after all, who had prepared Daly's f-word letter to union organizer Louis Celaya, which I had read in the *Chronicle*.

Ironically, Curt objected to Daly's stubborn refusal to let the clerical workers organize. Not that Curt was a softie. Hardly. But he was pragmatic. He had worked for and with unions for many years, and he knew how to handle them. He used to tell Daly that it was much easier to control employees when they were organized. With a union, everything was institutionalized. There was a proper way to ask for something and a proper way to complain. It was all spelled out.

"I used to tell him, 'With a union, I only have to deal with the business agent. It's better to have five business agents come to see me every day than all these employees with all their complaints,' " Steffen recalls. But Daly wouldn't have it. He wouldn't let go.

Now, just a month after the Celaya letter, Curt couldn't believe what was happening. Suddenly he found himself sitting with the other World executives before an audience of sixty supervisors at the kick-off meeting of an anti-union drive in which he would have no say. There he was, shoulder to shoulder with a dozen other officers of World Airways, in a manufactured show of management solidarity against the union. He stared out at the faces of the department heads and supervisors who filled the giant classroom. Before him, Tom Crosbie and Marty Levitt and Jim Bannon were prancing and dancing around the room, shaking their rattles and playing their war drums. And all he was supposed to do was listen and nod. It made him sick to his stomach.

Curt did listen, enough to know he hated every damn word we said and enough to know he was going to do what he could to work against us. When that first dog-and-pony show ended, Crosbie, Bannon, and I approached Curt to let him know what we would be needing from his office. We were going to want the names of all supervisors and the employees who reported to them, as well as all pertinent personnel information on each one. We talked to him dispassionately, as if giving an order to a waitress in a fast-food restaurant. Curt puffed his chest and stuck out his chin.

"Okay, you guys are here now. There's nothing I can do about that," he grunted. "But this kind of shit I can handle myself." With his whole body shaking, he barked a summary of his background—excluding the felony.

Crosbie responded coldly: "Okay, so you're the personnel man. Congratulations. Just understand one thing: we're running the show."

When Curt had left, Crosbie called me and Jim to a powwow. "This guy, he's not going to play ball with us. Watch out for him," he warned. "Don't give him too much. We may throw him a bone every now and then, but that's all. If he can do something to make us look bad, he will. Don't give him anything he can use." We were used to having to contend with wounded personnel directors, and generally it didn't bother us. We had learned that most executives saw personnel work as merely clerical—the administration of payroll, benefits programs, and the like—and that they generally resented spending money on it. Many of the companies that hired us, even relatively large ones, did not even have personnel departments. They saved their pennies by distributing the various tasks among the secretaries. Where there was an actual department designated as personnel or, more contemporarily, human resources, more often than not the function continued to be mostly bureaucratic. The human resources officers screened applications, put together the policy handbook, handed down judgments on leaves of absence, and produced tons and tons of employee-related paperwork. Personnel directors were just midlevel administrators, not leaders. I came to expect that the head of personnel would be the most incommunicative and unempathetic bureaucrat in the plant, possessing little vision and no authority. Rather than seeing human resources as a vital support service for employees—as the name suggests—our clients tended to consider the whole department a costly bother. As a result, we were able to completely overrun the personnel office, taking charge of the employees and appropriating even the most closely guarded information. The director might have grunted and groaned, but the way his boss figured it, it was about time the damn department was put to some use.

Curt Steffen was a little more problematic than most personnel chiefs. He whined plenty about our stepping on his toes, but our conflict with him turned out to be weightier than the usual battle over turf. Curt's objections to us were substantial, and he worked hard throughout the campaign to sabotage our strategy. Those people did need a union, and he knew it. So there he was, talking at Daly, telling him the workers would never swallow the bullshit we were churning out; there he was again, cursing our names and speculating on our high prices; and over there, ridiculing our message of love and our promises of change. Perhaps, had Curt been another type of man, he would have won. Perhaps, had he been able to harness his rage and suppress his pride, Curt would have been able to undermine us as he hoped. But Curt was a visceral being, one driven by passion and incapable of the self-control required to carry out a protracted war with an ice cold enemy. He was easy to provoke and not hard to disable, given the right weapon. Against Curt, our weapon was indifference. We didn't let him engage us in battle. We dismissed him, brushed him aside.

As exciting as it was to be working for Ed Daly, the real focus of my life was Alice. I thought about her day and night and spent much of my day hiding out in my office at World composing love letters or calling her on the phone. When Alice was working, I left messages for her at hotels in Boston, New York, Washington, St. Louis. When she was home, I was useless. I was so eager to be with her that I could hardly think straight. I knew she would be waiting for me, so I cut out of the office as early as I could and sped to fetch her from her parents' home. I romanced her the only way I knew how, by spending a great deal of money. We ate at expensive restaurants; I bought her fancy jewelry and sent her elaborate bouquets. We spent our nights together at Holly Road, drinking exotic liquors, bathing in the hot tub, and luxuriating in the peace and comfort of that Marin hideaway. Alice and I planned to marry in April 1974. With the wedding just a month away, we rented a small house in the charming bayside town of Tiburon, just down the hill from the Holly Road house, and began making plans for a honeymoon in Tahiti. The World Airways union vote was set for July, so the schedule seemed perfect.

It wasn't—not to Ed Daly, anyway. One night, around midnight, the phone rang. It was Dave Mendelsohn. I had been blabbing about my impending nuptials for weeks, so certainly the wedding was no secret, nor were my honeymoon plans. Those plans were the problem. Daly was getting nervous about the union drive, Mendelsohn told me; he couldn't have me so far away during the final stage of the campaign. What if the union did something sneaky? What if something went wrong? I had served as the emissary to Daly throughout the campaign, and he came to count on me as his window and his voice to the employees. He was very upset. Rather than honeymooning on a tropical island, would I consider using his cabin at Lake Tahoe?

It wasn't what I had in mind, but I agreed. I had been told that King Hussein had once stayed there, so I figured it couldn't be too bad. Alice and I were married amid the rococo elegance of Grace Cathedral atop San Francisco's legendary Nob Hill. That night, as husband and wife, we drove to Dollar Point in Lake Tahoe, in search of Mr. Daly's little cabin in the woods. What we found instead was a grand, six-thousand-square-foot mansion that rose up like a castle on a hill high above the lake. We arrived to find the cupboards packed with full liquor bottles, the refrigerator stuffed with fine food, and the beds all dressed in satin sheets.

Life was quite different for Edie Withington and her staff at Local 29. By 7 A.M. each weekday, half a dozen of the local's most earnest men and women had deployed themselves at the various entrances to the World Airways office buildings. Wrapped in heavy sweaters against the morning fog, they handed fliers to secretaries and file clerks as they hurried to work. The union folks then headed for their own jobs, only to return to the World offices at quitting time, when they would spend an hour or two trying to talk to the workers. Edie's nights belonged to the TraveLodge, one of a dozen motor inns that populated the ugly, mile-long stretch of Hegenberger Road linking the Nimitz Freeway to the Oakland Airport. There, in a stark meeting room, she would listen to World Airways office workers' troubles and try to convince them that Local 29 could make a difference. More often than not there were five or six anti-union employees at those meetings, workers who had been sent by me to disrupt the caucus and put the union on the defensive. Sometimes a couple of supervisors even showed up, a move strictly verboten by the National Labor Relations Act as an act of surveillance. But at World we were working with the railway act, and the chances of anybody making a stink about a couple of management types showing their faces at a union meeting were pretty remote. The anti-union workers made the going very tough for Edie and the rest of them. Sometimes they would shout and sneer. Other times they would ask questions—hostile, misleading questions. And sometimes they would just sit quietly, glaring at the participants and jotting down mysterious notes on little pieces of paper. Whatever tack they took, they always unnerved the employees, even if they didn't rattle the union officers. Every time they asked a question, they dropped a bit of distorted information.

"They insisted that joining the union meant you had to go on strike," Edie says. "They harped on union dues a lot. Then they said things like 'Figures don't lie, but liars figure.' It put a damper on the discussion, that's for sure."

The management plant is a standard presence at union-organizing meetings. Their job is manifold: disrupt the meeting so the union can't talk strategy; take the focus off workplace problems by turning the questions on the union; intimidate union sympathizers; report back to the management. Of course, if the anti-union workers are acting as spies, the railway act makes that patently illegal, but big deal. It's almost impossible to prove.

Edie Withington believed in her union. As a secretary at a Construction Laborers Union local and a union member for more than thirty years, she knew how unions worked and what they could do for people. She had seen lots of organizing drives and heard thousands of workers tell stories of injustice and abuse. So when she met with World Airways employees, she wasn't surprised to hear workers accuse their supervisors of favoritism, inconsistency, and a general lack of fairness. She knew those to be the capital sins of management, the corporate inequities that most often led workers to seek a union. Edie *was* surprised, however, at the depth of mistrust of World management and at the charges leveled against the chairman of the board himself.

"Daly scared people," she remembered, "particularly when he was drunk. Some thought he might even get violent. They had no job security. Management was arbitrary, capricious. They could get fired for anything or for nothing." Under those conditions, why weren't workers terrified of being identified with a union campaign? As Edie saw it, "They had nothing to lose."

Secondary to the issue of job security was the question of pay. In 1970 *Fortune* magazine listed Ed Daly among the twenty-five richest men in the world. Yet office workers at his company earned about 20 percent less than they would elsewhere, according to Curt Steffen, and their benefits package was meager. One former secretary remembers making $451 a month in 1974, which comes to about $2.62 an hour. The secretary liked her job in spite of the wages, saying her co-workers were like family. It was more than familial warmth, however, that convinced most workers to put up with World's paltry pay. For many, terrible wages were the trade-off for the company's considerable travel benefits. Even though World was just a supplemental airline, the company made available to all employees the enviable Interline Pass, the airline industry's premier perk. With the pass and the price of sales tax, World employees could fly their families anywhere in the world on any airline. World also allowed its employees to fly for free on any World Airways plane that was being delivered for charter service. If the company needed to send a DC-10 to Paris the following month for a European charter tour, for example, employees would be invited to sign up for a free trip. So dearly did employees prize World's travel benefits that the perk became a major obstacle to the union drive and a primary weapon for us. World employees didn't have much to lose to a union fight, except the travel package. So we warned the supervisors, "You know, there's no way Ed's going to let you keep your travel benefits if the union gets in." In our letters to the rank and file, the threat was more indirect; we preached that in contract negotiations the union would have to barter for every penny and every benefit, even the ones that workers already enjoyed. The message was clear.

The World Airways administrative supervisors were an angry bunch; it was a struggle to get them to campaign against the union. To better control the battle, we set our sights on eight key supervisors, who together oversaw more than two hundred clerical workers, almost half the voting unit. For those eight we prepared an intensified version of the campaign, with double doses of everything. We mixed sweet talk with warnings and saturated them daily, starting out soft and letting the tension build, until the threat of discharge seemed the only logical conclusion. "Can't you see what the union is doing to this company?" we teased. "We were like family. Now look. What's wrong? Don't your people trust you? What have you done to bring on this union thing? Well, you'd better find out. Go out there and talk to your people and get them to trust you again. (Pause) Of course, Daly isn't going to stand for having a union in here, you know that. If you can't control your own people, he's going to hold you responsible. What you tell me in these conferences is confidential, but I am under an obligation to report your effectiveness to my client."

We demanded that the eight, as managers of key departments, turn every single voter against the union. No exceptions. We didn't want stray sheep, and we didn't want unknowns. Everybody. And if they, the supervisors, couldn't convince their own workers to have faith in management, then they would have to answer to Ed Daly. Directly. He wasn't likely to be too understanding, either. On the other hand, Daly always rewarded loyalty, didn't he. Surely he would remember someone who worked so diligently on his behalf, perhaps with a promotion—or even a raise. Even later in the campaign, when we were letting less significant supervisors slide a little, we never loosened our grip on the target eight. Each was called in several times a day and asked for an accounting of every worker in his department. Each had to fulfill several assignments daily that brought him face to face with some of the toughest, sharpest pro-union workers in the office, over and over again. After a few months the routine had the supervisors begging for their jobs, not to Ed Daly or to us, but to the pro-union workers who seemed to hold their bosses' future in their hands.

After a few weeks it was clear that threats alone were not going to be enough, particularly with supervisors outside the eight-person bull's-eye. It had been mainly my job, both at the mass communions and in our private sessions, to give the supervisors hope that Daly was willing to change—to let go a little, to delegate a little, to be a little kinder, to fix some things. Some bought into the ruse, vowing to work against the union if we could extract certain pledges from Daly. But we needed more. We had convinced Daly he could sell the employees on a program of the benevolent father, and the employees weren't buying it. So we sharpened the other edge of the sword: having lured the supervisors into the confessional, we began to use their disclosures against them and their crews. Nothing made Daly fly into a rage more quickly than a suspected betrayal. He was lord, and he expected complete devotion from his subjects. When we began reporting employees' sins, the result was a wave of reprisals that pushed the infidels into a lonely corner. In a witch hunt, witches are always in great supply. Likewise, at World in 1974, traitors abounded. Disloyalty could be anything: a gripe, a snide remark, a little cheating with the time clock, a mistake, whatever we could use to raise Daly's ire and put pressure on a troublemaker. We tried to keep the source of the leaks secret, so that our captives would continue to feed us information. Still, people became wary.

"Marty had a reputation around the place," says Charles Patterson, one of Daly's vice-presidents. "People started saying, 'Look out for Marty. Watch what you say to him.'"

Curt Steffen got fired, sort of, for something he once said to me. He never forgot how it happened: "[Marty] would use anything you said against Daly. The interviews were tricky. They were setups. He'd lead you down this negative path, with things like 'Ed isn't always fair.' Then [you'd] say something, too, and he'd report it."

What Curt actually did was call Daly "a prick." I tattled. It gave me great pleasure. Curt had been a pain in the ass for months, and now maybe I could shut him up. Daly was drunk when I divulged what Curt thought of him; he fired Curt that same day. As often happened with Daly, however, by the next morning the transgression was forgotten. Curt was in his office piling his belongings into boxes when he got a phone call from the president's suite. "What are you doing down there?" a now sober Ed Daly demanded. "I need you up here." Curt was back on the job.

Once the campaign had settled into a routine, Crosbie, Bannon, and I found we had a lot of time on our hands. Some days we would lounge in our office for hours at a time and take turns making phone calls around the country. I called Alice, my parents, my friend Michael Krasny, or anyone else who could help me pass the time. Sometimes I found it frustrating, sitting there in a big fancy office with nothing to do. When Crosbie got on the horn to do his telephonic rain dances, I smoked and listened and clipped my nails. I was bored. After a couple of months we knew who was on our side and who wasn't, and we didn't need to interview every last supervisor every day anymore. The phone calls entertained us for a while; when we tired of that, Crosbie and I killed time talking about the Oakland Raiders or evaluating women. Eventually even those conversations ceased to be interesting, and it was time to get back to work. Crosbie would stand up, stretch noisily, and meander over to the door.

"Hey, it's pretty quiet out in the hallway. Maybe we should get someone in here. Who should we call?"

"What about Judy?" I suggested. "We haven't seen her for a while, and she's got great legs."

With the help of the in-house directory we had snatched from Curt Steffen's office, we summoned the person we had selected for the next hour's entertainment. A lot of the time the supervisors were grateful to be called. Those who were willingly carrying out our game plan saw our office as a haven from the work floor and a break from their routine. We engaged them in conversation, offered them cigarettes, swapped jokes, and used up a lot of time. One of our favorite comrades at World was the director of maintenance, a young hunk named Tom Ripa. Ripa looked like the actor Tom Selleck in his prime, muscles head to toe, a head full of black curly hair, a thick mustache, and a perpetual grin. He was our good buddy, our fraternity brother, a beer-drinking party boy with a hearty laugh. Great at guy talk. As maintenance director, Ripa supervised two hundred workers, but only six were clerical people. So, technically, he did not promise to be a key player in our campaign. But we liked Tom Ripa, and in the end he would come to play a role as important as it was bizarre.

At World Airways we never got to enjoy the cockiness that comes with a sure bet; this race belonged to Ed Daly, and he was constantly changing the odds. Still, about halfway through the campaign a company win began to look like a possibility. We had taken all the supervisors through the same basic program as the key eight; even with considerably less intensity, we had managed to convince them all that their jobs were in jeopardy should the union win. Sufficiently worried, the supervisors kept the pressure on their workers and after a few months managed to turn the campaign in our favor. We learned that the company-as-family argument appealed to many at World, so we never let up on the message of renewal. Meanwhile we had managed to keep the union on the defensive, forcing organizers to rewrite their game plan continually in order to respond to our moves and answer the questions we planted. Often, their answers were lacking. At their worst, they attacked Daly. That was the union's gravest error. So powerful was

Daly's magnetism that even those who claimed to despise him yearned for his approval and worshiped him secretly. To criticize Daly was blasphemy. It was a cruel irony: the campaign was all about Daly, yet the union didn't dare mention him.

After a series of miscalculations, Local 29 was looking clumsy and ineffective and desperate. At long last workers were losing interest and faith in the union; by our estimates, the company was leading by a handful of votes. In an NLRB election we might have felt somewhat secure. Our plan would have been to keep the warmth and love in focus until the last ballot was counted, then collect our check and walk away. But a Railway Labor Act election is done differently, and it wasn't going to be so easy.

Under the railway act, a union election is conducted by mail. Voters have two weeks to mark their ballots and return them to the National Mediation Board. That two-week time lag could be a problem anywhere, but at World it practically guaranteed a union win. There was no telling what Daly might do. He was live ammunition. We could go into the election with a solid majority, only to have it demolished by one rash Dalyism.

To make matters worse, on a railway act ballot there is no place to vote against the union. If an employee favors representation, he marks the box next to the union's name. If opposed, he simply does not return the ballot. We feared that in the peace and quiet of their own homes, with time to think it over, World employees might be inclined to follow the bias of the ballot and give the union their vote. The mediation board only has to receive a majority of ballots for the election to be valid, so Local 29 could win even if almost half the clerical workers threw their ballots away in disgust, assuming that those who did mail theirs in voted in favor of the union.

With just four weeks to go before we would turn the employees loose with their ballots, our side fell apart. Twice in the final stretch Daly mounted his notorious office raids, winning a few more for the other side with each savage incursion. But he saved his most stupid display for the end, just fourteen days before the election. At that crucial moment Daly apparently found himself overwhelmed by the urge to fire somebody. So he did. It might not have mattered if he had axed an irritating supervisor or picked on one of his executives, as he had so many times before. But, as if purposely trying to foil our operation, this time he chose a sweet, unassuming, newly hired young accounting clerk, someone guaranteed to inspire sympathy among the very workers who soon would be deciding whether or not they wanted a union. The reason for the firing made Daly's deed even more outrageous: the clerk paid a bill *on time*. That's right. World had a rule—unwritten, as far as I knew—that no bill was to be paid until the final day it was due. If an invoice called for payment within thirty days, the check was to be issued on the twenty-ninth day. Surely the new clerk had been taught the dogma, but for reasons unknown, she paid one bill on the twenty-third day of a thirty-day contract. Daly was merciless. Then, just in case his severity wasn't being given enough attention, the tyrant dashed off a lengthy, scathing memo berating the accounting staff and warning the others not to make a similar mistake.

We didn't know if we could rescue Daly's image from his latest blunders. What we did know was that we had only one hope: His Highness was going to have to ask his subjects' forgiveness. Crosbie and I knew our next visit to Daly's suite would not be pleasant, and we wanted to be prepared; we shut ourselves in our office and plotted. Together we drafted a letter of contrition that we saw as Daly's only chance to salvage the election. The letter was to be sent by Daly directly to the employees' homes, rather than being handed out in the office, in order to create an aura of intimacy, as in the confessional. We hoped a show of humility by Daly at that moment might be enough to rekindle the hope sparked by all the promises of the past months. The threats, we knew, would not be forgotten. We were loath to ask Daly to bend his knees even a little, but we also knew there was no other way. With the trepidation of apprentice exorcists about to meet the devil, we put a call in to Daly's office to say we were coming.

Daly could not have suspected the weight of the impending meeting; we had popped in three or four times a week for seven months in pursuit of his signature. By now it was all very matter-of-fact. This time would be different, though. This time we would fight. This time Daly would howl. Crosbie pulled out the letter and handed it to Daly, who was seated—as usual—behind his desk with his glass of Scotch. The two of us remained standing, like soldiers awaiting a reprimand. Daly read:

Dear Fellow Employee,
   I have taken the liberty of writing you at your home because of the extreme importance of my subject.

> For many months we have all had to endure the intrusion and annoyance of an outside third party. It has not been easy for anybody. But by now you have learned that the union can guarantee you nothing except that it will take money from you and perhaps take you out on strike. Your company is not perfect. No company is. We have made our share of mistakes in the past, and we may again in the future. But nothing can justify the damage that would be caused if we were infected by an outside agent. We will accomplish a lot more through a direct relationship than an arm's length one. And so I am asking you, from my heart: Please, give us a chance. Thank you for allowing me into your home with this most important message.
>
> Yours truly,
> Ed Daly.

As his eyes marched down the page, Daly's habitual scowl grew more pronounced. When he reached the middle of the letter, his face reddened. His cheeks quivered. Then he began to grunt. Finally he exploded. He slammed his fist on the desk and pushed himself to his feet, leaning toward us with rage. "What the hell are you thinking, walking in here with this crap?" he howled, throwing the letter on the floor. "I'm not going to sign that fucking shit. Get the hell out of here."

Crosbie and I were ready. "I don't think you have much of a choice, Ed," I told him coolly. "This letter is our only hope. Your people are angry. If you don't want them voting for the union, you have to make them believe that you recognize your mistakes." Then the clincher, the threat I always delivered when executives balked at playing humble: "Without this letter, I can't guarantee you the election."

In a reversal of our usual roles, Crosbie tried to be conciliatory, offering to change words here and there. But Daly would not be calmed. He ranted and fumed for nearly an hour. Then, finally, Crosbie struck gold; he came up with the only line that could freeze Daly's rage and transform it into glee. If we would add that one golden sentence, Daly said, he would sign. He even laughed as he penned his name. In the final edition, Daly's admission of imperfection was followed by the proclamation: "As you know, I never have and I never will bow to a gun at my head." Very John Wayne. Very Ed Daly. The letters were printed on Daly's personal stationery and put in the mail that night.

Within a few days supervisors began reporting that the "Give us a chance" letter was getting a warm reception. People really wanted to believe in one big happy World family, and they wanted to believe in Ed Daly. They also wanted not to see him angry again for a while. Things were going to be all right after all, they said with a collective sigh. Well, let's face it, he *has* been under a lot of stress lately. He really does care; I mean, Gawd, look what he did for the people in Baja after the hurricane, and look how he helped Helen out when her husband was in the hospital. Yeah.

Crosbie, Bannon, and I knew that the renewed romance with Daly was ephemeral; and we knew we had to concoct some gimmick that would short-circuit the railway act election system. We definitely didn't want those ballots sitting on people's coffee tables for two weeks, reminding them of World's problems. We were going to have to entice employees to rip them up. The election was a long shot, but not impossible: the two hundred clerks who worked under our eight target supervisors were crumbling under the pressure, as their bosses harangued, coaxed, and begged them to declare themselves against the union. Dozens of others were openly upset with Local 29's attacks on Daly and convinced by our benevolent father routine. That put the election within reach. Now we had to come up with a lure provocative enough to induce people to destroy their ballots. But what?

We happened to be tossing around ideas after a supervisors meeting one morning when Tom Ripa joined us. He was entertained by the problem and joked about it in his engagingly macho way. With a broad grin, Ripa quipped, "How 'bout if I let my girls know that if they bring me their ballots I'll streak the airport?" We all laughed. Just imagine: hundreds of young women forfeiting their union ballots for a chance to see a hunk like Ripa running stark naked across the airport. What a scream.

No one was more surprised than Ripa when I called him into my office a short while later to say I was taking his offer seriously. "You gotta be kidding!" he gasped. "It was only a joke."

Well, why not? I said. The mood was right. The employees had received the "Give us a chance" letter just a few days earlier and were still feeling forgiving. Half the workers were ready to nix the union anyway. The rest would be relieved by the change of pace, maybe even relieved enough to "give us a chance." Local 29 had lost its footing; maybe Ripa's heinie would be enough to push it over the edge. We called an emergency supervisors meeting and got the word out. Hear ye, hear ye: If more than half your employees rip up their ballots and turn them in to Tom Ripa before the voting deadline, Ripa will treat them to a show they'll never forget. To wit: a run in the buff. Well, the supervisors baited the hook with zeal. It was their only way out. So drained, so beaten down were my captives by then, that they would do anything to get this campaign off their backs. Grateful to finally have a product to sell, the supervisors hawked the promise of Ripa's body—and of a happy reunited company—like carnival barkers on commission. They goaded their weary subordinates: Step right up, folks. This is our chance to be friends again, to bury our differences. We need some excitement around here anyway, don't you agree? You're gonna love this.

To my surprise and delight, the workers swallowed the bait with gusto. Clerks and secretaries giggled as they egged and prodded each other. The pressure was off, finally. Throughout World Airways offices the sense of relief was palpable. Like magic, the hostility had dissolved. Seemed like old times again, workers whispered to one another, like before this union thing. World Airways was just one big family out for a little fun.

Eager to get it over with, girls and women hurried home to their mailboxes; nearly four hundred of them tore up their ballots and trotted them over to Ripa's office. And so it was that in the final days the World campaign was transformed into a circus. And so it was that we completely befuddled the men and women at Local 29, who stood by helplessly as the crowds abandoned the center ring for a silly sideshow.

We delivered Ripa as promised. Wrapped in a black fur coat and nothing else, Ripa was driven to a general aviation runway that lay in plain view of hangar six. At the foot of the air strip Ripa disembarked, shed the coat, and ran.

The Storm

It had taken me weeks of persistence to meet Ed Daly and months of constancy to gain his acceptance and approval. But it took just a moment to lose it all. As he did to so many others, Daly finally had me fired. In my case, though, it was deserved.

After World's stunning triumph over the union, Dave Mendelsohn had invited me stay on at the company as a symbol of a new era. The arrangement suited Daly, because my presence would make it look as though he really were trying to change things. Through me, Daly could show doubtful employees that he intended to keep the promises he made during the anti-union campaign.

The arrangement suited me for other reasons. First of all, it was a plum. Daly paid me $100 a day—that's $2,100 a month, which was as much as I made with Three M—and he let me keep the office I had used throughout the campaign. All he asked in return was that I show up every morning and that I conduct a management training session once a month—precious little for a guy who supposedly was committed to changing the way he ran his company. Daly didn't care how long I stayed or what I did, really, during my daily appearances, as long as the supervisors knew I was on the job. I did do the obligatory monthly workshops and also continued interviewing key supervisors to keep tabs on workers' postelection attitudes. But that only took an hour or two a day. The rest of the time, I was free to hustle other business, using the rent-free World Airways office as home base. The company's long-distance telephone line, which I also used for free, was like a present under the Christmas tree. I had a picnic with it. I called everybody I knew. It was a rare opportunity, a singular chance for me to set out on my own. I would have been a fool to let it pass me by. What really motivated me to stay, however, was Alice. I was passionately and obsessively in love with her; I was newly married and felt my marriage was my life. So consumed was I by desire for Alice that the thought of going back on the road with Three M sickened me. By then Alice was three months pregnant and had been laid off by American Airlines. How would I bear to abandon my twenty-five-year-old expectant nymph for days and weeks at a time? The very idea provoked in me intense and conflicting feelings of protectiveness, guilt, insecurity, and jealousy. The World Airways proposition gave me comfort.

So I quit Three M. Of course, it wasn't that simple or that clean. I left still owing the partners $5,000, an advance that I had requested so I could pay for the lavish wedding on which I insisted. It became an unfortunate habit of mine, borrowing money and never managing to pay it back. The pattern caused me to lose friends, burn business contacts, and spoil family relationships. I have always had a complicated and troubled relationship with money, as I have with love. No matter how much money I made, I never could get ahead. I have chased money—endlessly, it seems—and have been endlessly tormented by it. Money has acted as a cruel demon in my life, made all the more sinister by my drinking. In the years following my time at World Airways, the combination of money and alcohol would come to throw me into bankruptcy, force me back home to Mom and Dad, poison my marriage, and land me in prison. The real tragedy of it all is that within the world of labor relations consulting, I am not at all unusual. Alcoholism, bankruptcy, divorce, fraud: hazards of the trade, the secret résumé of the union buster.

The boys at Three M were not the forgiving kind. The way they saw it, not only did I steal the $5,000 when I left, I also stole World Airways, which they had been hoping to enlist as a post-election client. My sudden departure enraged them. "No one leaves us like this," Tony McKeown bellowed when I told him and Crosbie my decision. Who did I think I was? I was ungrateful, greedy, stupid. I'd be sorry. Harsh sentiments, I thought, coming from a gang like the big M's. But, hell, I should have expected it; that was the union buster's nature as I had come to know it. We were all predators, and everyone else was prey—everyone, including one another.

*　　*　　*

In January 1975 Alice and I had our first son. We named him Jason Edward—the Edward in honor of Daly. By the time Jason was born I was running a comfortable solo business from my World Airways office and was bringing home $6,000 in the good months. Through my contacts at World I picked up a couple of relatively small counterorganizing jobs that added $500 a day to World's $100. Jobs that were too big for one person I passed along to Three M, a gesture of goodwill born out of guilt. Alice and I really didn't need much money; I had no business overhead, and we paid no rent where we lived. A few months before, when the World campaign was ending, Alice had convinced me we should move into the cottage behind her parents' home in San Leandro, actually a chicken coop that my in-laws had expanded into a tidy house. A stint in the rundown little cottage was a tradition in Alice's family. Each of her three older sisters had lived there rent free during the first year of their marriages, and now it seemed it was our turn. The cottage, at 423 Sybil Avenue, had come to be known in the Campouris clan as the "423 Club." I didn't like the idea. For one thing, the 423 Club was dilapidated and horridly decorated; I knew how much work it was going to take to transform the ramshackle cottage into the kind of place in which a person with class would live. But Alice was very close to her parents, and I liked them. Besides, I could hardly offer a better plan at the time, so we moved in.

A month after my son's birth I was summoned to Daly's office for a special assignment. I was told that word of Daly's efforts to make World Airways a better place to work had spread throughout the company and had become a hot topic at Gatwick Airport outside London, home of World's European hub. Workers there, it seemed, were feeling slighted. Lately they had begun to grumble that they should be given the same attention as the folks at the home port. If supervisors in Oakland got to go to communications workshops and special interviews, why, so should the chaps on the other side of the Atlantic. Daly jumped at the invitation. He knew it would be smart to spread the "we don't need a union here" gospel as far and wide as he could while it was still a fresh topic. I was to leave for England the next week to do two weeks of supervisor training at the British connection.

Wow. London. This was a whole different kind of traveling, and I was thrilled. I was booked on a flight to London on TWA through a sweetheart arrangement that the major airlines offered each other's executives. The travel deal allowed VIPs to fly first class on any participating airlines, compliments of the host carrier. This time the big-shot VIP was to be me, and I was ready to swagger.

I arrived at San Francisco International Airport plenty early, knowing I would be pampered at the Ambassadors Club, a private TWA waiting area for passengers with big expense accounts and little tolerance for discomfort. I still had my membership in the club through Three M and wanted to indulge myself one last time before I was cut off. Ambassadors Club patrons were sheltered from the nuisances of airport reality with the help of such amenities as an exclusive ticket counter designed like an office reception area, stuffed armchairs, color televisions, and, of course, a cocktail lounge with a full bar.

I headed straight for the bar. There, surrounded as I loved to be by the trappings of the upper classes, I nailed three or four straight Scotches in no time, maybe five. I was feeling as virile as a young rooster when I strutted over to the reception desk to check in for my flight. There, a sweet-faced TWA ticket agent in a crisp burgundy uniform flipped through some papers. She clicked her tongue and, tapping her crimson fingernails on the desktop, dialed somebody on a black telephone. She hung up, looked up at me, then uttered the unutterable:

"I'm sorry, sir. First class is sold out. I can get you a seat in coach."

Excuse me? *Coach?* Clearly this little chickee didn't realize how important I was. Couldn't she see I was Somebody? I began huffing and puffing and yelling. "I'm from World Airways," I bellowed, pounding my fist on the clerk's desk. "Ed Daly set this up for me, goddammit. He's not going to be pleased to hear about this. Let me talk to your superior. . . . " TWA found a spot for me in first class.

For one week, life in London was bliss. World Airways had issued me a limo and a chauffeur—who just happened to have on his résumé a stint in Queen Elizabeth's secret service. The driver treated me like the royalty he had grown accustomed to. He took me sight-seeing throughout London and accompanied me to Harrod's, where, naturally, I bought a cashmere coat. I worked very few hours, as usual. It seemed my life had been blessed. Then the telex arrived:

Marty Levitt. You are to return to World Airways Oakland immediately. Report to David Mendelsohn immediately upon your return. Travel instructions to follow.

The second wire came the next day. It ordered me to board a particular stretch DC-8 that World Airways was shipping back across the Atlantic that night. The stretch DC-8 was an extra long plane sometimes used to ferry equipment and crew members back and forth for the charter flights. It was a big, big airplane, and it was completely empty that night except for me and my noisy little conscience. I had ten hours to think about what would happen to me when I got back.

I had imagined a much more fiery scene. Daly would be drunk; he'd rant, he'd curse, he'd pound his fist and throw me out of his office. Then, probably, he'd get on the phone the next morning and order me back to work. I could take that. But what I faced when I got back to Oakland left me stunned and wounded. There was to be no great story, no hilarious memory, no romantic melodrama attached to my exit from World. I was simply cut. It was dull and mundane and ordinary—and deeply humiliating. I didn't even rate a personal firing. Instead I was told to report to Mendelsohn, who dispatched his duty crisply.

"Ed heard from the president of TWA," he told me opaquely. I knew he wasn't through. I didn't try to stop him. "He said that you made some trouble at the Ambassadors Club. You know, Marty, our relationship with these airlines is very delicate because we're a supplemental carrier. We depend on the goodwill of the major airlines for our charter business. What you did has jeopardized a very important relationship. Because of this, we no longer want you to continue with World Airways."

And that was that. I never saw Ed Daly again.

At the 423 Club everything was small, including my kitchen. But that diminutive corner of home soon became my life. Once I left World Airways the kitchen at 423 Sybil Avenue came to serve me as both office and bar, as anchor and solace. The kitchen connection then set a pattern that persisted for more than two decades. After getting dressed in the morning, every morning that I wasn't on a job, I found my way to the black rotary dial telephone mounted on the kitchen wall. Alice served me coffee, rubbed my shoulders, and looked at me hopefully. And I got to work. It was fine with me that the only telephone at 423 was a wall phone, for I never could do a sales call sitting down. Before dialing the number of whatever corporate executive I hoped to seduce, I stepped into character. That character wouldn't sit, for he was strong and sure and energetic and emphatic—always in control. He had no time to waste and no patience with ambivalence. In that character there was no trace of the worried husband and new father who had just pissed away a good job and was forced to live in his in-laws' converted chicken coop. There was no hint of his deepening dependence on the bottle. That character had talked his way into and out of trouble all his life, and he knew just what he was doing. He stood staunchly, he paced, he gesticulated, he modulated his voice, and he never let go. That character knew his prey well, understood the greed, the ego, the fears, and the hatreds that drove them. He played adeptly to those frailties, weaving into his sales pitch a little sweet talk, a dash of sarcasm, a well-placed bit of advice, a dose of braggadocio, a whispered slander, and a stern warning. In time, the mark joined the con game, willingly becoming a player in the conspiracy.

For me, a sales call was always an adventure. With each call I saw myself entering an unknown jungle, and I had to plot my moves as I went. The subject of unions is a sensitive one at most companies; where a petition has been filed it becomes practically taboo. If I were to speak too directly too soon, or to the wrong person, I would scare away the executives. I had to hide in the grass and calculate each move, figure out how to go forward without stepping in a trap or frightening the prey. I knew when to hold back and when to launch an offensive. It was intuitive; I was a natural manipulator. For me, and for virtually everyone in the field of labor relations consulting, manipulation was a way of life. People were prizes to be won or commodities to be used; every predicament was a tacit dare. Could I outfox the fox? School, jobs, credit, taxes, lawsuits, sex: life was a series of games, not in the sense of entertainment, but games in that every circumstance was a contest that would produce a winner and a loser. I wanted to win, and I had learned how. Like an expert chess player, I was able to think many moves ahead, and that gave me control of the board. My drive to take control landed sales and carried me to victory in two hundred anti-union campaigns. It also, however, wreaked havoc on my personal life, as it did on the private lives of everyone who has been seriously involved in the anti-union business.

At 423 I spent the mornings by the kitchen wall and sometimes entire days. Later, in kitchens large enough to include a table, I established the table as my private domain. There, at those tables, I ate my breakfast, scanned the paper, smoked, clipped my nails, and made calls to prospective clients. There I ate my lunch, made more calls, and smoked and clipped some more. In the afternoons I started pouring drinks. As time went on I would become less and less fussy about the time and eventually would open my days with a couple of stiff ones. In 1975, however, I still enjoyed the illusion of self-control, so I worked all morning and drank in the evening, drank until I was free of that nagging, gnawing feeling in the pit of my stomach.

My first round of kitchen days at the 423 Club was brief. By chance I was released from World Airways with a couple of jobs already in my pocket. My trips to the NLRB offices had turned up a few organizing drives at northern California businesses, a couple of which were restaurants, and even before my shameful end at World I had hustled my way into a handful of well-paid jobs. The restaurant petitions were a fortuitous find. Not only did the work save me from idleness and probable poverty when World forced me out on my own, but it set me up as conquistador of a virgin market. Over the next couple of years I would come to be known by the operators of restaurants and hotels across the continent as the guru of union prevention. First, however, I was to take an ill-fated venture into life on the other side.

Within weeks of my dismissal from World Airways I began working a counterorganizing job at the Rusty Scupper, a nautical theme restaurant on the Oakland estuary. Unlike San Francisco, where tourism was the number one industry and hospitality workers had been organized for decades, Oakland was a relative newcomer to the tourist trade, and many of the newer restaurants and hotels were non-union. The local culinary union sought to bring to Oakland the kind of union strength then enjoyed by food and hospitality workers across the San Francisco Bay. Establishment owners were determined not to let it happen.

Throughout the two-month Scupper campaign I worked from home, composing "Dear Fellow Employee" letters at my in-laws' kitchen table and having Alice type them up. I worked energetically, eager to establish a reputation as a winner and thereby secure more work. As it turned out, the culinary union handed me rather an easy victory. Organizers were unprepared for the persistent, unforgiving war I waged on them; never before had they confronted such a tightly choreographed and unrelenting counterattack. They were dazed. It was clear that some changes had to be made in their organizing program, and within hours of the trouncing union officers came up with a plan they hoped would guarantee that such a shameful defeat would never happen again. On election night, during the management victory party at the Rusty Scupper bar, the union made me an unexpected proposition.

I was drinking alone, as I often did even at company events, leaning on the bar and swirling my glass of Scotch, when a large man I had never seen before walked up to me and introduced himself. He was Chuck Irvine, president and chief organizer of the Hotel Employees, Restaurant Employees, and Bartenders International Union Local 28, the organization I had just trounced.

"You must be the guy who ran the management campaign," he said. I nodded. "Well, I have to admit you did a hell of a job. You really kicked our ass. I've never witnessed a campaign like that."

Irvine laughed and slapped me on the back, then I laughed, too. He ordered me another drink and showered me with superlatives, calling my work "overwhelming" and "fabulous" and "masterful." Irvine and I spent a while indulging in macho flirtations, exchanging witticisms, and talking shop. Then came the proposal: with a smile on his lips but a cool look in his eye, Irvine whispered, "Our union is committed to organizing. But, judging from today, it seems we need help. We could use a professional like you. Have you ever considered working for the other side?"

The truth was, I hadn't. But the more Irvine talked, the more interested I became. I agreed to meet with the top man at Local 28, Irvine's father-in-law, the notorious Ray Lane. Lane was a slight man with a jumpy, uneven gaze; at first glance I dismissed him as an ineffectual weakling. I was laughably wrong. A few years later Lane would go to prison for embezzlement of union funds and smuggling. Lane's villainous exploits were chronicled in a 1978 *Reader's Digest* article entitled " 'You'll be a Hooker or Else.' "

The article owed its suggestive title to charges made by several of Lane's waitresses that, as a male union boss presiding over a largely female membership, Lane was an unrelenting tormenter and oppressor. In fact, the waitresses sued Lane for sexual harassment; he was ordered to pay $275,000.

When I met Lane the merger of three international unions—restaurant workers, bartenders, and hotel employees—which put Lane at the helm of Local 28, had just been consummated, and the depth of his corruption was not generally known. He invited me to lunch at an Oakland restaurant not far from my former World Airways office at Oakland Airport. There he put the rush on me: Come to work for the union, Lane said, and you'll find yourself quickly rising to the top. There's nobody else who can give us what you can. You'll see, before long you'll be playing a role high up in the international. Lane told me he had already mentioned me to the top people in the international and that they were interested in talking. I should think it over.

I was dizzy with excitement. I had never been courted like that in my life. I was thirty-one years old, and from the looks of it I was going to be able to write my own ticket. After just six years in management consulting I was suddenly dreaming of a career in organized labor.

It was a timely dream. The once floundering culinary union had become increasingly aggressive over the previous three years, since naming the politically cunning Edward T. Hanley, a forty-year-old former bartender and labor leader from Chicago, as general president. It was Hanley who, in 1975, *the year I met Lane*, had directed the merger of the culinary union with the hotel and bartenders unions to create a force capable of taking on the rich and powerful owners of the nation's largest hotel and restaurant chains. The next year Hanley's new improved union was to play a lead role in a five-union strike against fifteen Las Vegas hotel-casinos, which virtually shut down the city's famed strip for more than two weeks during the crucial spring tourist season and cost the businesses an estimated $150 million.

In years past the culinary union had been considered sluggish and ineffective; membership numbers showed that the union was losing ground even as the number of service jobs in the United States exploded. Between 1963 and 1973, the percentage of restaurant workers belonging to unions had dropped from more than 25 percent to 15 percent. But Hanley's 1976 Las Vegas performance would show that such numbers didn't tell the whole story. Even before Hanley's rise to power, unionism wasn't as crippled as restaurant management people thought. In fact, union membership was growing; it was just that hotels, restaurants, and bars were opening faster than the union could organize, so the *percentage* of culinary workers that belonged to unions remained small. With the Hanley presidency came a change in the way the culinary union operated, a change having to do with the political and financial clout the savvy young leader brought to the organization. During his first years in office, Hanley greatly increased the culinary union's organizing budget and heightened the organization's political profile with handsome contributions to sympathetic electoral candidates.

In California Hanley's clout was personal. Both as an individual and through the culinary union, Hanley had been a large contributor to the 1974 gubernatorial campaign of then–Governor Jerry Brown. Some political observers at the time thought it was the support of culinary workers that put Brown over the top in that close race against the incumbent governor, Ronald Reagan. It seemed to me, and to others in my field, that Governor Brown owed a big debt to Hanley and the culinary workers union. We figured payment could be called for at any time.

Until I was asked, the possibility of working for labor hadn't occurred to me. But suddenly it seemed the perfect move, the only move. I salivated just thinking of the possibilities, the money, the prestige and power I could enjoy. The next few weeks were a blur of lunch and dinner meetings—at union restaurants—as union officers tried to piece together a plan. Key to my hiring was Jack Kenneally, then general vice-president of the international and second in command to Ed Hanley. Kenneally told me that the union's elderly director of organizing was due to retire soon; he was hunting for an innovative young replacement who would bring excitement and creativity to the union's tired organizing process and thereby reach the young workers who were pouring by the thousands into new restaurant and hotel jobs.

"We're on a real youth movement," Kenneally told me. "We need some new energy."

By the time I found myself sharing pasta and salad with Jack Kenneally at Vince's Restaurant in Oakland, I really wanted the union job. And I knew how to get what I wanted. I dazzled him. Titillating Kenneally with revelations from my past campaigns, I convinced him that no one knew more than I about how employers fought unions.

"But could you work in a mirror?" Kenneally asked me. "For us, that's what you'd be doing."

Look, I told him, if I know why employers win, I also know why unions lose. I could turn that around. "I'm quick, and I'm slick, and I'm innovative," I said. "I think on my feet. I could pump energy into your organizing drives and catch the employers off guard."

Kenneally was thrilled. As we talked he grew more and more determined to get me. He wooed me with the promise, not of fortune, but of fame. "You could be a star in this union," he said. Kenneally returned to union headquarters in Cincinnati to sell me to Hanley.

Kenneally and Hanley had worked in organized labor long enough to be unremittingly suspicious of me. The two knew the risks: I was tainted property. I could easily turn on them and sell union information to the other side, they knew. I wouldn't be the first double agent in the union-management war. But, hell, the union was scrambling to organize, and what I was offering couldn't be bought just anywhere. Maybe I really could help. They decided to take the chance. Kenneally promised to keep a close watch on me and, if I didn't produce, to cut me loose. When Kenneally was ready to make an offer, the union flew Alice and me to Palm Springs—a sort of home away from home for the culinary union heavyweights—where they put us up for the weekend in a luxurious four-room suite at the Canyon Resort. Over a leisurely dinner of steak and wine that Saturday night, Alice and I charmed a handful of international officers and talked about the grand future we could have together. When the time was right, Kenneally asked me plainly, "What's it going to take to buy you?"

I had already decided on my price. I had been making close to $30,000 a year on my own, so I asked for a salary of $36,000 plus expenses, a full benefits package, and—a Marty Levitt must—a new car of my choice. Kenneally didn't hesitate; it would be no problem. The job was mine. Until the current organizing director retired, I would carry the title of "international representative."

I soon learned that getting hired by a union was a lot more complicated than winning a contract with a private business, where a sole owner or board of directors made the decision. After all those lunches and phone calls and plane trips, there was still work to be done. Unions consist of overlapping democracies, roughly analogous to state and federal governments, and union charters limit the ways in which the international can intervene in the affairs of its locals. That makes the organizations slow and cumbersome, but presumably more accountable to the local members, who pay for both levels of representation with their dues. In my case, while the international union had the power to hire me, it could not unilaterally install me in a local; local officers are elected by the local membership. Officials of the international had decided they would not anoint me director of organizing until I had proved myself at the grass-roots level, by winning a major organizing drive. And to do that, I badly needed a local to work from. Having decided to hire me, the international still had to figure out where to put me.

Conveniently, a spot turned up in Sacramento, thanks to a constitutional exception to local control called trusteeship. In the way that state governments can assume control of their insolvent school districts and cities, international unions are empowered to take over troubled locals by putting them into trusteeship. Not long before my talks with the culinary union began, president Hanley had put into trusteeship Local 49 of Sacramento and named his brother-in-law, Ted Hansen, as trustee. There would be no problem getting me in there.

From the moment I walked through the doors of the Local 49 office I knew I would not be staying long. The local was administered out of a drab little one-story building in downtown Sacramento. The office was small, the furnishings austere, the work endless, hardly comparable to the executive life-style afforded me at most companies. The guys at the international did their best to pamper their prize catch; they looked the other way when they got the auto leasing bill and found I had chosen a brand-new Lincoln Mark IV—turquoise, with a moon roof—and they paid for my meals and hotel room, no questions asked.

Upon my arrival at Local 49 I was given just one assignment: organize the Red Lion Inn in Sacramento. Period. The Red Lion had haunted the culinary union for years. A dogged non-union employer, the chain had managed to crush almost every organizing attempt nationwide and to force union supporters underground. In so doing, the Red Lion had earned itself the status of number two enemy to the culinary union, after the rabidly anti-union Marriott. Deliver Red Lion, I was told, and I would be on my way up the international ladder.

With that charge and nothing more, I was set loose. I had no fixed schedule, no reports to file, no boss at the local; in fact, no job description at all. All I had was an objective; how and when I accomplished it was up to me. The international gave generously, in hopes that their maverick organizer would help launch a brave new era for the union. I was an experiment, and they were willing to be flexible.

In contrast with me, Hansen and his staff were used to working long hours on a zillion tedious tasks for little reward. A handful of union officers and business agents worked out of the Sacramento office, supported by half a dozen secretaries and clerks. It was a busy local, responsible to some three thousand members spread throughout north central California. But, except for the secretarial force, there was rarely anyone sitting behind a desk. The business agents spent most days "out in the field," meeting with workers at the various hotels, restaurants, and bars assigned to them, attending grievance hearings, and seeing to their myriad other administrative duties. When employees at some non-union workplace sought to organize, Hansen and his crew of aging business agents had to squeeze the organizing drive in between everything else, often working day and night until the election.

To Hansen, my job was a luxury cruise, and my preferential treatment provoked some resentment. "Here we were all driving Chevys, and this guy drives up in a big blue Lincoln," recalls Hansen, who was elected secretary-treasurer of Local 49 when the trusteeship ended, and who continued to head the local into the 1990s. "I hardly saw him. As far as I could tell, he didn't do anything."

Yet for all the coddling, it was not enough. I hated Sacramento, considered it dull and unsophisticated. And local union work turned out to be far more tiresome, much less glorious, than I had envisioned. After six years of the corporate high life, my new job seemed like a grind. It was clear that union work at the local level would never afford me the kind of comfort I was accustomed to. Organizing was difficult and tedious, quite unromantic, really, hardly what I had imagined during my lofty conversations with Kenneally. Local 49 had little need for a showman and a great need for a steadfast worker and a true believer. I was neither.

I exhausted my well of inspiration during my first week on the Red Lion campaign, when I pulled a stunt out of my union-busting bag of tricks: passing myself off as the labor relations consultant I recently had been, I offered Red Lion executives a free two-hour communications workshop, purportedly as a sales pitch and sample of my wares. They took the bait. I got the entire management and supervisory contingent holed up in a hotel conference room; then union organizers hurried through the building, collecting workers' signatures on authorization cards. The ruse worked brilliantly. By the time the union people were discovered—and thrown out—we had enough cards to file a representation petition.

I was very proud of my stunt, but I never followed through, and the Red Lion organizing drive fizzled. By the time I decided to call it quits at the Red Lion, I realized that organizing was going to take a lot more than clever tricks. It would require a kind of miracle worker to round up workers from the bottom of the economic and social barrel—people who were frightened, isolated, vulnerable—and turn them into a united force willing to do battle with rich and powerful corporations. It would be a job that never ended, a job that could consume one's life. I worked magic, not miracles, and I wanted out. I may have had the guts for organizing, I surely had the brain, but I didn't yet have the heart. I saw myself doing a couple of quick hops up to director of organizing; I hadn't expected to be down in the trenches with laundry women and bellhops.

My scheme for quickly becoming a union big shot was perfect: I would organize Reno, the tourist capital of northern Nevada, which lay just a hundred miles east of Sacramento. Although the culinary union's strength in Las Vegas was legendary, Reno employers had managed to keep the union locked out. Operators of the city's scores of hotels, casinos, restaurants, and taverns were steadfast and united in their refusal to let their workers have a union. The way I saw it, if I could deliver Reno, my future with the international was assured.

There was another side, a personal side, to my Reno wet dream. Ever since I'd gotten the Sacramento job, Alice had been lobbying me to move the family to Reno so she could be close to her sister, Stephanie. The move would lengthen my commute, but not by much, and it would make Alice happy, which I very much wanted.

Doubly motivated, then, I began talking up my Reno plan to Kenneally. I could take on the whole town, I told him; I knew their game, and I could beat them at it. Kenneally loved it, and he must have believed I could do it, for not long after I was hired, the international agreed to advance me $5,000 toward the down payment on a $57,000 Reno home. I was on my way.

Then, on February 20, 1976, I got a phone call from Cleveland. It was Mother. Her voice was distant, oddly detached from the words she spoke: My younger brother, Harvey, was dead. He had killed himself. That afternoon, after being released from a methadone program and proclaimed free of his addiction to opiates, Harvey disappeared into the garage, closed himself in the car, pulled my father's gun out from under the front seat, and shot himself in the head. He was twenty-six years old.

Suicide. Harvey was dead. My only brother, the only one in the world. My brother, whom I never really knew. That shy, loving little boy in the background. That tender, troubled teenager hiding in his room. That forgotten young man. Dead. I tried to remember him. I couldn't. I couldn't see his face. Couldn't hear his voice. There was nothing. God—nothing. He was gone. And where was I? Where had I been? I had been busy. Very busy dazzling Mother and Dad. And Alice. And what about my parents? They had been busy, too. Busy building castles for me.

I went to Cleveland for Harvey's funeral. When I came home I was dead myself. I didn't talk about it. I couldn't even think about it. I couldn't think about anything or do anything. Most days I couldn't bring myself to get in the car. Some days I didn't even get out of bed. I never went to Sacramento anymore. I stayed home and drank and slept, or tried to sleep. Every so often Kenneally would call and ask me what the hell I was doing in Reno; I was supposed to be in Sacramento. I don't remember what I told him. It wasn't about Harvey, though. I couldn't bring myself to talk about Harvey. I was feeling guilty, angry, hurt, everything—nothing. I didn't know what to feel. I tried not to feel at all.

After a couple of weeks Kenneally had enough. I had, too. It wasn't working out, we agreed. Maybe it hadn't been such a good idea after all. The union wanted to cut its losses. We called the whole thing off.

Years later I concluded that things might have been different if I had been able to take time away from the hustle to grieve for Harvey, to reconcile my tortured feelings about his despairing life and lonely death. Maybe I would have developed a conscience and learned to live by it. But it was a trademark of mine to live on the edge; I never had enough money stashed away to see me through thin times. So the moment I lost my job with the culinary union, I had to begin looking for something else. There was no time for spiritual renewal. I had to make a living. So I stepped back through the looking glass and reassembled my credentials as a management consultant.

I had set my sights on Reno when I thought I would be doing union work; it didn't take much for me to recast the plan from the management perspective. There wouldn't be any serious organizing drives to battle, I knew, not in Reno. But with the union rumblings down in Las Vegas, perhaps I could convince hotel and restaurant executives to the north that they should have a "union prevention" program. I assembled my "we've got to make sure that never happens here" pitch and set out to woo the most powerful men in Reno.

The sales calls lifted my spirits. As long as I was in pursuit I could suppress my thoughts about Harvey, forget about the union and about my dwindling bank account and about my wife and tiny child. When I went into character, everything was possible; life was a thrill. And indeed, Reno hotel society gave me no reason to doubt my welcome. One after another, top executives invited me into their sanctuaries. They listened to me, absorbed, asked me a million probing questions. From the president of the Reno Employers Council to the manager of Harrah's hotel and casino, it seemed they couldn't hear enough. For some, my anti-union program was just the kind of thing they had been looking for. At least half a dozen of them almost made a deal right there—almost. They would run it by the board of directors and get back to me. There was no time to waste, they agreed.

After a couple of weeks I had plenty of lines out. I figured it would just be a matter of days before some big fish took the bait. No one called. I checked back with my most promising prospects. They were apologetic. The board still hadn't made up its mind, they'd get back to me as soon as something was decided. Nothing. I was perplexed. I was already bewildered by the rather sudden silent treatment I had received when I'd met with attorney Bill O'Mara, who represented several casinos. If it hadn't been for him, the Reno cold shoulder might have remained the biggest mystery of my career. Bill took a liking to me, it seems, for he decided to share with me the reason behind my failure to reel in any work. When our conversation turned to my lack of success in snagging any Reno employers, Bill walked over to his desk and pulled out a letter typed on a sheet of Reno Employers Council stationery. The letter, which apparently had been mailed out to all members, went something like this:

> Dear employer,
> You may be contacted by Marty Levitt, who claims to be a labor consultant. You should know that Mr. Levitt is, in effect, a double agent. He is on the payroll of the Hotel Employees, Restaurant Employees, and Bartenders International Union, and he is trying to infiltrate our private businesses. Mr. Levitt may tell you he is here to help Reno employers remain non-union. But he is really here as a spy. . . .

It was signed by the council president, Clinton Knoll. Now the only mystery that remained was where Mr. Knoll got his information. It didn't seem likely that the union people would have written the letter; they didn't yet know I was on the prowl in Reno. Maybe someone at the Red Lion in Sacramento had tipped him off. Well, the identity of the council's informant was to remain a mystery to me, but I had a pretty good nose and I smelled a rat. Bill O'Mara told me that, quite coincidentally, just days before I called, one of his clients had been contacted by another labor consulting firm regarding union prevention work. The other firm was a big outfit out of Chicago known as Modern Management Methods. Hmmm. Wasn't that interesting? I told Bill about my history with Three M, and he encouraged me to throw my hat into the ring. Why not? Bill didn't believe for a minute that I was a spy, and he said he would assure his client that I could be trusted. I knew Three M would be asking about $500 a day, so I set my rate at $350.

That was my final Reno mistake. I didn't get the job. But according to Bill, it had nothing to do with the letter. In fact, the way his client saw it, if I really did have some inside scoop on unions, all the better. The problem was my price. I was too cheap. The executives were interested in me, Bill told me, but my low price made them suspicious. There must be something wrong with him, they thought. If he really is some hot-shot union buster, why is he so willing to deal?

They went with Three M, and I never offered a deal again. From that day on I was the most expensive union buster in the business.

*   *   *

My little lesson in executive psychology was to serve me well in the future, but at the time it buried me. A month had passed since I'd lost my post with the union, and I wasn't any closer to making money. I didn't have any more tricks up my sleeve. Alice was frantic. The next time I saw Bill O'Mara it was for personal business; together we decided that bankruptcy was my only way out of the hole I had dug. I couldn't afford my house payments; I had bought all my furnishings on credit and still owed money on most of them. I also was still $5,000 in debt to the culinary union. I felt wretched.

As the bankruptcy case progressed, so did my drinking. Alice sniped at me constantly, and I shot back, my blasts becoming more vicious and more accurate with every drink. The bankruptcy proceedings, which I had hoped would put a quick end to my misery, instead tormented and taunted me for weeks. I began to think the bankruptcy courts were populated by perverts and sadists; what other kinds of beings could enjoy work that caused so much humiliation and misery? One day, when I was not at home, agents of the bankruptcy trustee assigned to my case came into my house and carted off everything with a resale value. They took my eight antique clocks—my most beloved possessions at the time—my new sofa and love seat and a stuffed easy chair. Our cars were repossessed. Then the bank foreclosed on our house and took that. Broke and homeless, Alice and Jason and I had nowhere to go but back to San Leandro, to the 423 Club, that emasculating little hovel in the shadow of Nanny and Papa Campouris.

The trip back to the Bay Area was symbolically perfect, straight out of an expressionist novel. A fierce snowstorm darkened the sky and froze our scowling faces; it also closed the Reno airport, forcing one pathetic little threesome to ride home through the bleak Sierras on a crowded, dreary Greyhound bus. With the wind and snow whipping the mountainsides, the heavy gray bus lumbered up the pass, then down again, for five gruesome hours. Then it deposited us at Oakland Airport. Alice and I had ridden in silence, I demoralized, she angry and afraid. The past year had taken away my brother, ruined my job, poisoned my career, devoured my money and my home, and soured my marriage. Where could I possibly go from here?

Back to the 423 Club. Reinstalled in the chicken coop, I didn't spend a long time wondering what to do. The pressure was on, and I had only one skill. I borrowed my father-in-law's car and drove to the Oakland NLRB. I got lucky right away, as I usually did, but not in the usual way. I picked up an organizing petition for a film company based in the quaint—and very wealthy—seaside town of Sausalito in Marin County, just down the coast from Tiburon. But when I met the owner of the company, a big, bearded man named Jack Burney, I met not a future client, but the man who would make me a star, the man who would help me become a big-time union buster, the most successful and most despised adversary of my onetime employer, the culinary union.

Burney thought big, and he moved fast. As soon as I explained to him what I did for a living, he knew there was money to be made, and he started calculating how to get at it. He wasn't interested in my counterorganizing service for his own company, wasn't particularly worried about the union drive. But he was interested in me.

"Look," he told me, "let's not waste time with a low-brow little consulting contract. How would you like to make films?"

Burney and I went into partnership almost immediately, with the idea of producing a series of union-busting training films for management. Our business relationship lasted barely six months, and we made only one film. But in that brief time Burney singlehandedly managed to remake Marty Levitt and revive my moribund career. For, more than a filmmaker, Burney was a marketing genius. He knew how to design a product, how to package it, and how to promote it. In the Burney-Levitt partnership I was the one with the raw material, the information we wanted to sell. But Burney knew how to lure the buyers. Burney knew, for example, that we had to focus on one industry if we wanted to dominate a market, if we wanted to, as they so elegantly say in marketeering, "penetrate." When I told him I had worked for the culinary union, he crowed. That was it! I would become the voice of union avoidance for the food and lodging industry. Under the Burney plan, the two of us would make films on union prevention aimed at the hospitality industry, then peddle the films at seminars and workshops that I would conduct. The seminars were my forte, my chance to shine; I considered them the heart of our enterprise. But to Burney, the day-long events were merely the vehicle for moving the important product—the films.

Burney christened our fledgling firm Synthesis—for the promise of a peaceful blending of management and employees. The logo he chose was even more audacious. As the symbol of our creative endeavor, he pirated the most famed detail from Michelangelo's Sistine Chapel masterpiece, the hand of God reaching down to touch the hand of Adam. So, thousands upon thousands of Synthesis brochures mailed to hotel and restaurant executives across the country implied with a line drawing what John Sheridan had dared to say out loud: we were doing the Lord's work.

With my career reincarnated, Alice and I moved out of the 423 Club and rented a little house in Kentfield, just inland from Sausalito Harbor, where Burney lived on his yacht. On May 1, 1976, Burney and I mailed out our first Synthesis brochure, hawking ten anti-union workshops to be held around the country the following month. We charged $150 per person and allowed only twenty-five into each workshop, the kind of intimate setting we said was necessary for our intensive training. The mailer was a marketing masterpiece and a classic example of union-busting promotional literature. Printed on a fourteen-by-eleven-inch sheet of heavy paper folded in thirds, the brochure was done in all-American red, white, and blue. On the cover, a collage of newspaper headlines and carefully chosen portions of articles screamed of the havoc wreaked by the hotel and restaurant union, particularly in the recent Las Vegas strike. In red letters on the upper left-hand corner of the cover, the pamphlet warned: "IT'S HAPPENING RIGHT NOW." Below, the newspaper clippings provided selective detail:

"Cooks, Bartenders Join Vegas Strike";
"The estimated loss in revenue to the Strip is in excess of $150 million and more than 250,000 visitors. It's practically impossible, now, to find a single member of any of the unions that admits voting to strike";
"End of a Tradition—Fosters to Quit Serving . . .
[Restaurant attorney Milton Maxwell Newmark] blamed the chain's financial troubles on "our attempt to conscientiously operate a 100 per cent union shop";
"NEW STRIKE OFFER."

Inside, the bombardment continued:

IT COULD BE ANYBODY, ANYTIME . . .
IT'S TIME TO DO SOMETHING. . . . It's time to immunize

your industry from union encroachment and combat the degenerative effects of unchecked union attack. . . .

HERE'S ONE POSITIVE THING YOU CAN DO: You can explore with the expert what's going on in the Hotel and Restaurant Employees and Bartenders International Union today, and what you and your own trained managers and supervisors can do to fight back. . . .

Synthesis Presents . . .
A CRASH COURSE IN
Preventive
LABOR RELATIONS
with Martin J. Levitt.

Having played on fear, we wrapped up our pitch with an appeal to the conscience. On the back of the mailer, beneath our godly logo, we took the soft approach, insisting that by keeping unions out, business managers would actually be showing their love. Yes, love, for their employees. We even quoted from Indian poet and philosopher Kahlil Gibran, whose work was popular in the 1970s: " 'Work,' wrote Gibran, 'is your love made visible.' " The final message was warm and inspirational:

> Deprive a man of the pride and sense of well-being he gets from doing meaningful work and doing it well—Deprive him of his rightful "say" in the affairs that surround and govern his working life, and you have trouble, more trouble than any of us need to see.
>
> We believe we can help management end the [labor vs. management] duality, and bring the employee to an "inside" position of involvement that makes a union totally outmoded.

The brochure was a magnificent piece of advertising, a brilliant blend of truth and distortion. It worked. My June seminars were filled.

My swift readjustment to my old career did not go unnoticed by the culinary union. When I reached the final seminar of the series, at the Hyatt Regency Hotel in San Francisco, fifty sign-carrying union members turned up to protest. That was only the beginning; the culinary union would follow me around the country for the next three years and picket nearly every Levitt event. But the San Francisco seminar on June 30, 1976, was my first rub with notoriety. The *Berkeley Barb,* the scrappy alternative newspaper that had served as the official organ of the Bay Area disenfranchised since the free speech movement a decade earlier, snuck a reporter into the workshop. Burney threw the young man out, then apologized and graciously granted him an interview in the hallway, in which he recited from our brochure. In the resulting article, the *Barb* called the Synthesis workshop a "secret, closed-door 'School for Union-busters' "; it referred to Burney as the "icing" and to me as the "cake" of the anti-union ruse. That was the first time I had been pinned publicly with the label "union buster." I was proud of the *Barb* article, so proud that I kept it in a scrapbook alongside letters of recommendation and gratitude from a score of executives—mostly from the restaurant industry—who attended my "school" throughout the late 1970s.

My partnership with Burney fell apart abruptly in July, when I decided I had tired of the relationship. Impetuously, I telephoned Burney and told him I no longer wanted to work with him, thus pulling the plug on our venture. It was a rash act, I decided later, but for once I was not going to pay for my lack of temperance. By then Burney already had planted the seeds of my future prosperity. Since my seminars were to serve as the distribution pipeline for Burney's films, he had wanted executives to feel that if they missed out on the seminars, they would be passing up a singular chance to control their business destiny. To do that, he had needed to make Martin J. Levitt a household name within the industry—fast. So he had called up a friend of his at Cahners Publishing, the Chicago megapublisher that counts among its titles various professional magazines, including one called *Institutions/Volume Feeding*, the premier trade journal of the food service industry. On May 15, as hundreds of restaurant operators were pondering the Synthesis brochure, *Institutions* magazine carried a special report on the growing strength of the culinary union under Hanley, an article that happened to quote a certain Martin Levitt. Ironically, my real media launching didn't occur until October, two months after I had broken away from Burney. By then I was on my own again, having incorporated the name Synthesis into a one-man union-busting firm for the restaurant industry called Martin Jay Levitt's Employee Synthesis Program. Then, on October 1, *Institutions* magazine published the second part of its report on the culinary union, this an in-depth analysis of the union's finances—which by then had become the target of a federal investigation. Packaged with the investigative report was a full-page article on counterorganizing techniques. There, between the features on Mexican restaurants and rangetop cooking, nestled an article titled "Management's Best Defense . . . " in which Martin Jay Levitt argued the case for preventive labor relations.

Thank you, Jack Burney.

Once the *Institutions* article appeared, I was swept up in a whirlwind of activity. Suddenly I was in great demand. Business came out of nowhere. Restaurant owners across the United States were scared, terrified that a powerful and sinister union might force them to loosen their grasp on their kingdoms. They wanted protection, and they were willing to pay for it. Restaurant executives clambered to my seminars in Atlanta, Chicago, and San Francisco that November and December. I decided not to limit attendance, as I had with Burney, and I drew one hundred eager participants to each event, for a gross income of $15,000 per event.

At the Chicago seminar I was approached by a man named Steve Miller, the director of educational seminars for the National Restaurant Association. Miller told me the association had conscientiously avoided training programs that dealt with labor relations, since its membership was hopelessly divided on the union issue. But after hearing me, he'd decided it was time for the association to provide some guidance, and he convinced me to go on the road under the auspices of his organization. Although the association paid me a small fraction of what I made on my own, I accepted the offer, figuring the exposure would feed my own business. I was right. One seminar inevitably led to another, so that I was almost drowning in the work—and the money. Quite accidentally, I had struck gold.

Even Jack Burney could not have realized what a glorious mother lode his restaurant industry mine would yield. The hospitality industry, I discovered, employed more workers than any other U.S. industry except construction, and in the 1970s it was booming, as were the other services such as finance, insurance, and health care. But in terms of union-avoidance consulting, the rest of the big service industries had been spoken for: Sheridan had begun rounding up banking and insurance firms fifteen years earlier, and Three M was the hired gun of choice at hospitals and nursing homes across the continent. Food service, it seemed, was the union buster's final frontier, and it fell to me.

The restaurant industry was true virgin territory and therefore quite a thrilling conquest. I found restaurant operators to be abominable managers: uninformed, unsophisticated, and often brutish in their treatment of workers. As an industry, food service was at least twenty years behind in employee relations. The pay stunk. Benefits were minimal, hiring and firing arbitrary, management training rudimentary, and decision making decidedly autocratic. I had seen plenty of poorly run businesses, but nowhere were the misery and anxiety of the workers more intense than at a badly run restaurant.

The reason, I suppose, is that a restaurant, more than any other business, tends to be a monument to its owner. In every detail, from the decor to the menu to the vacation policy, the privately owned restaurant is a commercial expression of the owner's ego. As such, there is no room for a second voice. An employee is simply there to do a job. His ideas are not of interest, his suggestions not welcome, his personal aspirations of no importance, and his well-being relevant only insofar as it affects his work. Clearly, restaurateurs had a lot to learn about employee relations, yet they might not have cared had it not been for Edward T. Hanley. Hanley's organizers were out in force, crisscrossing the country, rallying hotel and restaurant workers around the hope of a living wage and dignity on the job.

Their bosses came to me. From me they learned how to attack a union from every position on the board. They learned the secrets of staying in control and on the offensive during an organizing drive. They learned how to whip the union at the bargaining table, should management be unfortunate enough to have lost the election. And they learned how, later, to foment an ostensibly grassroots drive among union employees to dump the union, without getting caught by the laws that strictly forbid management involvement in decertification campaigns. Perhaps most important, the restaurant managers learned the tricks of evading the so-called union problem: by appearing to listen to their employees and to encourage openness, by making policies simple and clear, and by relaxing some rules. And yes, they were tricks. Sleight-of-hand. Perception was more than a tool for me: it was the whole game. Surely some real good could have come from what I taught had the proposed means not been so twisted by the desired end. But the objective was not to empower the employee, as I pretended, but to shut him up. Let him talk, sure, and let him feel he's being heard—in fact, actually listen to him when it suits you; there's nothing wrong with that. Just be selective. Give the workers just enough rope so that they believe they are off the leash, just enough to fool them into scorning the union. The golden rule of management control, as I taught it, was Incorporate dissent, institutionalize it. They would find, I promised my disciples, that dissension won't be half as attractive to the masses once the rebels are sitting down with the bosses. Like the clever parents who, wanting to cool their teenage daughter's desires for a leather-clad longhair, start inviting the objectionable beau to dinner, so the cunning manager should embrace his workplace rebels. Be grateful for them, I offered, for they are your most effective shield against the union. If you can convince the activists that they'll accomplish more, perhaps have more power, without a union, why, you've won the war.

By 1977 my day-long workshops had stretched into two-day affairs, and my firm had once again been reincarnated, this time under the name Employee Unity Institute. Although I still ran counterorganizing campaigns on my own, including a stint for actor Clint Eastwood at his trendy Carmel eatery, Hog's Breath Inn, most of my seminar work came through the National Restaurant Association. The association kept me busy, and each time I spoke, the demand for me increased. What I taught I presented as science, but really it was an art, the art of illusion. As an illusionist, I depended largely on the willingness of my audiences to believe. But as a businessman I knew I sometimes would be called upon to prove the truth of my claims, so I kept a stockpile of quasi-scientific data that I could tap whenever the need arose. The data I proffered were a mishmash of NLRB and Labor Department statistics, AFL-CIO reports, news stories, court decisions, survey results, and just about anything else that would seem to lend credence and import to my presentation. Most of my data were accurate, if incomplete and totally lacking in context; some of them I just made up. It hardly mattered. Since generally I spoke to managers who either were faced with or feared facing a union-organizing campaign, I was preaching to the converted. My task, then, was to persuade the listener to follow my way rather than someone else's; to hire me, not him.

The job of talking a businessman with no noticeable union problem into buying "preventive" services was a bit more challenging, but we consultants did it all the time. For those sales calls we made use of an incomparable tool—the employee attitude survey. With its sheen of cool scientific objectivity, the attitude survey, which later became known as the "opinion" survey, has made believers out of a multitude of timorous business administrators and won a great many clients for employee relations and management consulting firms, which of course is its whole point. I was introduced to the attitude survey early, by Sheridan, who taught his tadpoles to use the purportedly anonymous polling as a sophisticated version of the crass yet time-honored foot-in-the-door sales technique: the consultant would offer to assess the attitudes of a company's workers in a number of areas. The results inevitably and invariably pointed to some critical problems that required the consultant's immediate attention, for if left unchecked, a union-organizing drive was imminent.

It worked. It hooked clients so consistently, in fact, that in 1978 Three M purchased a union-busting firm well known in the health care industry called W. I. Christopher & Associates, which specialized in employee attitude testing. With the Christopher acquisition Three M added attitude assessment to its arsenal of employee relations "services." The attitude survey still reigns as one of the premier sales devices of latter-day labor relations consultants, including the host of former Sheridanites and Three M'ers, and their children, and their children's children. And why not? After all, how could a population conditioned to check the political polls before making up its mind on electoral candidates and social policy questions resist the temptation to find answers to its business problems in the same way? Along with a battery of astounding psychological tests purported to be capable of identifying a proclivity toward theft, union activism, or other "undesirable" behavior, the employee attitude survey is a shameful example of science twisted into service by industry.

Like any pretext used by the salesman to lure the buyer, the employee attitude survey is a sham, and I knew it from the start. After all, how often could consultants who earned their keep by solving problems in the workplace allow a survey to conclude that workers were basically happy? Yet not until I had been in the business for a decade, not until my reign as darling of the food service industry, did I come to understand the magnitude of the attitude-survey fraud.

While on the road for the restaurant association, I linked up with a trio who hoped to combine my influence in the hospitality industry with their areas of expertise to win a cozy station as the restaurant industry advisers of choice. The proposition came from Harlow White, a veteran of upper management from the Victoria Station restaurant chain. White had tired of corporate work, he told me, was longing to get into something more lucrative and free-wheeling, like consulting. He had these two friends, one a wizard with industrial surveys and personality assessments of all kinds, the other a seasoned management trainer, with whom he wanted to team up. Together they could offer one hell of a consulting package, didn't I agree? But there was one problem. Who was going to hire them? The food service industry was crawling with burned-out restaurant managers, chefs, executives, and accountants, all looking for consulting work. Restaurant people tended to be competitive and suspicious, White knew, perhaps because of the high mortality rate in their business. They would stick to familiar names, and Harlow White was not familiar to that many of them. That's what brought him to me. I had a name. He had an offer. We'd make it a foursome, he said, divide the business into four equal parts. I'd continue doing my high-profile union-avoidance seminars as well as the behind-the-scenes busts; White would offer general business advice; friend number one, Bill Rogin, would bring to us his Marin consulting company, called by the important name Education/Research, Inc., and peddle employee attitude surveys and personality assessments; friend number two, Marty Rabkin, would take charge of supervisor training classes. Together we'd have a full-service management consulting firm able to take on the big guys. Anything they could do we could do better.

The proposal appealed to me. How many times had I been forced to pass up potentially lucrative contracts because I was a soloist? I still grunted to myself when I thought of the big clients I had passed on to Three M in the months following my World Airways campaign—companies like Federal Express and General Dynamics. With the White-Rogin-Rabkin enterprise I could tap heavyweight clients without giving up my autonomy, which I cherished. There was also a soft side to my attraction to White's offer. I craved the involvement with other people that it promised. It is a psychological paradox with which I have struggled all my life: my drive for independence and my desire to belong. Since I left Sheridan I had been struggling to recapture the camaraderie and congeniality I had known there, like a drunk forever trying to re-create his first high and killing himself along the way.

Harlow White came along just as I was beginning to come unraveled by that and other hidden conflicts. Alice and I were living then in a palatial hillside home in Tiburon, which overlooked San Francisco Bay. It was an opulent place that bore ostentatious witness to my outward success and cloaked my inner wretchedness. I should have been happy. Instead I felt lonely and inexplicably frustrated. Alice was expecting our second child by then and yearned for a storybook home and family. She yearned in vain. My drinking had grown more persistent and more disturbing over the past year; I was a nasty drunk, sharp-tongued and unforgiving, and Alice both detested and feared me for it. Although by then a drinker as well, she preferred marijuana to spirits and harangued me continually to trade in the disquieting consequences of alcohol for the mellowing effects of weed. We had recurring quarrels over my drinking and her marijuana smoking, tussles that led invariably to a standoff over the ridiculous question of who had chosen the superior vice.

I never said so, but it disturbed me that I couldn't seem to stop drinking—that, in fact, I didn't even want to. And the more it disturbed me, the more I drank in order not to feel disturbed. But nothing got better. I was on the road a great deal and spent many empty hours alone, filling the time in hotel bars. When I was home Alice was distant—not cold exactly, but unreal. She seemed to be spending more time than ever at her parents' home, which irked me, for I felt I always had to compete with Papa and Nanny for my wife's affections. What I did not yet know was that another, much more sinister competitor was sneaking into Alice's life.

In Harlow White's offer I saw a chance to shake things up again, to whisk away the gilded cobwebs and start anew. My son Justin was born in September 1977; within the month I made a deal with Harlow and company, and before the end of the year Alice and I had traded in our Tiburon palace for a more modest home. I expected my new partnership to mean a drop in income, at least at the start, and I took the rare practical step of adjusting my expenses in anticipation of the decline. In December I moved my family into a brand-new home in an unfinished housing development in Novato, in inland Marin County, on a newly dug street with the unlikely and, it turned out, ironic name of Wyworry Court. Why worry indeed. Before Christmas I found myself lying in the psych ward of Marin's Ross Medical Center, having been driven by pleas of family and business associates to seek help for my drinking and, more to the point from their perspective, for the frightening personality changes that alcohol induced in me.

I entered Ross Medical Center an alcoholic and emerged a manic-depressive. That's what the doctors there said I was, and it was fine by me. The polysyllabic psychological label gave me a lift. Not that being mentally ill was so great, but it was a hell of a lot better than being a drunk. I was grateful. Just as cracks were beginning to form in my wall of denial, the Ross diagnosis came along to shore it up. So I wasn't a common lush, as I deeply feared. Not I. I had a very complex and, more important, solidly identifiable psychological problem.

As with so many other affiliations in my life, my association with White-Rogin-Rabkin was very short-lived, a matter of a few months. I can't say I learned a lot from my partners. On par I found the three of them utterly ineffectual. In one area, though, I must admit to having learned a great deal: that was the crafty design and use of employee attitude surveys. I saw firsthand just how survey questions are selected, then weighted to bring about the desired conclusions, the most important going something like this: "Growing within your work force, sir, are the seeds of employee discontent, which, when nourished by proponents of collective thought and action, of whom you have several, put your company at risk of a union-organizing drive." And I learned how the purportedly anonymous poll could be designed and administered in order to allow the employer to identify, if not the individuals responsible for planting the alleged pro-union sentiments within the work force, then certainly the departments in which the culprits worked. Even so, still delighted with my new partnership, early on I gave my blessing and lent my name to an industrywide employee attitude survey sponsored by *Nations Restaurant News*, a major food service trade journal and the number one competitor of *Institutions*.

I was sorry I did. Now, I imagine that some boss somewhere really does respect his employees and has used attitude surveys to find out what they need to make their work lives more bearable and their labor more fruitful. But I never met the guy. The guys I met wanted to know what their employees were thinking so they could control them better. My clients were interested in—or I got them interested in—heading off union-organizing drives, sometimes by identifying little workplace problems and making small improvements, but mainly by detecting union sympathies and weeding out dissenters.

From the hotel conference rooms and executive offices I inhabited throughout the late 1970s, it was impossible for me to assess the effects of my lessons on the outside world. But Ted Hansen, skipper of Local 49, was watching all the while. To Hansen, and to his colleagues and higher-ups in the culinary union, I had turned on them in the most vicious way and in doing so single-handedly kept hundreds of thousands of workers out of their union and in economic margins.

"He hurt a lot of people in my industry," Hansen said of me more than a decade after my restaurant work had ended. "He deprived people of medical plans and vacations. I know my industry; workers make small amounts of money. They're people who live on low incomes who do not have a lot in life. . . . With a union, at least they'd have a medical and dental plan; at least they wouldn't be discharged unfairly without someone looking into it. At least they'd have someone to turn to, to grieve to in case they've been wronged. Now they have no help."

My betrayal of the culinary union was not to be forgotten. In 1988, after I publicly renounced union busting, the international office of the hotel and restaurant employees union made sure I would not find it so easy to switch sides this time: culinary union executives quickly snuffed a consulting contract offered me by a local that wanted my help in organizing a New York Marriott Hotel; a short time later they blocked a book and consulting offer made to me by the AFL-CIO itself.

As I began my rise to national union-busting stardom, Three M had already reached its apex. The mid-1970s was the golden age for Modern Management Methods, and understandably, for by that time the nation was swept up in a renaissance of anti-unionism. During the previous decade union workers had made great gains in wages and fringe benefits and had won significant improvements in their working conditions in spite of the severe limitations that had been written into labor law at the behest of U.S. business. Because of the glaring contrast in the fortunes of union and non-union workers, labor's gains during the 1960s stood as dramatic testimony to the potency of collective bargaining. On the whole, American work life did not look good in the 1960s. Unemployment was a continuing national problem, aggravated by a mushrooming labor force and by the quickening pace of technology, which displaced thousands of unskilled and semiskilled industrial workers. Indeed, in the first half of the decade Presidents Kennedy and Johnson saw pervasive poverty and unemployment in the United States and undertook to attack economic strife with a host of social welfare and work training programs. Then, record growth in the labor force during the later 1960s and early 1970s created unprecedented competition for jobs, which kept wages down and relegated a great many of the new workers to low-paid non-union service jobs, in places like fast-food restaurants and hotels. Yet in the face of all that, employees covered by union contracts were generally well off and secure; a great many of them earned middle-class incomes, lived in the suburbs, and sent their children to college, just like their counterparts in management.

The advantages of union organization were clear to many, but labor unions had been built by and for blue-collar workers in industry and the building trades, and until the 1960s they didn't reach much farther. Then, in a dramatic shift that gained momentum throughout the 1970s, organized labor began seeping into business offices, fire departments, county hospitals, and public school classrooms. White-collar employees and public servants of all sorts joined unions in record numbers, making up the fastest-growing segment of the labor movement in the 1970s. Between 1968 and 1978 union membership among public employees tripled, to more than two million. Another two million public employees belonged to once sleepy professional associations that, in the previous decade, had been transformed into aggressive labor organizations.

The enlistment of the white-collar workers into the union ranks substantially upped the stakes of the war on labor. Business leaders knew they needed to send more troops to the front, and they justified the deployment with a recitation of the dangerous schisms in U.S. economy, things like the cost of the Vietnam War, foreign competition, plant closures, high inflation, the energy crises, recession, and growing unemployment. All that ravaged the American worker, of course, but it was American business that went crying and gnashing its teeth to Congress. The problem, our corporate captains wailed, was the damn cost of labor. Business leaders from all sectors organized to "control labor costs"—meaning cut people's pay—initially in the construction industry. Our illustrious executives focused on construction because, they alleged, high wages in the building trades translated into high-cost construction, which meant high-cost everything that came after—the age-old "ripple effect" as applied to anti-unionism. To invert the argument, then, if business could successfully undermine unions in the building and construction trades, it could well defeat the whole of organized labor. They were shooting for the moon.

Hardly the paranoid machinations of union leaders, the construction-wage stratagem was devised by an influential consortium of America's top businesses. Called first the Labor Law Study Group and later the Construction Users Anti-Inflation Roundtable—who could be anti anything called anti-inflation?—the organization claimed to represent more than 1,100 businesses nationwide in 1973, a membership that boasted such venerable icons of corporate America as AT&T, Union Carbide, Exxon, General Motors, B. F. Goodrich, Chrysler, and IBM. The Roundtable and its predecessor group were known to be instrumental in introducing dozens of so-called labor law reform bills before Congress, but their ultimate goal was the repeal of state and federal laws establishing minimum wage standards on publicly funded construction projects. In the bull's-eye lay the Davis-Bacon Act, a federal statute enacted in 1931 that requires the payment of wage rates and fringe benefits prevailing in a locality—and that generally means union rates—on any federally financed contract.

The Roundtable's agenda was weighty, but the group was not alone in its work. The organization clearly had the ear of some pretty weighty elected officials. Anna Stewart, an Australian federal researcher who in 1980 published a report on the U.S. business offensive against organized labor during the 1970s, excerpted this benign description of the consortium's efforts from an entry in the congressional record of January 11, 1976:

> The work of the Construction Roundtable has been largely concentrated on attempts to slow down inflation and restore management at the job sites with accompanying beneficial effects on wage costs on other industries and the economy generally. The work of the Labor Law Committee encompassed labor-related legal and economic issues. . . . It worked towards needed changes in labor laws, including those affecting construction. . . .

"Beneficial effects on wage costs"? "Needed changes"? That was hardly how organized labor saw corporate America's attempt to obliterate a fundamental wage protection law in effect for nearly fifty years. Happily, that was also not the way the U.S. secretary of labor saw it. In 1979 then–Labor Secretary Ray Marshall repudiated a federal government report inspired by the Roundtable, which called for a repeal of the Davis-Bacon Act and other prevailing-wage laws in order to control inflation. Marshall wrote:

> This report will . . . raise the specter among American workers that in the good name of the fight against inflation, there will be an open season on protective labor legislation for which they have fought for half a century. . . . The report states that these federal laws have an inflationary cost of 715 million dollars. However, the report candidly states that over two thirds of this estimate is based upon data which have no statistical validity. . . . I cannot believe that the American people would strip away this long-established and historically supported wage protection program from four million workers for inadequately supported reasons.

So the unions won a round—but very belatedly and only by a hair. That same year the mighty Chrysler Corporation declared itself on the brink of bankruptcy and appealed to President Jimmy Carter for an emergency bailout loan. The taxpayer loan was granted, but only under the condition that the labor unions representing Chrysler employees, primarily the United Auto Workers, agreed to substantial cuts in pay and benefits. Determined to preserve jobs, the UAW conceded; from the Chrysler bailout deal, then, was born the "concession bargaining" system that still dominated union contract talks a decade later.

Long before the Roundtable's proposals had even been made public, plenty of other formidable anti-union groups had been working to castrate American labor unions. Some of the organizations had been fashioned decades before, but there had been no time like the 1970s—except perhaps the 1930s—to kick some union butt.

As never before, the 1970s saw the institutionalization of the union-free movement. Employer groups from a wide array of industries formed alliances and began to incorporate into their credos the general principles of union avoidance. United in their fear of an organized work force, employers formed networks—both local and national—to spread the secrets of union busting through the ranks of American management and to garner support for anti-union legislation.

Of the dozens of national anti-union employer associations that came of age in the 1970s, one of the most notorious was the Associated Builders and Contractors, another child of the post–World War II anti-union movement. The ABC liked to affect a soft approach. Funded chiefly by non-union builders and related businesses, the group sent its well-dressed public relations team around the country to smile and promote what it called the "merit shop." The ABC defined merit shop innocuously—and disingenuously— as a system in which an employer hired and paid each worker according to his qualifications and performance rather than as prescribed by contract. The group doggedly insisted it was not anti-union; in fact, it said, union members were welcomed into merit shop jobs. But if a union member got a job in a merit shop but couldn't bring his contract, his pay rate, his work rules, his job security guarantees, or his grievance procedures with him, in what way did he have a union? The merit shop mumbo-jumbo was just a ruse to sweet-talk the public into accepting non-union, lower-paid construction jobs, and it worked. The association won a lot of backing in the 1970s; during the 1980s it went on to open, in several states, private training schools for carpenters, electricians, and other tradespeople in competition with the more exacting and lengthy union apprenticeship programs. By the mid-1980s the ABC boasted more than 18,500 members nationwide.

Also on the move during the 1970s was the employer-funded National Right to Work Committee. The committee had been around since 1955, lobbying and propagandizing across the nation for laws prohibiting the union shop, but in 1968 it established the Legal Defense Fund and began fighting union shop contracts directly, in the courts. In the 1970s the national committee began to spawn state organizations, a breeding frenzy that continued through the next decade. Some state groups hid their affiliation to the national organization—for eventually just about everybody recognized the committee as a rabidly anti-union lobby—by incorporating under distinct names, such as Californians for the Freedom to Work.

The granddaddy of this corporate anti-union conspiracy is the powerful, hundred-year-old National Association of Manufacturers. A tireless general of the war on organized labor, the association has fought unions since 1903 through a series of obliquely named affiliated organizations. By the late 1970s the association was so confident in the appeal of its anti-union position that it no longer bothered to hide behind euphemisms.

In 1977 the association unveiled its Council on a Union Free Environment, which was specially created for the task of defeating a major labor law reform bill proposed by President Jimmy Carter then being debated in Congress. Designed to plug the gaping loopholes that employers used to stonewall union-organizing efforts, Carter's bill held the rare promise of fairness to workers. The proposal was simple. Of its eleven major provisions, the most significant—and most threatening to employers—was the requirement that representation elections be held within fifteen days after the filing of a petition, where the union produces authorization cards from more than half the employees in the proposed bargaining unit. A quick election would render much of the union buster's arsenal useless and thus alter the landscape of organizing drives. It also could well alter the results: unions might actually win or lose based on the proportion of workers wanting representation. Imagine.

Well, employers could imagine, and they wouldn't have it. With the help of the National Right to Work Committee and the near unanimous backing of corporate America, the Council on a Union Free Environment was successful in killing Carter's reforms. Central to the business coalition's tactics was the proposal of an alternate bill, deceptively dubbed the Employees' Bill of Rights, which would have cleaned out what little gut remained in the National Labor Relations Act. Called "the bosses' bill" by labor, the counterproposal also lost, but never mind. What business wanted was to snuff the Carter bill, and that it got. Since then the council has continued its anti-union work, spending its members' money on campaigns to teach business leaders the craft of union avoidance; disseminate the image of union leaders as arrogant, incompetent, and criminal; block legislation favorable to labor; and lobby for laws that would cripple unions and make organizing nearly impossible.

It was in this stridently adversarial environment that Three M came of age and flourished. By mid-decade the anti-union consulting business was basking in the limelight, and the names Melnick, McKeown and Mickus figured among the best known and most revered in the industry. Beginning in about 1974 Three M enjoyed a six-year stretch of explosive growth and prosperity that was both unprecedented and, judging from how dismally they were managed, quite unexpected. In 1975 Three M employed at least twenty-five full-time union busters, twice as many as Sheridan had at his peak yet still a glimmer of what Three M would become. For by the end of the 1970s MMM would be dispatching nearly one hundred anti-union consultants out of half a dozen offices, including one in London. Australian researcher Anna Stewart reported that in the late 1970s MMM had put on at least two anti-union seminars for businessmen in her country. Naturally, the expanding Three M staff required more ample office space, so in 1975 the firm giddily abandoned its downtown Chicago headquarters for a grand and luxurious suite in a swank new office center in the affluent Chicago suburb of Deerfield. That same year Melnick, McKeown and Mickus changed their company's name to Modern Management Methods, Inc., in recognition of the firm's broadening market and expanding services, as well as the growing sophistication of its clients.

A great number of Modern Management clients may indeed have been sophisticated, but the boys and occasional girl at Three M were anything but. They were rough riders, cowboys, locker-room braggarts who broke balls by day and drank to their virility by night.

"There was a sort of romanticism involved with being a Three M gunslinger, coming in and busting the union," said Dave Parmenter, a Three M'er from 1977 to 1981 who later started his own consulting firm in Detroit. Parmenter was in his early thirties when he left the corporate world and signed on with Three M. He was easily seduced by the glamour and power of his new world and found the wham-bam-thank-you-ma'am pace of the work thrilling. "You're in, you hit, you hit hard, and you're out," he exclaimed. "It was fun then."

Fun? The Three M'ers were thugs, and their clients knew it. In late 1978, for example, after a successful Modern Management campaign at St. Elizabeth's Hospital in Boston, the NLRB issued thirty-eight unfair labor practice complaints against the hospital. The board charged the employer with threatening, intimidating, interrogating, and spying on workers and of suspending and discharging employees for union activities. Because of the severity of the charges, and because the vote had been a close one, St. Elizabeth was ordered to hold another election. But the fear instilled by the hospital administration during the union's first try did not dissipate with a simple election order. The union lost again.

In nearly five years with Modern Management, Parmenter said he rarely saw the founders. By then, Melnick and McKeown had assumed the status of gurus and, like Sheridan before them, had grown finicky about which parts of the work they deigned to touch with their own hands. Mickus had carved out a comfortable and prosperous niche in the seminar trade. During the 1970s Three M was best known for busting unions in the hospital industry, and by the end of the decade the Mickus seminars were sought by hospital associations across the country. But the hospitals were just a corner of the Three M business. In 1979 Mickus signed on as a star performer for an outfit called Professional Seminar Associates, which did not only for health care, but for the manufacturing, retail, insurance, and financial industries, what I was busy doing for restaurants and hotels.

Of the hundreds of consultants Three M has launched against working people over the years, few got rich off their exploits. They were paid well, no doubt about it, and they made good use of their corporate expense accounts. But the troops weren't about to become millionaires from a tour with Three M. As on any pirate ship, most the spoils of the Three M plunder were seized by the captain and his mates. Between 1977 and 1979, the most profitable years for Modern, the firm recorded nearly seven hundred counterorganizing campaigns, on top of the countless seminars, training camps, personnel consulting services, attitude surveys, and postelection clean-up services. In all, those jobs meant about a million dollars apiece for the principals of the firm over the two years. Court records of Tony McKeown's divorce from his wife, Ann, obtained and made public by the AFL-CIO in 1986, reveal that from 1977 through 1981 McKeown, the nominal president of Three M, earned about half a million dollars a year. Other documents show that even in fiscal year 1980, after Three M had begun an irretrievable financial tumble, Herb Melnick and Tony McKeown each were paid $545,983.32 in salary alone; Tom Crosbie reported a salary of $339,583.16; Ray Mickus, who made most of his money from independent seminars, was paid $107,692.33; and Ed Juodenas, with whom I would later work Cravat Coal, earned $137,500.08.

As the Three M staff doubled and tripled, so did the firm's competition. In the Sheridan tradition, many of Three M's new competitors were the discards and the disenchanted from the father firm, who were eager to make the kind of money their former employers did. Others were labor attorneys wanting a higher profile, fatter income, and greater excitement than the workaday world of the law seemed to offer. Still others were industrial relations officers and personnel directors from the corporate world who had sat through enough countercampaigns and union-prevention workshops to see that there was easy money to be made on the outside. Anybody can hang out the union-busting shingle—no license or degree or registration or even experience is required—and in the 1970s, just about anybody did.

Union avoidance was the hot topic and the hot business of the decade. Articles promoting anti-union personnel policies appeared by the dozens, in periodicals ranging from *Personnel* and the *Journal of Industrial Relations* to the *Harvard Business Review*. The number of anti-union consulting companies climbed into the hundreds, and labor law firms turned increasingly to the profitable business of counterorganizing. Union-evasion seminar programs proliferated, some targeting the public sector, where the most aggressive organizing was taking place. In 1979 a "quick count" by the AFL-CIO identified thirty anti-union seminar firms, the three most notorious being consultant Charles Hughes's Executive Enterprises, attorney Albert DeMaria's Center for Values Research, and Advanced Management Research, Inc., the seminar arm of the New York labor law firm Jackson, Lewis, Schnitzler and Krupman. As an indication of the acceptance gained by union busters during the 1970s, many seminarists managed to offer their fare on the campuses of colleges and universities, both private and public, quite a step up in respectability and authority from the hotel conference rooms of the past. Some universities—which, let us not forget, are employers as well as schools—actually sponsored the events and granted continuing education credit to program attendees.

All this union-busting activity took its toll on the labor movement, exerting steady pressure on workers to identify with management rather than with each other, and on supervisors to constantly monitor their subordinates' actions and attitudes. During the 1970s, union organizing increased, to be sure, but not as dramatically as efforts to dislodge and disable organized labor. Between 1969 and 1980 the number of decertification drives by union employees and disclaimers of interest filed by unions after winning a representation election grew by some 400 percent. What that says is that even when unions managed to win an election, they often lost at the bargaining table, finding it impossible to win the improvements they had set out to gain. So either the local union leaders or the new members gave up.

By 1979 business's assault on labor had created such intense pressures on American workers that anti-union activity once again became the subject of a congressional inquiry. The focus of the hearings before the House Subcommittee on Labor-Management Relations were the practices by employers and their consultants, including a certain Modern Management Methods, that interfered with workers' rights to organize. What the subcommittee heard was very disturbing, but what ired the good congressmen most was the revelation that public money was routinely used to pay for brutal—and often illegal—union-busting activities.

Three M, as a favorite union buster to hospitals, was one of the prime beneficiaries of the public treasury. Since hospitals receive money from many government sources, including the federal Medicaid program, a substantial portion of the hospital fees collected by Three M actually came from taxpayers. Now, it so happens that the costs of an employer's counterorganizing campaign are not listed as allowable charges to Medicaid, but for years Three M's hospital clients managed to get away with it by packaging union-busting costs with in-service training, which refers to training on site that purportedly brings some sort of benefit to patients or residents. According to testimony before Congress, a hospital watchdog agency in Massachusetts ordered six hospitals to return to the Medicaid program $250,000 in fees paid to Three M for their anti-union campaigns from 1974 to 1976.

This was just one small example of the ways in which federal money was used to interfere with the rights of workers to organize. Federal contracts and grants support a broad array of private enterprises, from weapons manufacturers to universities; American tax money, therefore, was being spent to oppose unions in all kinds of businesses, public and private. In the 1970s the Department of Defense was found to be partially financing the anti-union campaigns of its contractors, including Rockwell International as it was building the B-1 bomber, and to be reimbursing contractors for costs of fighting unfair labor practice charges that resulted from dirty campaigns. The engineering union involved in three Rockwell organizing attempts from 1976 to 1978 estimated that the federal government spent more than $1 million directly on Rockwell's countercampaign and possibly twice that amount in indirect charges. Since under the National Labor Relations Act federal labor policy is to "encourage the practice and procedure of collective bargaining," federal funding of anti-union campaigns would appear to be illegal.

Melnick and McKeown were called to testify at the 1979 hearings. Slick as they were, the two gurus must have found the attention embarrassing; certainly such notoriety was not going to help their conspiratorial enterprise, which thrived on secrecy. To be sure, during McKeown's divorce proceedings six years later his attorney charged that the congressional hearings had kicked off a severe reversal in Three M's fortunes, a downswing that was to continue throughout the 1980s.

Well, maybe. There was more to Three M's downfall than bad press, however. The exposure surely tarnished the image of Tony's once mighty firm. But let's be honest: Three M's clients knew exactly what they were paying for, just as Nate Shefferman's had known three decades earlier. The truth is, Three M planted the seeds of its own destruction the day it was formed. The firm was doomed to crumble under the weight of its own twisted code. By 1983 Three M would stand in near ruin, reduced to a fraction of its once gargantuan size, scrambling to hold on to clients and emptying its coffers into legal battles with former employees.

I am sorry to say that the spirit and method of Three M did not disappear with the fall of the father firm, however. Quite the contrary; as Three M collapsed, it sent spores out in a million directions to spawn hundreds of clone firms. During the wild growth of the 1970s Three M was a revolving door, plagued with a continuous exodus of consultants, almost all of whom went into business in direct competition with their former employer despite a noncompete clause that they had all signed upon joining Three M. Those abandoning ship came to include Jim Bannon in 1977 and Ray Mickus in 1981. In 1984 Herb Melnick himself would kick Three M in the teeth and strike out on his own.

Pathos

Like Three M, I was riding the crest of fame in the late 1970s. Not I exactly, but one-half of I, the public Marty Levitt, the character known to the restaurant world as one tough union buster. But as I was scaling mountains of glory, the other Marty Levitt was losing his grip. So dizzied was I by the glare of the spotlight, so impressed with my own ascent, that I couldn't seem to stop my private self from slipping into a chasm of wretchedness.

At home on Wyworry Court, life was miserable. Surely the neighbors wouldn't have thought so. Successful husband, beautiful wife, two little sons, nice house, great cars. And I loved Alice, loved her more than my career, however brilliant, more than life itself. More than anything, I wanted my darling Alice to be happy. I thought about her day and night, even as I lay on a hotel bed in some faraway city, flipping through the Yellow Pages in pursuit of a properly discreet "escort service." Even as I stood sweet-talking some lonely lady at the hotel bar in another strange city, beckoning her to share my bed with me. I really only wanted Alice, only wanted her to want me, to love me as I loved her. Nothing terrified me more than the thought of losing Alice. So I bought her things, lots of things: coats and jewels and dresses. And still she seemed unmoved. Somehow, somewhere, I had lost her.

Around this time Phil Lederer entered my life again, briefly. I contacted him to ask him to help my sister-in-law and her husband, a framing contractor, who were under fire from building trades unions for allegedly cheating on benefits payments. Phil said my timing was perfect, because he had had it with Three M. Not long before he got my call, Phil had been squeezed out of his own firm, Lederer, Fox & Grove, the darling of Three M. He had landed on his feet, though; in short order he had a new firm, Lederer, Reich, Sheldon and Connolly, and a string of big clients. Some of them were facing union-organizing drives, and Phil said he could really use me. He passed me some plums: I ran anti-union campaigns at American Automobile Association headquarters in St. Louis and at the Owens Corning plant in Compton, California; and I put on a seminar for the Institute of Scrap Iron and Steel in Chicago. But my heavy drinking and my troubles with Alice were wearing me down. I couldn't concentrate on my work, I was just going through the motions. I was an emotional wreck. I felt that any minute I would shatter into a million pieces; there was nothing to hold me together. When I could resist no more I turned myself over to the caring counselors of the alcohol treatment program at St. Helena Hospital, a church-run facility in the heart of California wine country.

From St. Helena I called Phil, asking for more work. He was kind, he wished me well. But I thought I could hear a trace of disgust in his voice. It was the last time I spoke to him.

One month after entering St. Helena, I emerged dry. I felt good, strong, happier than I had in a long time. The treatment program had jump-started me; with the momentum I stayed dry for four long, rough, glorious months. I thought I'd be sober forever. But something happened, or rather, something that had been happening for some time came bubbling to the surface.

Alice didn't talk about it at first. Instead it came seeping out late at night, all twisted and gnarled by marijuana and cocaine. Where is Alice this time? I asked Mary Quirk, our housekeeper, night after night. When will she be home? Who's been taking care of the babies? You? Did she say who she was going out with?

Alice always did come home, very late and very high. Let's have fun, she'd say; don't be such a baby. Then she'd smile, she'd vamp a little—a lot. Everything's okay, don't worry. I was just at a party. Let's make love.

The next night, she'd be gone again.

I didn't press her when I was sober the way I might have drunk; I suppose I didn't want her to tell me. But finally it had to come out: Alice was having an affair with a cocaine dealer she knew from our days in Tiburon.

His name was Jim. I knew him, too; he ran a coffee store in Sausalito and in fact had introduced me to the pleasures of freshly ground coffee beans when that epicurean luxury was still a novelty, even in California. Alice he had turned on to other vices, and she had succumbed gratefully. Maybe she could have kept her romantic entanglement a secret, or at least kept it unspoken, if she hadn't gotten into trouble. But when she finally confessed the affair to me, it was not so much that she wanted me to know the truth, but that she needed my help.

She had fallen into the affair when things didn't seem to be going well in our marriage, she told me. It just happened, it was a mistake, she didn't love him. It meant nothing. But now that she was trying to end it, Jim wouldn't let her go. She had managed to run up a debt to her lover, and he was, after all, a businessman. He wasn't about to release her until she paid.

I had to do something. I never knew the details of the mess, but I did know I would do anything to buy Alice back from Jim. Deep inside I was insecure little Marty. It still amazed me that I could get someone as beautiful as Alice. I wasn't about to let her go. I knew I had to find the money somehow, and while I was at it, I figured I'd buy Alice the one luxury she did seem to want: a big, glamorous 1970 Mercedes 280 SE convertible. I'd buy it, then she'd have to return to me. I had found one in Los Angeles for $10,000; this was my chance.

I was cool and matter-of-fact when I walked into World Savings & Loan and bought a $10,000 certificate of deposit with a bad check drawn on my old Wells Fargo account. I remained cool later that day as I sat down with the loan officer at the California Canadian Bank and applied for a $10,000 loan, offering my brand-new CD as collateral. The performance I gave that day was my best con job to date. I made the loan officer feel it was his lucky day. After all, I wasn't just any schmuck loan applicant. I was the kind of client bankers dreamed about: a bold and successful entrepreneur, young, sharp, and gutsy, with $10,000 socked away and the potential for who knew how much more. A big union buster— wow. The loan officer liked that. And here I just strolled into the bank and dropped my business right in his lap. It was too easy— he should have known that.

Within thirty minutes I had a check for $10,000 in my hands, and, as I had promised as part of my spiel, I promptly opened a couple of accounts at California Canadian. Alice got her buyout money as soon as I got home; she hopped in our BMW coupe and drove to Jim's to make the payoff. The two of us ended 1978 in a silent truce.

With money in the bank and my wife back by my side, I was feeling virile again, and I still hadn't taken a drink. The first payment on the loan wasn't due for a couple of months, and the demand for my workshops continued to grow. So what could go wrong?

Alice flew to Los Angeles with the money to buy the coveted Mercedes; she drove it up the coast to Carmel, where the two of us rendezvoused for a romantic getaway. Then I hit the road for a series of seminars, feeling sanguine and glad to be alive. Had I bothered to cover the damn loan payments, my fraud might never have been unearthed. But when the credulous banker watched the first due date come and go without finding a check from me, he started getting nervous. Then—and only then—did he bother to look into my collateral. All it took was a phone call. That's when he learned that there was no CD, no $10,000, no way to recover the loan. Surprise! Immediately he froze my accounts.

At the time my crime was discovered, I was just cranking up a two-day seminar for restaurateurs in Newport Beach, a sunny, affluent coastal town in southern California. On the afternoon of the first day, the banker repaid my surprise. There I was, deep in character, marching around the banquet hall pounding and regaling the troops, when who should appear in the back of the room but Mr. Loan Officer himself.

I faltered. It was the worst kind of nightmare for someone who kept two running identities so neatly apart. Suddenly my two selves stood face to face with each other in a potentially humiliating public confrontation. For an endless moment the two wrestled each other silently for control. I felt naked. I wanted to dart out the side door and disappear. But the cool character won the struggle: I kept my composure, even managed a smile, and casually called a break so that I could talk to my "important visitor." It was a painful conversation, for both of us, even sad. I always hated disappointing people and always seemed to be doing just that. The loan officer was, in fact, disappointed: more hurt, really, than angry. He took my deception very personally. With the look of a wounded lover, he told me, "Potentially, Marty, you're in big trouble." Not long after that he filed a complaint with the Marin County District Attorney's Office.

After I returned home I became positively self-destructive. I learned that Alice was seeing Jim again; maybe she had never stopped seeing him, how would I know. Anyway, I couldn't see how it mattered what happened to me. Without Alice I had nothing, I couldn't feel alive. I tumbled back down into the kind of morbid depression that had engulfed me after Harvey's suicide. I was numb, paralyzed, surrounded by gray. I couldn't think, couldn't feel, could hardly talk. Then I fell into the abyss.

After four months of sobriety I jumped in the beloved Mercedes, drove to a liquor store, bought a fifth of vodka, returned home in a rage, and got blind, stinking, fucking drunk. I lit a fire in the fireplace and started burning everything that reminded me of Jim, of Alice, of Alice and Jim, of my miserable existence. Then I drove off again, headed for Reno and God only knew what. I didn't get very far. The police pulled me over.

I spent that night in the Marin County Jail, and the next night, and two more nights. The police had a warrant for my arrest, thanks to the banker's complaint, so I was theirs until some generous soul came to post bail. Alice and my father did finally bail me out, but I didn't want any more help. I didn't intend to defend myself. Never mind, I told her, it doesn't matter. Maybe prison is where I belong after all, maybe it would be a relief. But Alice, whether out of guilt or love, insisted that I fight the charges, and in the end I relented, agreeing to talk to the attorney that she had found for me—through Jim, of course, who happened to know lots of criminal lawyers—and halfheartedly went about defending myself. In the meantime, the checks I had written over the previous weeks started bouncing like mad against the impermeable wall of the frozen accounts. By the end of the year I had amassed more than $7,000 in bad checks.

In April 1980, after many meetings with attorneys and probation officers, I pleaded guilty to four felony counts of passing bad checks and of intent to defraud. As part of my plea bargain, another eight counts, including two counts of grand theft—the actual bank fraud with which I was charged—were dropped. I, in turn, agreed to pay restitution for the rubber checks, to attend Alcoholics Anonymous meetings, and to repay an insurance claim of some $12,000 relating to a small house fire for which I had been responsible. The insurance restitution brought my total debt to nearly $20,000.

Originally the plea bargain had included an agreement that the DA would not ask for prison time. But on the day my plea was entered, I was sentenced to six months beginning in May at the Marin County Honor Farm, a country club jail for the common white-collar criminal of Marin.

I was thirty-five and going to jail. Amazingly, that wasn't the worst of it, at least not to me. Alice was by then involved in another affair, this time with the leader of a religious cult, a small but stormy man named Scott. The Bay Area branch of the cult, called alternately TWIG for The Word Is God, and The Way, had moved into the house two doors down from us on Wyworry Court. Not long after the group's arrival, a couple of the girl members had begun wooing Alice, inviting her to prayer meetings and Bible readings and social-spiritual gatherings. By then I realized that Alice was lonely and emotionally very needy; her hunger for a sense of belonging paralleled, I suppose, my own constant pursuit of fraternity and camaraderie. Yet I could not accept Alice's choices of friends, who always seemed dumb and ordinary, even crude, beneath her—or perhaps beneath me. Her involvement with the TWIG people irritated me to the extreme. I considered the religion a fraud and the followers simpletons, and I said so to Alice, endlessly. Yet the more I railed against the cult, the harder I pushed Alice into its bosom. Her visits to the temple became more frequent, her stays more lengthy, and inevitably she won herself a promotion from disciple to bedfellow.

With the countdown to jail time under way, I entered yet another alcohol treatment program. Jail, of course, was going to force me to stay dry, but a veteran AA member I knew in Novato had warned me that I would do a lot better if I started the battle in advance. No sense in doing it cold turkey if I had a choice.

I packed my things, did three weeks of a four-week alcohol program in San Jose, and then prepared to enter the honor farm. As my departure grew near, grief enveloped my household. My boys were two and five years old, too young to understand what was happening to their family but old enough to absorb and share in the sorrow. We cried a great deal in those final days.

The day my sentence was to begin, Alice drove me to the Marin Civic Center for processing. She brought along two girls from the cult who wanted to offer their prayers. All of us wept along the way. Alice and I both said we were sorry. She told me she loved me, that she would miss me. She said all the right words, then went home to her lover.

I served my sentence—four months in all, counting time off for good behavior and good work. During one Sunday visit at the honor farm, Alice served me with divorce papers.

In October 1980 I found myself in a familiar condition, sitting motionless in the family room of Mom and Dad's house in Beachwood. The TV was on, as it always was then, dispensing inappropriately gay sounds and colors. I rarely watched the silly thing, but I couldn't stand silence. So I sat, smoking, drinking vodka, and staring blankly at the screen, while the cheery bells and hollow applause of daytime game shows made a mockery of my misery. I hadn't wanted to go back to Ohio, surely not back to the nest, but as a convicted felon and alcoholic with no money, no home, and an explosive family life, I couldn't think of many people who would take me in. I had had to get a special dispensation from the judge in order to leave California and look for work elsewhere. My PO had whined and pouted about it, of course; he had wanted me within reach during the whole five years' probation so he could torture me personally. Luckily the judge was less rabid: as long as I continued to make the required $500-a-month restitution payments, and checked in regularly with the probation department in Cleveland, he didn't see any reason to hold me on the West Coast.

By the time I was a free man again, Alice had backed off on the divorce. I wasn't sure why. Was it out of pity or guilt or fear? I couldn't allow myself the luxury of believing it might be love, for the stiff coolness with which Alice had treated me during those long months on the farm had not softened. It had driven me crazy while I was inside. Yet I was hopeful. Maybe the trouble was California. Maybe if we just got the hell out of here, we could put our Humpty-Dumpty lives back together again. Alice was unsure. So I remained hopeful: she hadn't said no.

I made a halfhearted effort to find work. With my gleaming track record in the food-service industry, I figured perhaps I could land a job as the head of personnel with some big restaurant in town. I asked the National Restaurant Association for help; it obliged with a glowing letter of recommendation. But even that was not enough. The fact was, I had never worked as a personnel director in a restaurant, or in a restaurant at all, or in personnel at all, for that matter. When it came right down to it, I didn't have any ordinary job skills.

The weeks dragged on. Nothing. I called Alice almost every day and begged her to pack up the kids and join me in Ohio. I wanted us to be a family again. But her answer was always the same: "You don't have work. How are we going to live?" In California she had her parents, Nanny and Papa, to support her, but in Ohio it would be up to me. Clearly I wouldn't be able to do it. I was beginning to feel pretty pathetic and pretty ridiculous; there I was, thirty-six years old asking Mom and Dad for five dollars here and ten dollars there to get me through the day. I had to do something, and I knew what I did best.

Once I had decided, a calm optimism came over me. Mother drove me to the rapid transit station in neighboring Shaker Heights. It was like being in junior high again, getting a ride from my mom, then praying she would drop me off quickly, before any of the guys saw me. I thanked Mother for the ride, apologizing to her mentally for the adolescent embarrassment she was not even aware I felt. When her car disappeared I sighed with gratitude and relief. The train took me to Public Square, in the heart of downtown Cleveland; from there I walked the nine blocks to the federal building. The NLRB office was on the ninth floor.

When I asked the receptionist for the day's RC petitions, she didn't know what I was talking about. It was still a few weeks before the American people would put Ronald Reagan in the White House and a year before the new Republican president would turn union busting into a patriotic act by firing striking air traffic controllers. The great explosion in the number of union busters was still to come. By middecade the Cleveland NLRB office would have moved its "day file" to an auspicious site in the front lobby, and a long line of consultants and junior attorneys would be vying with one another for a crack at the freshest union representation petitions. But in October 1980 union busters still were getting the bulk of their work as I always had, through their network of labor lawyers.

I asked to speak to the duty officer. She wasn't sure where the petitions were kept; she thought they might be somewhere in the back. I followed the befuddled bureaucrat into a stuffy storage room. There we located a file drawer crammed full of petitions. Three were fresh, filed just the day before. On the note pad I always kept in my pocket, I jotted down the particulars of all three, the company name, the executive to contact, the description of the proposed voting unit, the name of the union and its organizer. Then I hopped back on the train and headed for home, opting to walk the four miles from the Shaker Heights station to Beachwood rather than calling Mommy to come pick me up.

With three hot petitions in hand, I felt intoxicated. My ego quickly swelled to its pre–honor farm mass. At my kitchen table command post I began poring over my NLRB notes, in preparation for the sales calls. I fell into character quickly, hungrily; as I did, a rush of confidence and guile swept over me. I smiled to myself. Well, what do you know? The son of a bitch is back.

Copeland Oaks

Petition

Name of Employer: Copeland Oaks, Inc., Sebring, Ohio
Type of Establishment: Retirement home
Employer Representative: Claude L. Roe, executive director
Petitioner: Service, Hospital, Nursing Home & Public Employees
  Union, Local 47, Cleveland, Ohio, affiliated with Service
  Employees International Union, AFL-CIO
Union Representative: James Horton

Jim Horton entered the world in the midst of the Great Depression. As the third of sixteen children born to a black Alabama coal miner and his wife, and as their eldest son, Horton learned about work early. He also learned about unions. Horton was in grade school in the 1940s, and his papa was in the UMWA. The United Mine Workers of America, historically one of the most militant unions in the country, was roaring and growing under the raging leadership of John L. Lewis. Once a month, more often when there was trouble, the elder Horton awakened Jim at dawn and dragged him from their rural cottage to the early morning union meetings in Birmingham. Jim learned a great deal from watching his father; he grew up thinking of union men as hardworking and serious. And he grew up believing in loyalty.

At age seventeen Jim left home. His parents had enough mouths to feed, and it was high time. He said good-bye to Alabama still clutching the dream that he might one day play major league baseball. But soon after he arrived in Cleveland Jim's boyhood fantasy dissolved, overshadowed by more pressing matters, like the need for food. He took whatever jobs he could find, first at a chemical company and later with the B&O Railroad, and then he joined the air force.

Jim's discharge from military service four years later brought with it the GI Bill and the promise of higher education. But first things first: he had to make his way once again in the civilian work world. In 1959 Jim Horton was hired as an orderly in the psychiatric ward at St. Luke's Hospital, a stately Methodist institution in downtown Cleveland. Jim was just twenty-five years old, and the pay of $1.30 an hour didn't seem so bad, not at first. He was industrious, bright, capable. He wouldn't be staying long.

He started taking classes at the Ohio School of Broadcasting and at the Arma Lee Barber College as well; he planned to have a real career someday. But six years later Jim was still at St. Luke's, making just a few cents an hour more than when he'd started. In 1962 Jim had married, and within a few years he had fathered a son and a daughter. He started looking around the hospital. What he saw disturbed him: hundreds of workers, most of them blacks and other minorities, toiled for years at heavy, dirty, emotionally draining jobs for rock-bottom pay. The workers were frightened and distrustful, even of one another. They had no protection from the disciplinary whims of their erratic supervisors, no job guarantees, little hope for promotions, and no hope at all of one day earning a living wage. The more Jim saw, the more he wanted to know, so he started poking around, asking questions. And the more he heard, the more determined he became that something had to change. Jim found janitors and nurse's aides with ten, fifteen years at the hospital who still made well under two dollars an hour. He found a capricious wage structure that totally disregarded experience and seniority. He found long entrenched work rules that discouraged groups of employees from gathering. And he found a system of selective threats and promises that encouraged employees to compete with one another rather than to cooperate. That's when he decided to do something.

Jim couldn't know that his call to Local 47 of the Building Service Employees International Union would touch off a terrible two-year war, not only in the corridors of St. Luke's, but throughout all of Cleveland. The year was 1966. Nonprofit hospitals were still eight years away from being written into federal collective bargaining law, so there was no way to force hospital management to recognize a union it didn't want. Jim was an optimist by nature, but he also was a realist. From his father he had learned what it could mean to fight for unionization. He knew the hospital bosses would not be polite in their counterattack, and he knew workers might be forced to strike. And he knew that in a strike, many workers would suffer; some would lose their homes, families would be torn apart, people would go hungry, workers on both sides of the line might grow violent. So at that first meeting with Joe Murphy, then president of Local 47, and with other union officers at the Lancer Steak House, what Jim wanted most of all were assurances that the union would protect and support his people for the duration of the struggle. "I've got five hundred people out there," he told the union men. "You'd better be serious."

Satisfied that the international would stand by his workers, Jim accepted a thousand union authorization cards and went about the business of organizing. Through clandestine chats in the locker room, he rounded up a committee. He started working overtime so he could talk to people on different shifts and from different departments. "We had to move fast and quiet," he said. "I was in a hurry."

Within five months the union had managed to sign up almost all of the hospital's service employees. In the meantime Joe Murphy was working the political angle, meeting with hospital management and the Methodist clergy in an effort to convince them it would be best to recognize the union. But they wouldn't budge. The talks dragged on and on for more than a year, and still nothing. Then came the strike. One Tuesday afternoon at exactly one-thirty, five hundred hospital workers dropped what they were doing and marched down to the lobby. It was war.

Twenty-four hours a day seven days a week, picketers announced to the world that they wanted a union and vowed not to go back to work until the hospital agreed to negotiate. Outsiders joined in, uninvited, the Communist party and the Black Nationals, opportunists who saw the strike as a medium for their own political agenda. Fights broke out, a couple of homemade bombs went off. A court order was handed down, limiting strikers to three picketers per entrance. The community was outraged, terrified. The youngest and the oldest workers crossed the lines and went to work—the youngsters because they didn't understand, the older people out of fear. Still, the majority stuck to the strike: janitors, orderlies, aides, and food service workers all scraping by on their $25-a-week strike pay and charity from local churches and labor groups. Joe Murphy went to the Catholics, he went to the Methodists, and he went to Mayor Carl B. Stokes, the first black mayor of a major U.S. city, pleading for help. At last, in 1968, a year after the strike had begun, the Cleveland City Council passed a law requiring nonprofit hospitals in the city to hold a representation election if a majority of workers signed union authorization cards.

Victory.

A couple of months later Jim Horton was ordained an organizer for Local 47 and thrown right back into the trenches, this time in charge of nursing homes. Jim must have caught his adversary off guard, for he organized a dozen Cleveland-area homes in the first year. His pace slowed after that, but by the time he was named director of organizing in 1976, Jim Horton had brought workers from twenty nursing homes and twelve hospitals into the Local 47 fold. In the summer of 1980 he got a call from someone at the Copeland Oaks retirement home.

The sixty-mile drive out to Sebring lifted me into another world. With greater Cleveland far behind me, I meandered along narrow rustic roads that I had never even known about as a boy. For thirty miles along softly curved roadways my eyes feasted on the colors and patterns of the countryside: pastures and rolling hills, aging oaks and red-leafed maples, rickety fences and lazy cows, whitewashed farmhouses. My car—an old Chrysler my dad had bought for me—seemed to float. Silence enveloped the land, a silence at once earthy and divine, so filled with peace that the jabbering of my radio talk show seemed sacrilegious. I clicked off the radio and, for the first time in as long as I could remember, savored the feeling of solitude. For one glorious hour my mind had only the low rumble of the engine to distract it from its serenity. I chuckled to myself; it seemed proper that a retirement community would be built out on this road, along the pathway to Paradise.

My reverie was shattered by my arrival in Sebring. One look around and suddenly I wasn't feeling at all joyful. "Where the hell am I?" I said to myself. "And what am I doing there?"

Once the hub of Ohio's pottery industry, Sebring was now a patchwork of abandoned brick factories and boarded-up storefronts. The town proper was a two-block ghost town. I saw a dilapidated shop marked "Cafe" that appeared to have a couple of customers, and I noticed a well-stocked hardware store. But otherwise there were no signs of life. I cruised down the main street, peering up side roads. God, did anyone actually live there? I couldn't imagine. I checked my directions again, hoping that I had somehow missed Sebring and wound up in the wrong town. No such luck. I had started this trip hopeful that the Copeland Oaks job would buy me a new start in life. Now I was beginning to doubt that the place would be able to afford my $750 per diem. I checked the directions another time. I still had a couple of blocks before reaching the address; I'd just have to wait and see.

Then, out of nowhere, it appeared. Two stone pillars rose up from atop a low hill and stood guard over the entrance of an elegant estate. A cast-iron arch announced *Copeland Oaks, a Cope Methodist Home.* Beyond the columns, a long driveway stretched through the middle of a great green lawn, leading to a stately, colonial-style brick hall, its porch guarded by six whitewashed wooden columns. The large central building was surrounded by charming ranch-style homes, built of light orange brick, which were woven together with a maze of trim lawns and immaculate walkways. Beyond the buildings a blue lake shimmered in the amber autumn sun. The parking lot was discreetly tucked away to the side, so as not to intrude upon a visitor's view. A smile flitted across my lips. This was going to be okay.

The doors of the central building opened onto a magnificent foyer. The plush carpet muffled the buzz of a motorized wheelchair that carried a white-haired woman past formal sitting areas to the elevator. Two young women in crisp white knee-length dresses and thick-soled white shoes padded silently across the lobby, whispering serious secrets. They stepped into the elevator with the elderly woman and greeted her with cheery hellos. The door closed on the harmonic blend of the three voices.

I told the receptionist, who also smiled, that I had come to see Claude Roe. When I first contacted Claude he had given me the pat brush-off: "We already have a labor attorney." My months away from the action hadn't rusted me a bit, and I had responded enthusiastically:

"That's good to hear. I'm not a lawyer myself, and I wouldn't work without one. You need labor counsel."

That had bought me another minute. Then my supervisors-as-great-communicators pitch had rolled off my tongue as if I never had another thing on my mind, as if I had never been a desperate husband, an alcoholic, a criminal. I was sailing. Roe had seemed reassured by my confidence.

"You've tweaked my interest," he admitted. "Why don't you give my attorney a call."

I did, and I landed a meeting with Roe and attorney Lou Davies for the next day at Davies's office in Youngstown. The meeting was friendly; Roe and Davies seemed to like my approach. Still, Davies couldn't quite understand what I would be doing that he couldn't do just as well himself. So I applied a tactic that few salesmen—particularly union busters, who tend to be stingy and suspicious—are willing to use: I handed out free advice.

"Look," I said, "whether you hire me or not, there are certain things you should do to make sure you keep the advantage." Then I told them about the Excelsior list strategy, about not giving the complete names and addresses of employees on the list that they are required to prepare for the NLRB and the union. "Make it as hard as possible for the union to get to the people," I said.

They liked that. I was sent out of the room so Roe and Davies could talk things over. When I was called back in, Davies told me it had been the Excelsior list detail that clinched the sale.

Claude—"Dr. Roe" to his staff—came gliding through the lobby to greet me. He presented a most intimidating figure. A round, bald head rode stiffly on square shoulders atop a stately frame. The face was chiseled into a permanent scowl, the nose held at a slight upward angle in an expression of mild distaste for everything below. The body moved stiffly, frugally, as if every gesture had a sacred purpose. A Presbyterian minister and doctor of divinity who for career considerations was in the process of converting to the Methodist faith, Claude shunned his minister's costume, preferring the gray business suit of a banker. Affixed to his lapel was a small gold pin bearing the acronym MENSA. The brooch bore witness to Dr. Roe's membership in that international organization of the intellectually gifted and served as a constant reminder to all of his native superiority. Although I came to think of him as a sincere, if opaque, man, to Copeland Oaks workers Dr. Roe was considered stern and aloof. When the executive director greeted me with a pleasant look on his face and a crisp handshake, it was a rare show of enthusiasm that at the time I couldn't fully appreciate.

It was no secret that a decade earlier Copeland Oaks had stood on the brink of financial ruin. And it was no secret that Claude Roe had been the one to salvage it. When Claude was hired away from a string of Presbyterian nursing homes in New Jersey in 1972,

Copeland was $11 million in the hole. The home reserved a large portion of its rooms for needy residents, who paid a fraction of the $500–$600 monthly fee out of their Social Security or Medicare income, with Copeland subsidizing the rest. Over the years those subsidies had become more and more of a burden to the facility. As a nonprofit home, Copeland did not have a steady source of income; it depended on donations and bequeathals from good-hearted citizens and grants from churches and foundations. Without constant rainmaking, the well had run dry. It took Claude six years to abolish Copeland's deficit, but by 1980—through a combination of higher fees, fewer subsidies, and endless, endless fund-raising—the home was enjoying a healthy annual surplus, known in commercial business as a profit.

Claude was clearly proud of Copeland's amenities—saw them as a personal tribute to him—so before we got down to business he took me on a tour of the kingdom. The elegance of the home continued to amaze me; I had worked at hospitals and nursing homes before, but this was different. The central building I had entered housed the Copeland corporate offices and a hundred residential apartments, but in decor and character it was more like a swank hotel. In addition to plush apartments and a regal sitting room, the main building boasted a lovely chapel, a dining room that was more elegant than most fine restaurants, and a recreation area that was a health club with billiard tables. A separate physical therapy room with specialized equipment and whirlpool bath was also available to the esteemed residents of Copeland.

Attached to the rear of the main building was the lumber-and-cement shell of a skilled-care facility that was then under construction. The new section, called Crandall Medical Center, was designed both as a hospital for current Copeland residents and as a home for other elderly people too feeble or ill for Copeland. Crandall was expected to be operating within a year, with Claude Roe as executive director.

Outside, strolling among the private homes—which Copeland called "villas"—I felt that I was a guest at an exclusive country club. I didn't mind revealing to him that I was impressed. "If I retire and have to go to a nursing home, this is where I want to be," I exclaimed. Claude knew the comforts of Copeland well. He and his wife lived in one of the more exclusive villas—for free.

Satisfied that I was sufficiently appreciative of Copeland's charm, Claude called a meeting with Davies. The executive director was clearly nervous. During the previous months, as Claude was all over northeastern Ohio meeting with church foundations, wealthy Christians, and other potential benefactors of his esteemed retirement home, Horton and his team of organizers had quietly spread the promise of a union to the weary Copeland employees. By fall Horton had assembled an inside organizing committee of thirty women and two men, which crusaded swiftly and silently for the support of the other workers. By the time Claude heard the rumblings, the union had signed up 60 percent of Copeland's hourly employees, about 170 nurses, nurse's aides, housekeepers, janitors, cooks, and waitresses. Signed authorization cards at the ready, Jim Horton had put in a call to Dr. Roe.

It was a phone call Claude will never forget, for it was the opening salvo of a nasty nineteen-month war. Horton was brief and courteous. He told Dr. Roe that Copeland employees had expressed an interest in union representation and asked for a meeting with the director so he could prove that a majority of employees had signed authorization cards. If Dr. Roe would agree voluntarily to recognize the union, both sides could save themselves the trouble and expense of an NLRB election, and they could get right to work on negotiating a contract.

Well, Dr. Roe had no intention of meeting, and he certainly wasn't negotiating any contract. Why should he? The union was after him, not the other way around. *He* didn't need a union, and he didn't want one; it was just going to cost him money and get in his way. He couldn't see how he had anything to gain by sitting down with union people. No, Mr. Horton, said Claude. There will be no meeting. We have nothing to discuss. If the union wants Copeland Oaks, it is going to have to come and get it.

Claude's pronouncement that the union was going to have to fight for Copeland was a perversion of the truth so sublime that most people would not catch it; possibly even Claude himself was unaware of the deception. The truth is, unions do not fight to "get" workers. They fight on behalf of workers. At Copeland the truth was employees were asking the union to represent them, not the other way around. The truth was Copeland workers had called Local 47, not the other way around. The truth was Copeland workers were unhappy with their treatment and wanted changes. The truth was Horton and the other organizers were trying to help Copeland employees get what the employees wanted, which was an organization that would look out for their interests. The truth was in vowing to fight the union, Claude was vowing to fight his own employees, to do battle with laundrywomen and maids and cooks.

Funny thing was, Claude thought himself a kind man. Really.

He announced proudly that Copeland paid as well as the other retirement homes in the area—that is to say, a few pennies above the minimum wage—despite a history of horrific financial trouble. He boasted that the employees were like family to one another, as if that were somehow his doing. There were fewer than three hundred workers at Copeland, most of them simple, modest women from Sebring and the surrounding towns and villages. They knew each other's children, they shared each other's secrets, they attended each other's Christmas parties. Claude himself claimed to know all his employees by name, although I never saw him greet any of his subordinates, by name or otherwise. Amazingly, he imagined that he was loved and respected and believed that the employees thought of him in fatherly terms. He was appalled at the suggestion that he had not done enough for them. If that union really thought it could turn his girls against him, well, it was welcome to try.

Claude, Lou Davies, and I locked ourselves in Claude's office for our first strategy session. Before we began drawing battle plans, I turned to Claude and offered my congratulations for his having sidestepped the first of what I called union "traps": the proposed meeting. Claude's refusal to meet with Horton had been impetuous, I knew, driven by ego, not wiles. He was raw, a union hater to be sure, but not an educated one. Now his schooling was about to begin. First lesson: The union must always be thought of—and publicized—as devious. Every move must be interpreted as sneaky, every motive treated as suspect. I told Claude that Horton's meeting invitation had been a ploy to trick him into recognizing the union. Unions will do that, you know, I said. They'll slither up to you with some pretense or other, then they'll stick a pile of authorization cards under your nose, and before you know it you've bought yourself a union. Thank goodness you had the instincts to run, Claude, for had you not, you might be sitting across the table from the SEIU right now instead of me.

Claude gasped. How could that be? he asked.

Here's how, I said: if, being a good-hearted and fair man, you had sat down with union organizers on Copeland Oaks premises, you would have taken one step toward recognizing the union. If, being a reasonable man, you had taken them up on their offer to look at the authorization cards, you could have automatically waived your so-called "good-faith doubt" that the union had the support of a majority of the workers, and the NLRB could have ordered you to negotiate. Imagine! The union would have snuck right in under your nose.

Claude let out a stream of air he seemed to have forgotten about. Good for you for not falling for that one, I told him. But watch out, this was just the first trick. There will be hundreds of land mines buried along the way. Unions are desperate for members, and they'll resort to all kinds of chicanery to fill their rosters. That is why you must not say or do anything in this campaign without checking with Mr. Davies and me.

Claude looked grateful. He was all mine.

What I told Claude, and later all the Copeland supervisors, and all supervisors in every anti-union campaign, was another perverted truth. I started with the facts of the law, then put a spin on them to make the whole process seem quite unholy. Yes, labor law does allow unions and employers to agree on union recognition without going to an NLRB election. In fact, before the NLRB will even accept a union's petition for an election, the union must already have asked management if it will recognize the union voluntarily. It has to ask. Louis Celaya asked Ed Daly. He had to. Later, Jim White would ask Mike Puskarich at Cravat Coal. He would have to. Horton asked Roe. He had to.

Companies wishing to save some money and avoid the antagonism generated during a representation election campaign can answer "Yes" and agree to recognize the union by checking the authorization cards in the presence of a neutral witness, thereby acknowledging that the union represents the majority of workers. It's very simple, and it's very cheap. And it's almost never done. Why? Because bosses don't want to negotiate with their workers, that's why.

Now, suppose a card check, as the process is called, did not automatically constitute recognition of the union. What would happen? Well, management would jump at the chance to see the cards, wouldn't it? What anti-union boss wouldn't love to have a peek at union authorization cards and get the names of all those sonsofbitches who signed them? After its little reconnaissance mission, management could tell the union, Forget it, no deal, and go back to the company and kick butt. How could the union protect the employees who had signed cards? It couldn't. And how could the union ever win an election? It couldn't. So the law seeks to ensure that bosses will not play dangerous card games by prescribing that, under certain conditions, a supervisor's looking at authorization cards may constitute de facto recognition. Naturally my clients never heard the truthful version of the law, nor did they care to. When you're at war you do well not to identify with your enemy.

With my little band huddled around me in Claude's office, I scanned the SEIU petition for clues to my opening strike. As expected, I found an opening in the union's definition of the bargaining unit.

Local 47 sought to represent more than 250 Copeland workers, all the facility's housekeepers, laundrywomen, maintenance men, cooks, waitresses, dishwashers, nurse's aides, beauticians, and vocational nurses. That left me only about a dozen executives, department heads, RNs, and miscellaneous office people to carry out my countercampaign. At a glance I knew that wouldn't do. There was no way I could count on a handful of supervisors—and I had to assume some of them would side with their workers—to conquer twenty times that number of employees. Not with a strategy that turned on direct, one-on-one confrontations with the workers. The more frequent and more intense those confrontations, the greater the chances that my troops would succeed in breaking the workers' resolve. As a general rule, I juggled bargaining units so that no supervisor would have to handle more than fifteen subordinates. I would do the same at Copeland; the only question was where to strike.

Nurse's aides made up the largest employee group; the SEIU petition put the number at ninety. Claude suspected that the aides also were the most solidly pro-union, and it turned out he was right. Yet Copeland's nursing management consisted of one director of nursing and just three RNs. I knew four people would never be able to grind down that many union supporters no matter how earnestly they carried out my campaign. They were going to need help. I zeroed in on the thirty vocational nurses, called LPNs (for licensed practical nurses). I had worked hospital campaigns before, so I knew the general hierarchy of the nursing world. It was a running joke inside hospitals that RN stands for "real nurses" and LPN means "let's pretend nurses." But in terms of what most people think of as nursing, down-and-dirty patient care, the real work is done by the LPNs. Copeland's LPNs were responsible for the day-to-day care of the residents; the RNs administered the drugs, and the LPNs did just about everything else. They dressed the wounds, exercised the limbs, drew the blood, took the temperature, fed the mouths, and listened and listened and listened. And they wanted a union. Several LPNs had been involved in the organizing from the beginning, and a few still were part of Horton's organizing committee, which met weekly at a coffee shop in the town of Alliance, thirty miles east of Sebring.

There was little to suggest that LPNs should be considered part of management, but I needed them and I deemed that they would be. Because there were only three RNs at Copeland, I knew the nurse's aides answered directly to the LPNs. The LPNs were the ones who told the aides when a patient needed to be taken to the toilet or bathed or fed or when bed pans had to be emptied or messes needed to be cleaned up. That was a start. I also learned that at Copeland some LPNs were designated as "charge" nurses, meaning they were in charge of the swing shift or the graveyard shift on a particular day. That was even better. In truth, just because a worker sometimes directs the activities of another does not mean she should automatically be excluded from a union. But the ambiguous language of labor law regarding the definition of a supervisor leaves plenty of room for games. I was a good player, and I knew I had a chance at capturing the LPNs. According to the National Labor Relations Act, a supervisor is someone who can hire, fire, or transfer employees or—and here are the magic words—"who can effectively recommend" any of those things. All we would have to do is argue that the LPNs could make recommendations about the duties and assignments of their aides.

I told Davies we needed to get the LPNs designated as supervisors if we were to have a chance to defuse the organizing drive. Davies was doubtful. It would be difficult, he said, shaking his head; there was no legal precedent. Nevertheless, he conceded that I had provided him with a logical argument and said he'd be glad to give it a whirl. I smiled. It was going to be a pleasure working with Davies, I decided. He was serious and professional, a fine attorney from a traditional Youngstown law firm. But he was obviously willing to try new things.

As Davies prepared to go to hearing on the unit issue, I launched my campaign. I set a kick-off for the next day, in the home's Williamsburg Lounge, a cozy sitting room adjacent to the chapel. Naturally I wouldn't be letting the LPNs in on the meeting while they were still part of the union movement, so my kick-off would be an unusually intimate affair, including only the twelve managers I knew I had. If the board found in my favor, terrific; I'd do another kick-off for the LPNs. If not, well, I was in trouble, and I'd better get started. When Davies filed his objection to the voting unit, he simultaneously filed a challenge to the jurisdiction of the NLRB at Copeland. It was a bread-and-butter delay tactic to argue that the labor board had no business overseeing union elections at a company for some obscure legal reason. But the stratagem was no less effective for its ordinariness. As long as the board went on debating and deliberating on that issue, the union would not get the Excelsior list, making it hard for them to contact all the potential voters, and no election date would be set. All the while, we would have the run of the place.

The board's ruling came fast, in less than a week. Although the union had fought the reclassifying of LPNs as supervisors, the NLRB saw it our way. I got them. The LPNs were mine. I relished the victory even though I knew it was a mixed one. Throughout all my years running anti-union drives, I never found a group of supervisors more resentful of my campaigns than nurses. As a class I have found nurses difficult and ornery; considering what I was all about, that is very much to their credit. Nurses, no matter how low paid, consider themselves professionals. The way they see it, their job is to care for the patients, period. They do not willingly accept assignments that interfere with that sacred mission. Typically, nurses resist even those administrative and managerial tasks that are part of the usual health care routine. When burdened with a duty as imposing and obnoxious as an anti-union drive, they can be positively defiant. And when it so happens that the nursing staff is overwhelmingly in favor of organizing—as it was at Copeland—they can make a real mess of things. And I have to be particularly nasty. I knew my brigade of newly drafted LPNs would be troublesome. Nonetheless, their conscription into the ranks of management gave me the numbers I needed and, if nothing else, automatically robbed the union of a few dozen votes.

As soon as Lou Davies told me the nurses were in, I skipped over to Claude's office. The LPN issue was a delicate one, and I had to make sure that word got out in just the right way. We didn't want the nurses thinking for a moment that management had pulled a fast one. Oh, gosh, no. It was time for a little preventive PR.

My yellow legal pad in hand, I sat down with Claude and composed a letter in longhand. It was addressed to the licensed practical nurses at Copeland Oaks retirement home and phrased very neatly. The language was dry, à la Claude Roe, but the tone was a bit warmer. The letter informed the nurses that they had been determined by the federal government to be supervisors. The words implied innocence on the part of Copeland management, which was portrayed as astonished by the revelation that the federal government, not the administration, got to decide who was a supervisor and who was not. The letter then waxed humble, recognizing that the management had no choice but to obey the law. In that spirit, the letter went on to explain that the role of supervisor brought with it certain obligations, not the least of which was loyalty to the company. Therefore Copeland would dutifully incorporate the newly knighted LPNs into management's pro-company campaign. I passed the pad to Claude, who gave the letter a quick reading, then looked at me with a quizzical smirk.

"I want the nurses to hear that we're not manipulating them," I told him, pronouncing the word *manipulating* with special care. He nodded.

I took my composition to Claude's secretary, Betty Miller, and asked her to type it up on a Copeland-Crandall letterhead. Then Claude signed his name importantly at the bottom.

The next afternoon, the letter having been distributed and, no doubt, much commented on, the nurses filed silently into the Williamsburg Lounge. They held their eyes steady, their faces stiff and expressionless. Dressed in crisp white pant suits and dresses, they ranged in age from their late teens to their late fifties. I sensed their strength at once. They didn't seem hostile, really. No, they were tougher than that. Hostile is easy. I can take hostile and twist it back on itself with a few quick moves. But I could see that first day that the Copeland nurses were a little more wily, a little more in control, than most groups of unwilling managers. Their opaque expressions and occasional smirks told me they were impervious to my exhortations and only mildly entertained by my cleverness. As I paced the room quizzing the crowd, I silently evaluated my students' anti-union IQ and made a mental list of potential troublemakers. The list was long.

In the beginning, some of the most vocal support for the union came from the LPNs. They contributed to the strategy meetings, they helped pass out authorization cards. Their familiarity with the workings and personalities of Copeland and their understanding of the nursing home business had given SEIU organizers the kind of detailed intelligence that is invaluable to a union effort and very difficult to obtain. The nurses were determined to get that union. They felt they were neither paid nor respected as skilled professionals. Tasks and shifts were assigned, perquisites and punishments meted out, at the whim of the trio of RNs who ran Copeland's medical department, the director of nursing, and her assistants. Accordingly, the quality of each nurse's work life depended on the personal rapport she maintained with three distant and, some said, hostile administrators. A chosen few had it made. The rest suffered.

But the moment they were drafted into management, the LPNs had to give up the union meetings. At the kick-off I warned them that they could be fired for attending. Not Copeland's rule, mind you, but the federal government's rule on surveillance. I told the LPNs they didn't dare go anywhere near the organizing meetings, no matter how close their friendships with the union "pushers." Friendship could be very dangerous at times like these, I said. In war alliances had to be redefined. The nurses were management now, and they had to be careful not to let their emotional ties lead them into a union trap that could harm the company. I taught the nurses the facts of the law: that management presence at union meetings destroys the "laboratory conditions" in which the NLRB insists that union-organizing campaigns take place and thus risks an unfair labor practice charge against the company. If any of them were to let that happen, I said, she would be held responsible. She would be fired.

Naturally my main interest in keeping the nurses away from union meetings was to deny organizers their support and their information. But this time I had labor law on my side. What I told them was essentially true. What I didn't tell them was that I had nothing at all against spying. When I needed spies I would send in my anti-union rank and file, my circle pluses, my grunts. Perfectly legitimate.

I knew my hold on this new group of hostages was tenuous, no matter how powerful my performance, so I decided to set them to work right away. I had started my letter campaign without the nurses, but now that they were mine I wanted them involved every second. Before releasing the LPNs, I gave them their first assignment. I passed out a letter written in question-and-answer format, an old trick I used to create the illusion that an actual dialogue was taking place. The opening read:

Dear Staff Member: Several of you have been asking some very important questions concerning the current union situation. Here are the *factual* answers to your questions:

Following were three questions and Claude's—that is, my— lengthy and emphatic answers. Of course, no employee had asked a thing. I had made those questions up, a fact of which Claude might or might not have been aware. As controller of information, I regulated not only what the employees were told, but when they were told it, by whom, and in what form. I certainly wasn't going to wait for a bunch of cooks and maids to ask the right question at the right time in the right way. In that very early letter, I began my ground war against the integrity of collective bargaining, the heart of union representation. With cunningly worded answers to contrived questions, I presented collective bargaining as a protracted, risky, and possibly futile process and warned employees that "unions have been known to trade away whatever it takes" to win costly little plums for themselves.

That first Q&A letter walked a tightrope over the realm of the unlawful. For example, had I written, "Bargaining starts from scratch," my letter would have been illegal and the union could have filed an unfair labor practice complaint. That's because those exact words have been tested in the courts and determined to be against the laws that govern representation elections. So, big deal, I picked other words. But I said the same thing. I wrote, "Nothing is automatic in a union contract. Everything is subject to bargaining (horse trading). . . . "

It is also illegal for a company to refuse to bargain with a union that has been duly elected by the workers. So I didn't say Copeland would refuse. I just let the readers know that the company would make it very hard on the union to win anything. I wrote: "We would not be obliged to agree to anything or to make any concessions. . . . "

Before taking the letter to Claude for his signature, I cleared it with Lou Davies. I didn't mind breaking the law, but things would go so much more smoothly if we could just slither in and out of the loopholes. Davies said it was fine. The letter closed with the admonition, "*Remember:* A bird in the hand is worth two in the bush." Trite, but crystal clear.

Later on in the campaign I had Claude set up a question box by the time clock. I designed the box—a shoebox-size container covered with white paper and decorated with big red question marks, with a slot on the top through which discreet questioners could deposit their queries on folded scraps of paper. Claude then invited all employees to use the box to ask questions about the union drive—anonymity guaranteed. It was a revival of an old Sheridan trick. Perhaps the box actually would attract a question or two that would point to some frailty in the organizing effort or show us what the workers feared. Handy, but that wasn't the point. The question box really served as a cover for my tightly orchestrated information campaign; I made up most of the questions myself. In my earlier years I had occasionally been challenged upon claiming that workers had been asking a certain question. A feisty supervisor would stand up in a meeting and complain, "Wait a minute. I never heard anybody out there ask that. Just who do you say is asking that question?" or something similar. I would always have an out in claiming respect for the purported inquisitor's privacy and refuse to identify him, but the confrontation itself was undesirable. It planted the possibility in the minds of otherwise docile supervisors that upper management might, in fact, be scamming them. With the question box in place, no one would know who was asking what, and I could float "questions from the employees" as I saw fit. Any doubt about the legitimacy of the inquiries would be limited to some private mutterings.

I was living in two worlds during those early days of Copeland. By day I played the heavy. I held the fate of nearly three hundred workers in my hands, and I gave the orders. I handed out praise and punishment as I saw fit, showing mercy one moment, ruthlessness the next. But when night fell I was a little boy again. Back at my parents' house I sat in the family room, watched TV, smoked, played with my nail clipper, drank Scotch, scratched cryptic calculations on my legal pad, and telephoned Alice. After begging and pleading with her every night for nearly a month, I could tell she was beginning to relent. She started talking about wanting to get away from the cult, away from Scott. Yes, she said, maybe we should try to be a family again. God knew the boys could use having you around. But she was afraid. What if he didn't let her go? He had said he intended to marry her. What if he came after her? He could be pretty scary. Besides, she said, she didn't have the money to move all our stuff.

Then I got a brilliant idea. Alice was glad I was working, but that wasn't enough to get her to move away from her mom and dad. But if she had a job as well, she might do it. "Alice," I said, "I could really use some help on this campaign. There are too many supervisors for me to handle alone. Most of them are women, and I get the feeling some of them would be more comfortable talking to a woman. You'd be perfect. You're sweet, you're compassionate, I'm sure they'd open up to you in a way they just won't to me. I can tell some of them are holding back."

Alice was intrigued. She was a torn woman, restless from being home all the time yet committed to her fantasy of being the storybook wife and mother, which required her to be home all the time. She also was held back by her poor self-image. She couldn't imagine who would want to hire her, and she never tried to find out. But one thing I knew she was good at, and that was nurturing. Alice was a caring mother, a talented and energetic homemaker, a gifted gardener, a giving friend. She was even an enthusiastic wife when times were good. I figured I could parlay all that native empathy into a stint at Copeland.

"To hell with Scott," I said. "He wants to marry you? Well, I already did that, and I'm the one who doesn't want to let you go. Come back to me. We can work together like we did in the old days. I love you. I love you, Alice. I need you."

At long last, Alice gave in. All right, she said. Get the money for the move and I will fly out with the boys. We'll be there before Christmas.

I had sold Copeland Oaks at my going rate of $750 a day, and the campaign promised to last a few months at least; I knew I had money coming. But because my sales pitch had been somewhat a show of self-assurance, I hadn't wanted to ask Claude for a retainer. So I was still as broke as the day I had left California.

During the early weeks of the campaign, Claude and I had become quite good friends. Wherever I was, I liked to develop a personal relationship with the top man; it helped me retain control by averting resentment. But with Claude, the relationship grew more rapidly than usual. I often spent the afternoons in long conversations with him that inevitably grew quite intimate. I felt comfortable revealing my sins to him, undoubtedly seduced by his station as a man of the cloth. When I stepped into his office and closed the door, it was as if I had entered the confessional. I barely knew Claude when I began telling him about Alice's affairs and my drinking and our constant warring. He listened and counseled and consoled and seemed earnest about his desire to help me straighten out my life. He had been married to his wife, Gladys, for four decades, and still seemed very much taken with her. He said often that he wished I would someday know the happiness that came from a long, enduring marriage. When I appeared in his office one December morning and asked if he could pay me a ten-day advance so that I could move my family out to Cleveland, Claude didn't hesitate.

The executive director called in his comptroller and ordered him to draw me up a check for $7,500. Immediately.

I didn't have a bank account and, after my bank shenanigans in California, had little hope of getting one. I was still puzzling over how to cash Claude's check when a moving van pulled up in front of my parents' house.

Alice and the boys had made it to my parents' house a week before Christmas.

Within a couple of weeks I had identified the few supervisors who were willing to work extra hard for me—or, as they put it, "for the home." Through that handful of good soldiers I set to work establishing a network of rank-and-file employees who would serve as spies, informants, and saboteurs. Those so-called loyal employees would be called upon to lobby against the union, report on union meetings, hand over union literature to their bosses, tattle on their co-workers, help spread rumors, and make general pests of themselves within the organizing drive. I rarely knew who my company plants were, and I didn't at Copeland. It was cleaner that way. Nobody could connect me to the activities, I steered clear of the reporting requirements of Landrum-Griffin, and the workers' "pro-company" countercampaign was believed to be a grass-roots movement.

My intelligence network informed me early on that, although Jim Horton was the man in charge of the Copeland drive, and probably had a lot to do with the campaign's methodology, he was not the most visible organizer. Horton and four other union officers cooperated in the Copeland effort, that drive being one of the biggest ever for Local 47. The name known to most of the workers was Phil Ganni.

Ganni, a gruff old man with a round belly, was an interesting anomaly. He was not an organizer, not on staff at Local 47, not even a member, not a Copeland employee. He was, quite simply, a good friend. Ganni was a former Sebring auto worker on permanent disability, and he was a devoted union man. Many of the women who worked at Copeland happened to live in his Alliance neighborhood, and he talked with them often about their jobs and their troubles. When the women started asking him how to go about getting a union, Ganni said he'd be glad to help. It was Ganni who placed that first call to Local 47 in the summer of 1980. It was Ganni who first met with Horton at an Alliance coffee shop to talk strategy. It was Ganni who first started assembling an organizing committee through his neighborhood friends. It was Ganni, more than anyone else in the early days, who went knocking on doors and setting up meetings and making phone calls to his friends. After the union petition was filed in late November, Ganni stayed on, working as a link between the union organizers in Cleveland and his friends in Sebring and Alliance. To the women at Copeland, Ganni was quarterback, coach, and cheerleader all rolled into one. For many weeks he worked the organizing effort as a volunteer, putting in full days and long nights out of sheer conviction. Eventually Local 47 paid him a stipend for his trouble.

From the reading I was getting through my supervisors, Local 47 was running a straight campaign, nothing dirty, no wild promises, no rabble-rousing. I was always grateful when a few union people did something really tacky or really stupid, like start a fight or slash somebody's tires; it made things so easy. All I had to do was say, "Just look. Are those the kind of people you want representing you?" But it wasn't going to be like that at Copeland. I was going to have to commit Local 47's sins myself.

One target was Ganni. I never used his name, didn't throw too big a spotlight on him. I had been told that the Copeland workers generally liked and respected Ganni, those who knew him, so I knew an all-out attack on him would be unwise. But I also knew that some of the women considered Ganni somewhat of a blowhard; they had been heard wondering aloud, "Who does he think he is?" That gave me an opening, not to topple him—he wasn't *that* important—just to nurture the germ of doubt about him that already existed.

I started spreading the word through supervisors that Local 47 apparently couldn't handle the Copeland organizing drive itself. It had come to my attention, I told them, that the union was paying someone to go after the "pro-company" employees. What kind of a dirty trick was that? I asked. Just like a union. When things start getting rough, send in a goon. I began referring to Ganni as the union's "paid bounty hunter from Alliance" and eventually included that reference in a letter. This bounty hunter, I wrote, was working in collusion with "inside union pushers" and "high-paid professional unionists from up in Cleveland," all of whom *"have lied to you in their efforts to fill their pockets with your money."* In that way I painted a picture of the cold, corrupt, big-business union that so many of my victims had heard about ad nauseam growing up in the small towns of the Midwest. Of course, those union types were lying, I implied. Whenever I mentioned the union people, I was sure to note that they came from far away in the big city. Big cities mean bad guys, crime, sleaze, big money, Mafia.

For the record, as director of organizing Jim Horton was paid about $600 a week in 1980; his fellow organizers earned slightly less. An okay salary, but for a man of fifty-two hardly big money. I never found out what Ganni was paid.

Ganni's closest contact within the union was not Horton, but another black man, Art Worthy. Softspoken and earnest, Worthy won Ganni's trust immediately, and he became the union face to Copeland workers. When Ganni sent letters to the local, they were addressed to Art Worthy. When he set up meetings, he made sure Worthy would be there. When he called, he wanted to talk to Art. Worthy had gotten into organizing during the 1960s, after working as a construction laborer for many years. His first organizing jobs were with the Construction Laborers Union, but he switched to hospitals in 1971 in order to help Local 47 bring a union to service workers at Huron Road Hospital in East Cleveland, where many of his relatives toiled. Worthy stayed with Local 47 after winning Huron, and he even worked for a time as business representative to St. Luke's, Horton's old stamping grounds. Worthy and Horton got on well, and although there were three other field organizers assigned to Copeland, the campaign was essentially theirs.

Every week Horton or Worthy sat down to discuss strategy with the thirty-odd inside organizers from Copeland. The duo also ran union rallies and informational meetings at hotel meeting rooms and restaurants in Sebring, Alliance, and the surrounding towns, and they put out union circulars. The organizers from Local 47 kept in touch with Copeland workers the best it could, with the dogged assistance of Ganni, and tried their damnedest to defuse the hostility and defend their union against the charges being launched daily under the name of Claude L. Roe.

From their years on the front lines, Horton and Worthy had developed a very definite organizing style and a strong sense of strategy. The first rule was Stick to your own game. Horton was adamant about it. You don't let the company and you certainly don't let a hired union buster dictate the issues and determine the direction of your own organizing campaign. It's a good rule, a smart rule. But it's also a difficult one to follow, impossible if there's someone like Marty Levitt on the inside, immersing the workers hour by hour in the issues *he* wants to address. The union doesn't get to come inside. The union gets to talk to the workers only after they've heard eight hours' worth of the other side, sometimes accompanied by threats, sometimes by tears.

"[Copeland] was the toughest campaign I've ever done—the most painful," Horton said years later. The reason: Organizers seemed always to be following my lead, always responding to charges, always defending the union. At Copeland Horton never had a chance to run the organizing campaign the way he knew it should be run. Not that it was the first time he had come across a professional union buster. He had dealt with union busters many times before, had lost a lot, but also had beaten them often enough to figure he knew their game. Horton and his fellow organizers had gone to workshops on union busters, seen films, planned counterstrategies. He knew enough to warn union supporters at the early Copeland meetings, "Watch out. Whoever's writing the letters for management is going to put half-truths in there, just enough so it's not a lie." The union buster Horton knew best was a fellow named Jack Hickey, an independent consultant based in Columbus who had followed Local 47 from campaign to campaign for years. Hickey's style was rougher than mine. He routinely called in security guards to intimidate workers, for example. Hickey was brusque, and, according to Horton, "turn[ed] people off along the way." But organizers had yet to experience the Sheridan cum Three M cum Levitt war of saturation bombing, and I caught them quite unprepared.

"[Marty] confused the workers. . . . He got them doubting us, challenging us, using up our meeting time," Horton said.

A union meeting might go two, three, four hours. More often than not, during the Copeland effort, Horton and Worthy were forced to spend that time straightening out the twisted disinformation sown by me.

"Marty put us on the defensive," said Horton. "Some of the rank-and-file workers knew his name. But most of them just knew him as 'that man,' the man they had heard about from their supervisors. They would always say, 'That man, he told us this. . . . ' He would always say something halfway. He might leave out something or make one little change that would make what he said wrong. Then we'd have to spend the whole meeting explaining it."

In the end, maybe the people's immediate questions would be answered, maybe. But there would be more to come, and more, and more, ad infinitum. Of equal importance to me, organizers would have had no time for planning, no time for campaign strategy, no time for talking about the issues that really concerned the workers. The union would have gone nowhere.

Copeland's cleaning crew was a tight-knit and hardworking group. Every morning at 7 A.M., as the day shift came on, the group of eighteen housekeepers and laundrywomen met in the ladies' locker room. There they received their assignments for the day and discussed any special preparations that had to be made. The meeting was routine, but to the women there was something very comforting about starting the day together like that. It was a time of laughter and gossip, and it gave the crew a jump start at the top of a day of hard, dirty work. It was a cherished time. After the meeting the housekeeping crew split up in pairs and scrubbed and polished and vacuumed its way through every apartment and villa in the complex, in an energetic endeavor to defend Copeland's reputation as the cleanest retirement home in the area.

Presiding over the morning roll call like a stern but loving mother superior was Kathleen Taylor, director of housekeeping and laundry. Kathleen was an odd, rather anachronistic character. She covered her tidy matronly figure in prim frocks adorned with the lace cuffs and high button-up collars of the previous century. She always kept an embroidered cloth hankie tucked neatly under one cuff. From our first conversation Kathleen painted herself as the beloved auntie to all her employees, to whom she referred as her "girls." She took care of them, she said, mothered them. Kathleen treasured the morning roll call perhaps even more than her crew; she took personal pride in the quality of her "girls' " work—and personal interest in the details of their lives. She relished the gossip, the confessions, the conspiracies, the glimpse inside the homes of each of her subordinates. And she imagined that her "girls" loved her in return.

She was wrong. Although Kathleen had a couple of loyal friends among her crew, my conversations with her co-workers revealed that by and large, the girls scorned her. They considered her mothering overbearing and intrusive, her leadership autocratic and arbitrary, and her personal style ridiculous. They said she played favorites. They called her a busybody, a snob, and a witch.

There is an element of truth in almost everything the union buster says. One of the truths is that where an organizing drive is taking place, one will invariably find lousy supervision. Kathleen was a dedicated employee, a loyal soldier; but she was one crummy supervisor. She was bossy, she was manipulative, she was nosy, and she was unfair. The trouble was, she didn't know it. Copeland's housekeeping crew was a feisty bunch, outspoken and unafraid and, from what I could tell, quite solidly behind the organizing drive. I wasn't going to have Kathleen fired; the girls didn't hate her enough for that to have been useful. But I knew I had to wake her up from her delusion if she was going to do me any good.

"Kathleen, do you know what your girls are saying about you?" I asked her during a one-on-one session a few weeks into the campaign. She couldn't imagine. I held her eyes with mine and said with a tone of pity: "You're a fool if you think your girls look up to you. They don't even like you. In fact, they laugh at you. They even make fun of the way you dress, did you know that? The lace and the high collars, and the hankie and all. They call you a snob. They say you think you're a fashion plate, and they mimic the way you talk. I hope you don't think those girls will be loyal to you. They won't. They're stabbing you in the back right now."

Kathleen was dumbfounded. How could it be? How could she not see it? She had always treated the girls the way she would want to be treated if their roles were reversed, hadn't she? She showed them respect, and they respected her in return. Didn't they? Kathleen's eyes filled. She pulled the hankie from her sleeve and dabbed the tears, sniffing to hold back a full-blown cry. She was all mine.

"Look, Kathleen," I offered. "You still have a chance to make amends to your girls. Talk to them. Find out what it is you've done to make them call in the union and tell them you're willing to change. Assure them that they can come to you with any complaint, and let them know you'll really listen. Apologize for any mistakes you've made, even if you don't know what they are." Then my voice turned hard. "At the same time, be sure they know this: It's a onetime offer. Warn them that once the union takes over it's out of your hands. From that moment on there will be no more flexibility, no more chances for change. Everything will be regimented, impersonal. Tell them that they won't be able to speak for themselves, and you won't be allowed to answer. Every little detail of their workday will be determined by some union man up in Cleveland."

That did it. Kathleen would do anything to fight off this personal attack. She would do anything to defeat the monster that would take her workers away from her. I was sure she would not stray; I was equally sure she would not be very effective. I would have to work around her.

After a month or so at Copeland I found myself having to work around quite a number of management people, not the least of whom was Claude L. Roe. As is true at most companies, the poor supervision on the floor of Copeland Oaks was more than a matter of a few bad hires. The trouble was endemic to the organization and would not be cleared up with a couple of training workshops. Rather, Copeland's erratic supervision was a symptom of a diseased organization; the disease spread downward, from a cancer afflicting the top.

One after the other, the supervisors hinted at it. "Dr. Roe, he's so . . . smart. People are afraid to talk to him." "The girls don't . . . feel very comfortable around him." "He doesn't seem to, well, care very much about us." But it was Claude's secretary, Betty Miller, who made me see just how much the employees dreaded her boss. Betty was likable and intelligent. She had the run of Copeland; she saw things; she heard things. What she heard most was that Dr. Roe was quite unanimously despised. The girls thought he was mean and sour. His presence was oppressive. Everyone was happiest when he was away. I tried, I tried my damnedest to lighten Claude up, get him at least to greet people when he was packed into an elevator with them. But to no avail. I couldn't even talk Claude into opening his anti-union letters with "Dear Fellow Employee." Too cozy, unprofessional. Claude did not consider himself a "fellow" to any of the workers. He was their boss, and they were his staff.

Because of his refusal to bow his head even slightly, I found it necessary to pop open my "Give us a chance" letter earlier in the Copeland campaign than I would have liked. Ever since World Airways, the tearful, apologetic plea had become a mainstay of the final days of my campaigns. The letter tended to be most effective at that time, when everybody was exhausted from the fight and therefore vulnerable to an apparent call for a truce. I decided not to take chances with Claude. I packaged the plea into his third letter, being careful not to give it too much emphasis lest it be recognized for the ploy that it was. Claude's "we are not perfect" passage followed the claim that he was not afraid of the union, along with a trio of lies that purported to explain why, in that case, Copeland management was fighting so hard to defeat it.

"WE ARE CONCERNED," I wrote.

"WE ARE CONCERNED *that a self-serving group of outsiders* does not *trick* you into putting *your future* on a bargaining table.

"WE ARE CONCERNED about seeing you give up your individual right to speak for yourself.

"WE ARE CONCERNED about losing the proud tradition of *direct relationships* and *flexibility* that has allowed Copeland Oaks to be so very special."

Then came a brief admission that Copeland management might, indeed, have made some mistakes and the declaration, "But we genuinely believe we *deserve a chance!*"

It was total crap. Claude was not concerned, he was afraid and he was angry. Union representation did not threaten to deprive the employees of any of their so-called proud traditions, if there were any, but it did threaten to deprive Claude of his autocracy.

I never stopped trying to soften Claude's severe bearing. I began to see the old grump as an amusing puzzle; it was a personal challenge to make him laugh—hell, smile even. But I wasn't going to risk my campaign for a little fun. So while I scratched away at Claude's opaqueness, I enlisted a pair of his top aides to be the face of Copeland to the people.

My ace was Bill Hogg, the home's resident Methodist minister and the director of community relations. Bill was friendly and warm—naturally. Unlike Claude, who liked to hole himself up in

his executive suite, Bill spent his days roaming the halls of Copeland Oaks, visiting residents, chatting with the workers, conducting
chapel service. I heard often in my interviews that the girls wished
Bill Hogg were the director instead of Dr. Roe. Bill—they called
him Bill—joked with them, ate with them, *was* one of them, really.
Except that Bill was also a good company man, and that meant he
would fight their organizing drive.

I had Claude sign the letters to employees. But when it came
to personal appeals, I sent Bill. Bill's whole shtick was bridge building—that's what community relations was all about. He brought
people together to sup in peace. When Bill characterized the union
as an invader that would tear friends apart, people listened. I knew
they would listen even better if God could be insinuated into the
fight. So I arranged for a pivotal staff meeting to be scheduled in
the Copeland chapel. There, Bill delivered a most eloquent, most
passionate anti-union homily from the pulpit.

Helping Bill out with any gender-related issues was Gerry Sposato, Claude's assistant director. Gerry was a dour, straitlaced lady
in her early forties, drab, proper, and hardly fun-loving. She did
not really fit my job description for the new, reformed manager,
but she was useful in her own way. Gerry knew a great deal about
Copeland, about Claude, about her fellow supervisors, and about
the workers. She was the first to tell me what the housekeepers
thought of Kathleen; she also informed me that the nurses felt oppressed by their boss, Anna Moracco, and knew the complaints of
the kitchen staff. Gerry knew how things worked, who influenced
whom. And she had managed to survive in a position of authority
without making too many enemies, an admirable feat in the small
town inside a small town that was Copeland. The girls didn't love
Gerry, maybe, but they didn't hate her, either. In general she had
their lukewarm respect. I badly needed a spokeswoman. Gerry
would have to do.

With Claude distracted by the administrative demands of his
post and Lou Davies busy with corporate legal matters, I was free
to execute my battle plan as only I knew how. My high command
in place, I dug a deep trench down the middle of the work force,
ordering supervisors to cease all the informal socializing with the
rank and file. It was an assault on the very playfulness that made
work at Copeland bearable and an implied harbinger of things to
come should Copeland be "unionized." I wanted supervisors and

subordinates alike to wrestle with the irritations of an organizing drive every day and to hate the union for it.

"Your workers have declared war on you. And a war changes the rules we live by," I told the supervisors. I warned them that the union would use their friendships with workers as a weapon. They would twist an innocent social conversation between a supervisor and an employee into an accusation of spying or intimidation, and the unwitting supervisor would find herself dragged into court.

"Be careful of what you say and where you go and who you are with," I said. "In a union drive you can't trust anybody, not even your best friend. Just wait: you will see the nicest people turn into liars and thieves."

I allowed the morning housekeeping meetings to continue, for I thought them a useful forum for my purposes. I decided I could use the sessions to remind employees every day of how wonderful life at Copeland used to be before the union came along and screwed things up. The morning meetings were to go on, but without the joviality and spontaneity of the past, without the warmth. Kathleen was to keep things strictly business.

Otherwise, all social gatherings between ranks were verboten. I wanted to be sure the workers felt the tension of the union battle first thing in the morning. I told my troops they should not attend parties or baby showers or even go out to dinner with rank-and-file employees until the union election was behind us. For their own protection, I said. Anything could be a trap, anyone could be the bait. I even discouraged them from attending the Christmas festivities in their own departments.

The new rules came as a shock to supervisors, particularly the LPNs. To many Copeland employees, their co-workers had been like a second family. Most of the women led poor lives inside tiny houses in dull, small towns. Their greatest joy was coming to work, taking care of the old people, and spending the day with friends. They gossiped and giggled as they worked, they celebrated one another's birthdays, they sent flowers when a co-worker was sick. My rules put an end to all that, clouded the atmosphere, turned it dark and grim. Nurses were afraid to chat with their aides; aides and housekeepers fell silent when a nurse walked into the apartment in which they were working. Laundrywomen and waitresses could be seen ducking into elevators or scooting down the hall to avoid the inevitable, oppressive conversation with a supervisor. Friends stopped speaking.

After four weeks of countercampaigning, the supervisors were beginning to break down. In that brief time they each had been forced to drop whatever they were doing several times a day to attend group brainwashing sessions or probing interviews with me. They had reported on their friends in exhaustive and embarrassing detail—to a stranger—and they had harangued those friends as well. Collectively the supervisors had made hundreds of individual letter deliveries, complete with the memorized explanations and probing questions and relentless follow-up that I ordered. In return they had been growled at, insulted, pushed aside, pleaded with, scolded, laughed at, cried to, and stonewalled. Many were having to skip lunch to get everything done, union-busting assignments on top of their regular duties, which were not lightened for the sake of the campaign. They were going home tense and angry, too upset to eat. They found themselves snapping at their husbands and yelling at their children and having a hard time getting to sleep at night. They were miserable. And it was only the beginning. There was so much more to come—more than even I knew.

During those first few weeks of the Copeland campaign, I had delivered my standard program; but all the while I was searching for a secret weapon and an Achilles' heel. Every company seemed to have one of each. At Copeland I found both in the old people, the heart and soul of the home. The Copeland employees loved those old people, every last one of them. Some of those old folks were cranky, some were ill, and some wouldn't talk at all. Nursing home work could be dirty, unpleasant, emotionally trying, sometimes demeaning. But for many workers, their relationships with the old men and women of Copeland transformed a mundane job into a vocation. Nurses, nurse's aides, housekeepers, cooks, waitresses, all of them, what they wanted most was to please the old people, to make their lives a little more comfortable. It didn't take much: a witty conversation, a special favor, a little time spent looking over pictures of great-grandchildren or admiring vintage jewelry. It brought the workers great joy to know that they were making the old people's lives just a little better, and it made them feel important. It was no accident that Copeland employees were so tender with the elderly residents; Claude had incorporated love and respect for the old people into every job description. When a worker was hired, even for the kitchen or the laundry room, she was told, "We are here for the residents. They pay your salary, and they are the most important part of your job. Talk to them. Take a little time out for them. Show them you care."

To me, those elderly residents were the "victims" I needed to make the union look truly evil. And I planned to use them. I figured that the Copeland organizing drive would not survive a threat on the old people. If I could convince the workers that the union would somehow jeopardize the well-being of the beloved residents, the pressure on union proponents would be unbearable. So, without saying a word to Lou Davies or Claude about my motives, I devised a dual strategy that totally subverted the Copeland mission.

First I blockaded the direct relationship between the line workers and the residents by imposing new formalities. Early on, I had Claude decree that "out of concern for the peace of mind of the residents," supervisors were to see to it that the old people were shielded from the hostilities of the organizing drive. They were not to be involved in any way. The supervisors were to make sure they would not be by prohibiting their subordinates from conversing or socializing with the residents. There would be no more lingering in the residents' rooms after a job was done, no dialogue except that which was necessary for the job. Lower-level employees would no longer be allowed to run errands or do special favors for the residents; if the residents needed something, the supervisors would be glad to get it for them. Workers were to stop addressing residents by their first name or nickname—as many of the old people preferred—and use only "Mr." or "Mrs." and the surname. It seemed a superficial change, but the new formality had a profound psychological impact. When "Dovie" became "Mrs. Jones," the old woman cried.

The official reason for these changes was to make sure the old people would not be manipulated or badgered by union people, used as propaganda tools. The real reason was that I wanted to manipulate them myself.

The sudden silence of their onetime confidantes made the old people nervous. They wondered to each other, "What next?" Naturally management blamed the new protocols on the union, explaining ever so patronizingly that the rules were being enforced for the residents' own protection. Protection? they wondered. Protection from what?

Once the seed was planted, the weed of fear just seemed to grow. It was easy to scare the old people into thinking that if the union got in, the residents would lose everything they held dear about their home at Copeland. Through my network I got the word out that life in a unionized nursing home would be Spartan and unpredictable. There would be pages and pages of regulations. There would be strikes, violence. What would happen to the old people while their caretakers were walking the picket line? The union would demand higher wages, and Copeland would have to raise its rates to pay salaries. What about the residents who couldn't afford to pay more? Where were they going to go? And what if worse came to worst and Copeland was forced to close its doors?

I didn't want to leave my propagandizing and fear-mongering to the shifting winds of rumor, however reliably those breezes had blown so far. I had a plan. It had come to my attention that there were a number of former corporate managers residing at Copeland, including a handful of retired CEOs. If I could get those savvy business types to bad-talk the union to their fellow residents—unofficially, of course, and spontaneously—I would be able to hit the workers from all sides. Every door the women opened as they went through their workday could lead them into another harangue or yet another plea. I mentioned to Claude that I would like to talk to some of his retired executives. He said he could do better. There was a residents committee at Copeland that met monthly to discuss matters of concern to the old people. Claude arranged for me to talk with the committee president, who happened to be a former management person; a few days later I met with a group of committee members. The committee agreed to send a letter to employees telling them they were afraid of what might happen to them if the union got in and asking them to please stop the union drive. I wrote the letter, the committee members signed it. From there the message of fear was spread to the entire residential community.

The old people's response was even more fiery than I had hoped. Several of them barked at the aides and housekeepers whenever they came into the apartment or harassed the kitchen help: "What the hell do you want a union for?" Others pleaded, "How could you do this to us?" Some even broke out weeping and fretted, "What if you go on strike? What's going to become of us?" Naturally Claude and Bill Hogg calmly assured the residents that they had no need to fear, that Copeland management would do everything in its power to keep them from harm. The message was clear: You folks have a damn good reason to be afraid, and the reason is the union.

As Christmas neared, life was becoming more and more unbearable around Copeland Oaks. My timing seemed perfect. I always liked to have the strife and dissension most intense around the holidays; it gave me great material. The union petition having been filed just after Thanksgiving, I had been cheated out of one of my favorite union-busting holidays. Thanksgiving, a time to be grateful for one's bounty, no matter how humble, was the perfect time for distribution of what I called my "count your blessings" letter. I considered that particular letter one of my masterpieces; it had always been a real crowd pleaser and astoundingly effective. I was not about to do without it at Copeland. So I recast the piece as a Christmas message. To ensure that the employees would accept the letter as sincere and spontaneous, I distributed it under the name of Gerry Sposato rather than Claude L. Roe. Written in a more fervent tone than the letters bearing Claude's signature, it was one of only two anti-union circulars in which I could replace Claude's rigid "Dear Staff Member" opening with my preferred, egalitarian greeting: "Dear Fellow Employee." No one would have taken the heartfelt plea seriously if it were said to spring from the impenetrable Dr. Roe. No, it was worker appealing to worker, sister to sister.

With my words, Gerry told her colleagues that the union had destroyed the loving working relationship among Copeland employees through a strategy of "divide and conquer." She charged union proponents with lying to workers about what the union could do for them and warned that the union might trade away the wonderful benefits of Copeland employment to which they had become accustomed. She repeated the charge that contract negotiation was nothing more than horse trading, and that the horse trading inevitably would require giving something back. The Christmas letter reinforced the continuing message that the union could guarantee nothing. It was true, in essence: in fact, the union would not be able to win a better life for Copeland workers unless the management agreed to give it. However, standing in the way of that better life was not some greedy union officer, but a gaggle of Copeland managers headed by Claude L. Roe.

Gerry's Christmas letter closed with a plea: "Christmas is a time to count our blessings, and I have attached to this letter a partial list of what would have to be put on a bargaining table and negotiated for if this union somehow becomes your bargaining agent."

The following page carried a typed list of twenty-six "blessings" and the implication that some or all could be lost in the collective bargaining process. The list ranged from such niceties as free meals and snacks; to protections that were required by law, such as workers' compensation insurance and disability pay; to inconsequential items like free parking—hardly a hot commodity in Sebring—and the availability of vending machines. Pay was not mentioned, nor were seniority rights, nor was health insurance, nor was respect, nor was consistency, nor was fairness, nor were working conditions, which were the actual issues on which the organizing drive turned.

At the foot of the page was a cartoon I had clipped from the local newspaper, then altered to reinforce the idea in a humorous way. The cartoon pictured a smug-looking Santa Claus, arms crossed in front of him, with a little boy seated in his lap. The boy was handing Santa a pencil and a piece of paper bearing the initials IOU. Santa, his eyes closed in an indication of intransigence, was saying, "I'll do my best kid . . . but I'm not signing anything." On Santa's hat I had penciled in "seiu #47." Below the cartoon I had written an emphatic "Vote *No!*"

The letter was distributed on Christmas Eve. Unbeknownst to Claude, a few days later, while a bedraggled Christmas spirit still lingered in the frosty air, I dispatched a contingent of commandos to scratch up the cars of high-profile pro-company workers and to make threatening phone calls to others. I bade farewell to 1980 with a letter from Claude taking the union to task for such barbarous scare tactics.

I could not know yet that my anti-union campaign at Copeland would go on for a full year and a half. All that time, while purportedly saving Copeland money, Claude paid me more than $15,000 a month. It would take a Copeland housekeeper two years of sheet changing and bathroom scrubbing to earn that much money. But the employees would never know about that. And that number doesn't count the perquisites like free meals, mileage expenses, and, toward the end of the campaign, a free room, which cost Copeland $1,000 a month in lost income. Nor does it count the thousands of dollars in attorneys' fees. The employees would never know about that.

Alice came to work in mid-January, at a rate of $500 a day.

By that time I had figured out which supervisors would work for me and which ones I could brand as "useless"—at least I thought I had. Into the useless category I lumped two types of supervisors: those who clearly sympathized with their workers' organizing effort and those who, without knowing it, had such little credibility with their subordinates that it would be foolish of me to allow them to carry the company message. I knew from training and experience, however, that I could not simply ignore those supervisors, no matter how little use they were to me, particularly that second group. If I were to slight them, they might turn on me and, one never knew, maybe even develop a following among an ego-bruised middle-management corps. Yet as a one-man band I had many much more crucial parts to play than theirs and didn't want to waste my time nurturing their delusions. Whenever there were several consultants on a job, we simply traded off the distasteful task of meeting with the pests. But at Copeland I was alone. How was I going to finesse this? Then I got a brilliant idea: I would dump the pests on Alice.

Of course, I never phrased it in that way, but that is essentially what I did. I set Alice up in a sort of shell campaign that paralleled mine and began funneling half a dozen benign but "useless" supervisors into long daily interviews with her. I didn't care what the supervisors said during their hours with Alice, and I didn't much care what she told them. I just wanted them to talk and talk and feel that we were listening. In that way I yanked everyone I didn't want to bother with out of the campaign without them even knowing it.

I introduced Alice to the supervisors during the first meeting of the new year 1981. Admonishing my audience to give her the same respect they gave me, I told the crowd she was not only my wife, but my partner, and said we would be working the remainder of the campaign together until the election, the date of which, by the way, still had not been set.

Alice managed a sweet smile and a soft "Hello" to the crowd, but she was feeling faint. She had been a nervous wreck during the drive to Sebring and had tried to talk me out of using her. She wouldn't know what to say, she told me. What if they asked her questions she couldn't answer? She didn't know anything about unions; she couldn't think on her feet the way I could, and she knew it.

What Alice didn't know was that none of that mattered. I hadn't dared tell my dear wife the true plan. I had told her the same story I had told Claude: that some of the workers might feel more comfortable talking to a woman, and that she was a natural. For the ruse to work, I needed Alice to be wholly genuine in the interviews. I needed her to console and commiserate and cry with true empathy. Alice being a guileless lady, she would have been incapable of pulling off the job if she had known it was a hoax.

"Alice," I said, "don't worry. You'll be great."

And in fact, she was. One of the first supervisors to have a session with Alice was Kathleen; she, like several others, bonded with my wife in a way she never had with me. My wife's sessions were filled with tears and hugs and heartfelt words of encouragement. Everybody felt better; nobody got in the way.

With the useless supes off the road, I had more room to maneuver with my special forces. Usually I counted on a handful of elite warriors to carry the campaign for the ineffective supervisors. But at Copeland all I needed was Judy Stanley. Judy was the resident social worker at Copeland, a plump, plain-faced twenty-nine-year-old from the nearby Quaker town of Beloit. She was more highly educated than most of her co-workers, having received her bachelor's degree in psychology as well as a license in social work. She fancied herself a real pro with people and aspired to a position of authority within the Copeland organization. Judy admired me. She was intrigued by my keen, totally intuitive lock on human psychology. And she was loyal like a puppy. Judy was single, homely, and—I thought at the time—destined to be a spinster forever. Copeland was her family and her life. Her job meant everything to her, and she would do anything if she was convinced it was for the good of the home. Helping me shoot down this union, I convinced her, was the best thing we could do.

I took Judy under my wing, and I turned her into a one-woman SWAT team. I taught her, trained her, molded her into a perfect little soldier. In her job as social worker, Judy roamed the Copeland complex, meeting with residents to help them untangle upsetting problems, which usually involved some intimidating government bureaucracy like the Social Security Administration or the IRS. She set her own daily schedule, and she knew just about everyone. As soon as she knew the rhetoric and the false logic of my campaign, I commissioned her as the mine sweeper. She followed the tracks of the less able supervisors, reinforcing my anti-union message—emphasis on my the-union-will-tear-us-apart theme—delivering the promise of harmony and making a plea for another chance. People listened to Judy, it seemed; she was articulate, she was sincere.

Judy bought into my program so eagerly, believed the ruse so completely, that I was almost sorry for her.

On January 19 the NLRB finally decided that it did, in fact, have jurisdiction over Copeland, and the workers had a right to hold a representation election. The board set the election for one month later, February 19. Then, and only then, was the union entitled to get the Excelsior list—my severely edited version, of course. After five months of work, then, and only then, were organizers able to find out the names and addresses of everyone in the voting unit. Then, and only then, would the union have the chance to contact all the workers. I had my offensive ready: the same letter that informed the workers of the time and place of the upcoming election also warned them to expect intrusions from a desperate and bothersome union.

Election day began at 6:30 A.M.
Snow covered the ground.
The sky was still dark when the NLRB agent arrived about a half hour before the voting was to begin. Claude greeted him at the big white doors, showed him into the Williamsburg Lounge, and disappeared into his office; management was not allowed near the polling place during voting hours. In the lounge, the agent was joined by the designated election observers—half a dozen pro-union workers and half a dozen management people—who would make it their job to be sure nothing slippery occurred during the balloting. The two contingents huddled on opposite sides of the room, whispered, peered over at the enemy. Then the agent called their attention. He was about to perform the legally required ballot box ritual that I always referred to as the "magic act."

The agent stood behind an oak table, and the observers assembled before it. He picked up what looked like a thin pile of brown cardboard sheets and, with a flick of his arm—pop!—flipped the pile into the form of a two-foot-long rectangular tunnel. The agent held the tunnel straight out at the level of his chest, allowing observers to look through it straight to his gray suit. Without saying a word, he solemnly passed a fisted hand through the space. Keeping the tunnel parallel to the floor, he moved it in a slow half circle, parading its emptiness before everyone in the room. That accomplished, the agent turned the tunnel vertically and quickly folded the lower ends upward to create a bottom. He turned the box on its side and showed it to the observers once again, proving to the suspicious that there was still nothing inside. Setting the box on the table, he then folded down four upper panels, making a slotted top.

The agent checked his watch. A line had formed at the doorway. With ten minutes to go, he set up the portable voting booth at one end of the room. He instructed one observer from each camp to take a seat on either side of him at the table. He took out his copy of the Excelsior list, which he would check to be sure no one voted twice. The rest of the observers stationed themselves about the lounge. At 6:30 sharp the agent let the voting begin.

I stayed with Claude in his office throughout the morning vote, listening to him identify wild-bird calls on an Audubon Society recording. At 8:00 A.M. the polls closed; they would reopen again at 2:30 P.M., half an hour before the afternoon shift was to begin. When the morning session ended, the agent sealed the ballot box as prescribed by law, taping the edges and corners and having the observers sign the tape. Then everyone left the room.

When I wandered into the lounge a little later, I was surprised to find the box sitting unattended on the top of the oak table. The agents usually take the box with them wherever they go, even to the rest room. I looked at it, looked around the empty room, looked behind me at the closed door. It would be easy, I thought. I wouldn't have to stuff the box; all I would have to do is make it clear the box had been tampered with, and the election would be held invalid. Then the union would have to go through the organizing drive all over again. I would blame the union for whatever I did to the box, which would give me the added ammunition of the union's obvious criminality.

I milled around the room, pacing like a tiger. I had called the election a winner, and for that reason I couldn't decide whether it would be worth the risk. My internal struggle was interrupted by a very flustered board agent, who came racing back into the room, his face flushed. I was nowhere near the box.

The second voting time ended at 4:00 P.M., just as the sky outside was beginning to darken. It had been a long, tense day. Supervisors were even more on edge than their workers. For the voters, election day held hope and promise, even after all that had been done to them. Not so for the supervisors. For them it was the moment of truth, the day they would discover if they were still despised, as they must have been when their workers called in the union. It was the day they would learn whether their co-workers were their enemies or their friends. Of the dozens of employees who showed up for the vote count, most were supervisors. They, all of them, needed to see it through to the end. Those on the morning shift didn't go home—they grouped in the Williamsburg Lounge. Afternoon workers stopped by on their breaks or wandered through on their way to care for a patient. Out in the hallways there was nothing but silence.

The agent took his seat behind the oak table, flanked by an observer from each side. He punched the seal, tore open the ballot box, and began to count. One by one he unfolded the ballots and read them aloud; one by one the observers marked "yes" or "no" on their tally sheet. At first, each call provoked a gasp from one side of the room, a muffled cheer from the other. But as the count progressed, the room fell silent. It was too close.

When the last ballot had been counted, the agent announced the results. The room erupted.

"Oh, my God," someone exclaimed.

"All *right!*" cheered someone else.

Judy's eyes filled. Kathleen covered her face. A trio of nurses wept aloud. Across the room, another group of girls squealed and wrapped their arms around each other. "Hey, we got 'em!" a voice proclaimed. A sharp hoot ripped through the room. A couple of girls dashed out the door. Suddenly there was clapping and cheering breaking out all over Copeland.

The union had won.

Bloodletting

Claude didn't blame me.

Still, I was sorry. If I had thought there was even a chance we might lose, I would have told him. Just good business. The only kind of surprise I liked was a win much bigger than the one I had predicted. This way it was embarrassing. True, we lost by only five votes, but I hadn't expected it to be anywhere near that close. Every pro-company employee had voted; I had made sure of that. So where had I gone wrong? I was dumbfounded. I never mentioned it to Claude, but I kept thinking about that unguarded ballot box, about how I could have taken care of things right there.

On election night Claude and his wife invited me and Alice out to dinner. What a good sport, I thought. Many CEOs might have snarled, "Thanks for nothing," and slammed the door in my face. But not Claude. Claude bought me steak and wine, and we spent a good long time licking our wounds together at the finest restaurant in Alliance.

"I was buffaloed," I confessed to Claude as we took our first sips of Cabernet. "I really believed I had it counted right. All I can figure is, an awful lot of the girls must have been lying. I'll bet it was the nurses."

I had lost before—not a lot, three or four times, maybe—but never without realizing it in advance, never without having the chance to prepare my client. It felt terrible. I apologized to Claude a dozen times; he absolved me many times over. What a good sport.

We made small talk about other details of my life: the brick house Alice and I had rented in the old University Heights district of Cleveland; the Jewish day care and private elementary school we had found for the boys in order to evade the urban public schools; how hard it had been for Alice to share the castle with my mom during the weeks we all had lived together in Beachwood. But the conversation always wound its way back to the election, to the union, to what went wrong. Claude was conciliatory.

"It was a great campaign, Marty," he said. "I wouldn't have wanted you to do anything differently. In fact, if you're willing, I'd like you to stick around for a while and work with the supervisors."

It seemed that Claude was taking the high road, accepting that the union had beat him and going on. He would have me run monthly workshops to teach the supervisors how to handle the union, keep tabs on the grapevine maybe through a rotating roundtable, and let it go. Could it be? Hardly. By the time the waiter was grinding black pepper onto my tossed green salad, I realized that old Claude was not a good sport at all. He hadn't said it yet, but I knew that as far as he was concerned, he hadn't lost. This thing wasn't over; it had only just begun.

I agreed to come in the next morning to meet with Claude and Lou Davies, and when I arrived, Davies was already there. Claude was seated behind his desk, looking grave. This time there was no small talk, no merriment. Barely had the door shut behind me when Claude announced in a solemn voice that there was not to be a contract at Copeland Oaks. He turned to the attorney and commanded him to be Copeland's representative at the bargaining table.

Lou leaned forward on the chair he occupied facing Claude's desk. He looked into Claude's cold eyes, shook his head slowly, and refused. "I can't do it, Claude," he said, almost whispering. "I know you don't intend to bargain in good faith. For me to go to the bargaining table with no intention of reaching a contract would be unethical. It's called surface bargaining, and it's against my professional code of conduct."

Claude frowned. He hadn't counted on that. He sat silently for a moment; then a smile flickered across his lips. He turned to me.

I knew instinctively what he was thinking, and I nodded in agreement. But, of course: unlike Lou, I was not bound by any code of ethics or any professional canons and therefore would not have to worry about my behavior at the bargaining table. In fact, for the purposes of my résumé, the naughtier I was, the better. The worst thing that could happen if I got caught surface bargaining was that the NLRB would order Copeland to bargain in good faith. And even the good-faith order was unlikely, because a charge of surface bargaining is very difficult to substantiate. The union people would need witnesses; I would have as many as they. The union people would need documentation; that would be hard to come by if nothing was happening. All I would have to do to defend myself would be to show that I had agreed to *something,* that some progress had been made. The law imposes on management and a newly elected union a "duty to bargain" for twelve months, and no more. I figured I could jerk off the union for a year, no problem. I told Claude I'd be glad to do it.

Claude also wanted me to go ahead with the supervisor training and the employee discussion groups as I had planned, in preparation for Copeland's certain return to monarchy. That was fine with me. For one thing, it meant one more day each month that I would pocket $750; that was on top of my daily fee for handling the negotiations. What's more, the supervisor meetings would give me the perfect forum for spreading my version of what was happening at the bargaining table and other important lies.

I called the first meeting immediately; I wanted to seize upon the intense emotions aroused by the company's humiliating loss. Many of the supervisors were shaken by the pro-union vote, as if it were a personal tragedy. I had taught them well. They were in anguish. They felt betrayed. They were hurt, confused, angry. But for the moment the targets of their passion were many: many of the women were as angry at Copeland and at Claude and at me as they were at the employees and their union. If I was to revive the anti-union drive from its startling knock-out, I had to collect all that rancor and aim it squarely at the workers who dealt the blows. And I had to do it quickly, before the supervisors could come to consider that life in an organized company might not be so bad.

Two days after the big upset election one hundred dispirited nurses, secretaries, and department managers assembled in the Williamsburg Lounge. No one spoke. Some still wore the telltale puffy eyes and red noses of a long crying spell. Others were pale and walked with a hypnotic stare. They looked beaten, dejected. Looking out at the faces of my grief-stricken troops, I realized that many expected to be scolded. They would not be. I did not want them contrite, not now. I wanted them angry.

The days of the this-is-all-your-fault tack and the give-us-a-chance tack were behind us. I would have no use in the postelection campaign for the soft emotions. There would be no more begging and pleading, no apologizing, no wooing. Now there would be nothing but fire.

So I told them, in steady, modulated tones, "Ladies, I know this is a very trying time for most of you. You have worked hard, and I have to say, you did one fantastic job. Truly. So, hold your heads high. You have nothing to be ashamed of. The only people who should be ashamed are the traitors who voted against their company. After all you did these past three months, listening to them and talking with them and trying your level best to make your company a better place, those creeps went right ahead and stabbed you in the back. They lied to you. They told you they were your friends, then they turned around and voted against you anyway. Well, now they're going to pay. We will show them that we spoke the truth in the campaign. And they'll see they made a terrible mistake. They wanted a union, let's give them a union."

Already the mood had shifted. The meeting room was abuzz. Nurses began whispering to each other, quite a few were smiling, some were even chuckling. With a lighter touch to my voice now, I reminded the supervisors that all the union had won was twelve months, nothing more. It had not won a contract. "We have lost the battle," I said, "but we have not yet lost the war."

The negotiation of a first contract is very delicate, so the process is highly controlled by labor law. Company executives who have just been forced to recognize a union—after spending tens of thousands of dollars to defeat it—rarely walk into their first bargaining session with open arms. To protect the inchoate contract from sabotage by an embittered management, then, labor law sets rigid rules of conduct for the postelection period. The purpose of the rules is to impede management from undermining negotiations, whether through subtle bribes, veiled threats, or an outright propaganda campaign. As with most labor laws, however, the rules are largely ineffective. Worse: the hands of a union buster can quite easily twist those rules into a precision weapon against the union.

During the postelectoral battle, I would not be able to send letters to the rank-and-file employees as I had during the counterorganizing campaign. Any memo or letter coming from management that even hinted at criticizing the union could be interpreted by the labor board as an attempt to undermine the union and ne-

gotiations. That would make the company look like the bad guy—
which I didn't want—and could pressure Claude into actually
negotiating, which he did not want. There was nothing, however,
to stop us from talking to the supervisors. We would continue our
propaganda war all right, we just wouldn't put it in writing. Once
again the supervisors were taken hostage.

I looked out at my audience. It was hungry. Hundreds of eyes
were upon me, begging me for relief from pain and emptiness. I
began the feeding, slowly at first, then picking up the pace as my
captives became accustomed to their new meal. In one hour I had
to whip every vestige of remorse and forgiveness out of all those
loving hearts and refill the empty space with spite. Labor law was
going to help me accomplish my aim. All I had to do was take
every rule that suited my game plan and stretch it to the extreme.
I would ignore the spirit and enforce the letter of the law so far
beyond its intent that it would double back on itself and end up
destroying the very process—and the very people—it was written
to protect.

My strategy was predetermined by the campaign that had just
ended. Throughout three months of war I had made many a hor-
rifying prediction of what could happen to Copeland should the
union win the election. Now I would make sure that every last one
of the dire forecasts came to pass. I had warned that the cherished
"direct relationship" between supervisor and worker would come
to an end. I had warned that the two sides would see each other,
and treat each other, as enemies. I had warned that all flexibility
in scheduling, in duties, in everything, would disappear. I had
warned that negotiations could be prolonged and uncertain. I had
warned that Copeland would stagnate during those negotiations;
there would be no workplace improvements, no pay raises. And I
had warned that there could be a strike, that there might be violence, that the residents would be in jeopardy. Now it was time to
deliver.

"I can't imagine that many of you have been in the army," I
quipped to my audience, looking the younger ones in the eyes. I
knew them all so well, now. I smiled, and the levity was received
with gratitude. "It doesn't matter," I said, chuckling. "You don't
need to have been in the army to know about drill instructors. How
many of you know what a drill instructor is?" Hands shot up
around the room. I let a sly smile rest on my lips. "Good. I thought
so. Well, that's what I want you all to become. Starting today, you

are drill instructors. Shore up your departments. You are the bosses, you make the rules, and you keep everyone in line. It's clear to me—and it should be clear to you—that you can't trust your workers. You were lied to, you were betrayed, and you can't know for certain who did the lying and the betraying. So everybody gets the tough treatment.

"The employees wanted the structure of a union," I continued. "That's what that vote was all about. Well, we'll show them how it works. Flexibility will disappear. There will be no give and take, no favors, no compassion, no bending of rules."

I decreed that supervisors were not to talk to any subordinates—at all—except to give orders. Any personal ties to their employees that had survived the organizing campaign were to be severed immediately. "From now on, there's no room for understanding. Everything," I said, "everything will be done by the book."

Funny thing was, until I appeared at Copeland, there was no book. Claude had never bothered to put employment policies in writing—indeed, in many areas there were no actual policies. At my insistence, during the previous months, Claude and his helpmates had thrown together a handbook that spelled out the mundane details of Copeland employment, such as work hours and duties, discipline procedures, management rights and responsibilities, and absentee policies. Where rules and procedures did not exist, something was made up on the spot for the benefit of the handbook. The policies were then typed up on looseleaf sheets and collected in a three-ring binder—a precaution that I routinely recommended so that management could rewrite any policy in a moment. Now, suddenly, this hastily prepared shell manual was to become the bible.

Claude declined to include in the manual a number of niceties, preferring to think of them as unearned perquisites to be doled out and taken away at his whim. I took some favorites away immediately. The first to go was the morning and afternoon breaks, two coveted fifteen-minute respites from the daily tedium. Gone. No more idleness at company expense. Then went free meals, a real blow to the workers. Technically such changes could be illegal, if the purpose of the changes was to undermine the union. Labor law recognizes the elected union as the sole and exclusive bargaining agent for wages, hours, benefits, and working conditions and encourages management to maintain everything in those areas at status quo until a contract is agreed to and signed by both sides. My answer to that was: So what? If the union wanted to file a complaint about the changes, fine, let the labor board decide. In the meantime the changes would go into effect.

Where the status quo guidelines did not suit me, I ignored them. Where they did suit my purpose, however, I made sure they were enforced with a vengeance. In the area of pay, benefits, and working conditions, Copeland employees hungered for improvements. All Claude would have had to do to grant a pay raise while negotiations with Local 47 were in process was get the union's okay. The union might have hated to let management take the credit for a pay increase, but it would hardly have been able to refuse. The new members would never have understood. Same thing for any other improvement, from upgrading medical insurance to fixing toilets. Management had only to ask. Well, Claude was not about to *ask* the union for anything, and I wouldn't have let him if he had been so inclined. No, the workers were just going to have to wait and curse the union as they tightened their belts. A de facto wage freeze had gone into effect at Copeland three months earlier, the day the union had filed its petition. But because raises at Copeland were sporadic and minuscule at best, the action—or, more accurately, *in*action—went largely unnoticed. That was to change. After the union vote, Claude extended the freeze indefinitely.

We had the supervisors make a lot of noise about the lack of pay raises. The noise went something like this: "Copeland Oaks would like to give everybody a raise; in fact, a raise had been considered for this month. But the federal government says we can't raise wages as long as negotiations are pending." Then, the personal touch: "I know you need the money, Nan. But there's nothing we can do about it. Our hands are tied—by the union."

My final order to the troops on that first day of phase II was that they be particularly rigid with the known "troublemakers" who had gotten everybody into this mess in the first place. Also referred to as the "red-hots," those union pushers were bad seeds, I said. They were not to be left alone for a moment, lest they breed even more misery. "Bird-dog them," I ordered. "Wherever a troublemaker goes, a supervisor must go, too; into the ladies' room, down to the lockers, to the dining room, out on the grounds, into a resident's apartment. A troublemaker must never have a chance to talk privately with other workers, and she must never, ever, be left alone with one of the old folks. We can't take that chance. No telling what she might do." The union couldn't do much about all that, for their role now was limited to bargaining. The only right they had won was the right to try to negotiate a contract.

As I revived the ground war, I also recast the war of delay. This time the delay revolved not around the hearing room of the NLRB, but around the bargaining table. As word of the wage freeze and evidence of the new military order spread throughout Copeland Oaks, so did the message that, so far, the union had done nothing. In fact, union officers were busy drawing up a proposed contract. But they had not contacted Copeland and clearly felt no pressure to move quickly. Why should they? After all, they had no idea they were still at war. They thought they had won. I did not call the union, nor did Claude. We just went about unfolding our in-house drama and waited for the union to come to us. They only had twelve months, and the clock was ticking. We were in no rush. Time was on our side.

Six weeks after the election, Claude got a letter from the union attorney asking the executive director to schedule the first bargaining session. Claude wrote back saying that all future correspondence should be sent to his representative, Martin Jay Levitt; he gave my home address and telephone number. Since I was required at Copeland only two half days a month then, I had resumed my kitchen table routine. Eventually I found a handful of other union-busting jobs to keep me busy, but for the first couple of months after the Copeland election I spent most of my days at home drinking and just passing the time.

In mid-April 1981, about a month after Claude had received the union letter, I got a call from Local 47. "We need to start negotiations," said the voice at the other end of the line. "Can we meet out at Copeland Oaks? It's gonna be tough for our committee to get all the way up here to Cleveland."

Instinctively I said no. Why? Partly because I didn't feel like driving out to Sebring and partly just to make things difficult on the union members. "Dr. Roe doesn't want any bargaining to take place at his facility," I lied. "It might be upsetting to the residents."

In that case, said the union man, we could use the conference room at union headquarters in downtown Cleveland. He mentioned matter-of-factly that the members of his negotiating committee would naturally need paid time off in order to attend negotiations.

"I'm sure my client will have no trouble granting time off," said I, "but I can also assure you it won't be paid."

I had some demands of my own. I told the union man that I required Joe Murphy, president of Local 47, to be present at every bargaining session. "I'm not interested in bargaining with anyone less than the president of the local," I said.

The voice answered, "That's going to be very difficult. Mr. Murphy has a very busy schedule."

I retorted, "Well, so do I." Pretending to check that schedule, I then told my union contact that the first date I had available was in two weeks. We set the meeting for 4:30 P.M. on a Wednesday. Before hanging up, I said I needed the names of every employee on the negotiating team so that I could arrange time off for the meeting. For most of the workers, that wasn't going to be necessary, I knew. I had been careful to schedule the session after the end of the day shift, to make it a hardship for the workers, some of whom surely would have to get back to their families. The real reason for obtaining the names was to give me time to arrange for the immediate supervisor of each committee member to be present at negotiations.

By the time I met Jim Horton, Art Worthy, and Joe Murphy face to face, two months had passed. Two down, ten to go.

I walked into the first session twenty minutes late and as blustery as ever. Behind me were six stern-faced supervisors. I had instructed the bosses to take the seat directly across from their subordinate, if possible, then to keep quiet. They thought they had been invited along to observe the proceedings so that they could report the facts to their crews. In truth they were there only to intimidate. I told them nothing about negotiations, nothing. When Kathleen Taylor walked in, the face of one committee member fell. Then in walked Anna Moracco, director of nursing, and I saw another face grow pale.

I took my seat. Jim Horton introduced himself; the union attorney, Mel Swartzwall; and Joe Murphy. The attorney handed me a typed list of demands. He asked, "Do you have anything in writing?"

I didn't. I growled, "It's not my obligation to bring something in writing to you. That's your job."

The union people remained unruffled, but everyone else in the room shifted on their seats and glanced at one another uneasily. Not about to waste precious bargaining time, the attorney suggested, "Well, since we're here, let's get some routine things out of the way. We'd like union shop and check-off—"

I stopped him there. The union was asking Copeland to agree to require all employees to pay union dues and to deduct those dues automatically from paychecks. "Wait a minute," I told him. "We're not prepared to consider that yet. Remember, this was a close election." I decided to keep the meeting short, a show of how futile bargaining could be and to frustrate all those inconvenienced people. Saying I needed to review the union proposals before I could proceed, I suggested we call it a day.

The union contingent was eager to set the next meeting time. I was not. I said my calendar was jammed, and that I'd have to look it over and get back to them. I then reissued my demand that Murphy attend every bargaining session. The entire union side of the table protested; having to work meetings around Joe's packed schedule was going to bog things down. But I insisted: this being a first contract, it was of utmost importance that the president of the local be involved. I unilaterally adjourned the session, rose, and told the union I'd be in touch by telephone. My contingent of supervisors stood and exited behind me.

I called a supervisors meeting at Copeland the next day. I wanted to be sure I got my story out on the wire before the union had a chance to deliver its version. "We'll be first with the facts," I had told the supervisors, and I was holding true to my promise. There was little to report, I said. I told my audience about a gruff, sour union president who, now that he had won the election, didn't want to do the work of negotiating. I told them about the predictable demand for union shop and check-off but said nothing about the twenty-four-page, detailed proposal the union had prepared for that first bargaining session. In fact, I never even read the proposal. I had no idea what they were asking for, didn't need to know. I had no intention of ever talking about it.

I didn't call the union back as I had said I would. Two weeks passed, and Jim Horton called me. I was brusque. "I've been busy," I snapped.

The union wanted to schedule the next meeting as soon as possible; Horton wanted to know if we could meet at Copeland Oaks this time. Out of the question, I said.

"It's a hardship on those working people to travel up to Cleveland," he protested.

I agreed to consider an alternate place but left it up to him to come up with one. We left it at that.

Jim Horton called me back a little while later with the name of a roadside motel fifteen minutes outside of Sebring. We could use the meeting room there, he said. Now, let's set a date. He suggested the following Tuesday; I reminded him that I expected Joe Murphy to be there.

"Mr. Murphy's not available on that day," he replied, "but we're ready to go."

I balked. "If he's not available, then I'm not available."

We finally agreed on a date two weeks later. Before signing off, Horton reminded me, "Oh, and Marty, bring a counterproposal this time. Something in writing."

"I'll see what I can do," was all I would say.

When I walked into the second session with my team, the union people were a bit more aggressive but still terribly polite. They asked for my counterproposal immediately. I said no, I did not have a proposal ready; but in the next breath I assured them I was prepared to negotiate. To keep the talks going and create a patina of "good faith," I agreed to a handful of routine items. In negotiating lingo, I "initialed off" on a series of penny items such as recognition of the union, equal opportunity employment, and the like by scrawling my initials alongside the sections. It was a cursory gesture, which took care of but one page of the union's twenty-five-page proposal. It meant nothing, but it bought me some time and created evidence that I was, in fact, willing to negotiate. The process took all of five minutes, at the end of which there was nothing left to do, since I had not yet responded to the proposal handed me a month earlier. The union people looked perturbed. Swartzwall began to grumble. Then Murphy took over, waxing genteel before his newly won members and their bosses.

"Come on, Marty," he cajoled. "You know we need a written proposal from you if we're going to get anywhere. What do you say?"

I feigned cooperation, saying in a mellifluous voice, "I'll do what I can to put something together." We set the next session for two weeks thence, same place. I let the union pick up the tab for the room.

The following meeting was like a gift sent from the great Union Buster below. Naturally I brought not a scrap of paper with me. But the other side would never know that. When I entered the meeting room—late, as usual—I noticed Joe Murphy was not present. After the management people and I had taken our seats, I called the oversight to the union's attention.

Horton responded apologetically, "Mr. Murphy had a last-minute conflict and regrets that he cannot attend today's session."

That did it. They had handed me my bluff. "What?" I boomed, full of indignation. "We had an agreement!"

The union attorney told me to shut up, the other committee members tried to be more conciliatory, but I wasn't letting go. With the help of Lou Davies I had boned up on the myriad ways in which unions protected their right to represent workers, just in case I was forced into a bargaining session; I had planned to waste that day arguing over the technicalities of union membership. But this was better.

I jumped up from my seat and bellowed, "If your top man can't bother to be here, I'm not wasting my time." I turned to my stunned committee and announced, "We have nothing more to discuss." On cue, my troops rose with me, and we all marched out of the room, leaving the union team in shocked silence.

Four down, eight to go.

Back at Copeland my war machine was steamrolling along. I met with supervisors regularly in order to add a few strokes to the portrait I was painting in their minds, the portrait of an inept, uncaring, and potentially dangerous union. Under the blessed banner of "communication" I reported on the pathetic bargaining sessions, I floated rumors, spread fear. I also spent one morning a month with supervisors delivering my training program. The class plans were simple: one thirty-minute canned film on responsive management or positive reinforcement or the team approach or some other overblown management concept, followed by an apparently freewheeling discussion, which, on the heels of the film and in the context of the continuing anti-union drive, was quite easy to guide toward certain desired conclusions. So straightforward was the system that a trainer was barely needed, except to run the projector and keep the talk from falling off the track.

After a few sessions I began handing the work over to Judy Stanley, whom I was grooming to carry on for me when my job at Copeland was done. Most of the information in the training films as well as the ideas circulated during discussions could be considered harmless. Some might even have been useful, had they not been tainted by the narrow and belligerent motive of keeping the workers unorganized and under control.

On a separate morning each month, I had Judy conduct the rotating roundtable discussions with rank-and-file workers. Since I was acting as negotiator for Copeland, I still chose not to speak with employees directly. It was to my strategic advantage that the rap sessions were moderated by a low-brow middle manager like Judy, who, although classified as a supervisor, was nobody's direct boss and was not seen as a threat. The workers would open up to her, I figured; at the very least they would not be afraid to open up to each other in front of her. I sent Judy into each meeting with a tightly choreographed program designed to make workers feel good by letting them voice their complaints and to squeeze intelligence out of the fecund employee grapevine. At the start of the discussion, which was attended each time by a different worker representative from each department, Judy assured the group that whatever they said would be held in strictest confidence. Although she might need to report what was said so that management could accomplish the improvements the workers sought, she would never, ever, divulge the source of any complaint. Any notes she took would be totally anonymous. She promised, and she meant it. After each session, when Judy reported to me not only every detail of the discussion, but the names of her sources, she never imagined that I would break her trust and use the information against the employees.

Out on the floor, the atmosphere was even more oppressive than during the organizing effort. "After the union passed, that's when they blasted us," remembers former housekeeper Jean Householder. Jean was a prominent and fearless union supporter. A one-time friend of her boss, Kathleen Taylor, Jean ran the organizing drive in the housekeeping and laundry departments. A thirty-nine-year-old with twelve years at Copeland, she was an election observer and a member of the negotiating committee. She was also one of the chief targets of Copeland's postelectoral bloodbath. I saw Jean, and about twenty-three other key union proponents, as the biggest impediment to my campaign to discredit the newly elected union. Those two dozen women were keeping workers informed almost as well as I was; they could be counted on both to rebut my disinformation and to inspire nerve-racked employees to stick with the union. I figured that if I could get them out of the way over the next few months, while maintaining the unofficial impasse at the bargaining table, I just might be able to fuel a worker revolt against the union.

I knew, and Claude confirmed, that employee turnover in nursing homes was quite high. Nine, ten months from now, as much as one-third of Copeland employees could be new hires. They would not have voted in the representation election, and they would have been hired in part for their verifiable anti-union inclinations. With no strong union leaders left at the job, a union decertification campaign could spread quickly.

Claude bought off a handful of the former union activists right away, through minor promotions. But what I really wanted was for Jean and her pals to quit. To that end, I made sure they could not enjoy one minute of their workday, the pressure on them and the hostility toward them would be so intense. Supervisors, co-workers, and residents would gang up on the remaining twenty and blame them for everyone's unhappiness. The target twenty would draw lousy shifts and find themselves with the most despised assignments; they would be harassed, shunned, and punished until life at Copeland became so unbearable that they would decide they owed it to themselves—and to their loving families—to find another job. If that didn't work, of course, they would have to be fired.

The Jean plan was boilerplate harassment, but it was nonetheless effective for its lack of originality. A harassed worker feels totally alone, no matter how many tens of thousands of workers have been similarly harassed, in a different time, at a different place. Immediately following the union win, Jean was paired with her direct supervisor, the assistant director of housekeeping and laundry, Betty Rusky. The pairing had a double aim: one, of course, was to subject Jean to the constant hostility of her ego-injured boss. The other was to underhandedly double Jean's workload. Since Betty was constantly being pulled off the floor for meetings—with me, with the department heads, with upper management—Jean was constantly having to clean their twelve rooms and change the linens in twelve others with no help. When they were together, Jean and Betty labored in tense silence. One morning, on one of the rare occasions Jean was cleaning an apartment alongside her boss-partner, she believes she overheard the elderly resident whisper to Betty, "What about these union people they're telling us about? They say we're supposed to lock our doors against them at night." Betty put her index finger to her lips, glanced over at Jean, and whispered back, "Shhhhh. She goes to negotiations with them."

After a few months Jean could take no more. In March 1982 she quit her job.

Sharing the bull's-eye with the twenty "red-hot" Copeland women was one man—in fact, a supervisor, Fred Moracco. Fred, a big-bellied fellow nearing sixty, was the director of maintenance and husband of Anna Moracco, the nursing director. Fred knew Copeland Oaks better than Claude, better than anyone. Heck, he had built the place. When Copeland was under construction in the mid-1960s, Fred had been the project foreman—and the union steward. A union laborer since the 1940s, Fred quit construction work and left the International Laborers Union in 1968 to take the job as Copeland's head maintenance man. With that move, he forfeited the pension he had been building with the union at ten cents an hour for twenty-five years. But that was okay. He was taking a step up.

So Fred was a veteran union man. He was also a good friend to the hardworking ladies of Copeland Oaks and quite unashamed of his support for their union effort, his wife's managerial loyalty notwithstanding. I didn't pick up on Fred's empathy with the workers during my interviews with him before the election—he was a good poker player, apparently. I knew he wasn't carrying out my orders to interrogate his eleven subordinates on their union sympathies; and he sure wasn't doing any lobbying on management's behalf. But Fred was such a cranky guy, independent in that defiant, midwestern, blue-collar sort of way. I figured his stubbornness was just his nature, and although I tormented him about it endlessly during our one-on-one interviews, I didn't let it worry me much. Whatever sympathy Fred had for the organizing effort he kept quiet; he even joined the other managers in signing my final anti-union letter.

But after the union win, Fred let his views be known: the union had won, for God's sake, now let it go about its business. Fred refused to comply with my postelection directive to snub union supporters. "I'll talk to whoever I want to," was his gruff retort. Fred did more than talk. When he passed union organizers in the hallways and on the grounds, he was always sure to give them a thumbs-up: "Way to go! I don't blame you for what you're doing. It's about time. You deserve it. Keep up the good work."

Fred's outspokenness annoyed me, to be sure, but not as much as it annoyed Claude Roe. I saw Fred as a loudmouth; Claude saw him as a Judas. As time went on, Claude became more rabid and more irrational in his contempt for Fred. Dr. Roe, who was most self-consciously patrician under usual circumstances, became suddenly and uncharacteristically rash whenever the conversation turned to his maintenance man. The minister's ire bubbled over into the most inarticulate and decidedly un-Christian accusations, peppered with raw expletives. I delighted in these lapses of self-control and enjoyed baiting him on the subject: I listened as he speculated on how Fred must have collaborated with union organizers, and I joined him in defiling the traitor. To me, those conversations were pure entertainment and not to be taken seriously. I liked Fred. Claude, however, had never been more serious, and he was building his case.

Where the payoff theory came from, I do not know. On March 25, 1981, Claude called me into his office to inform me that he believed Fred Moracco had been on the Local 47 payroll. I knew what that meant, of course: Fred was to be fired.

A little before four that afternoon, Claude summoned Fred to his office. When his maintenance man appeared, the reverend Claude pushed a sheet of paper and a pen across his desk and dryly ordered Fred to sign it. It was a resignation letter.

Fred read the words on the page, looked quizzically at Claude, and refused. He had no desire to resign, and Claude had given him no reason why he should. Fine, said Claude. Then you're fired. Get out. As of now you are trespassing.

The next day Anna quit in protest of her husband's ill treatment.

Claude did not choose to share with Fred the reasons for his sudden dismissal. He did share them, however, with the rest of the Copeland work force and with the public at large. A few days after the firing, he called a meeting of employees and residents. He confirmed that one of the department heads had been let go and, using a parable as his cover, implied that the miscreant had been stealing from the company. Over the next few days vague references to theft solidified into a specific charge, and soon everyone was debating whether or not it was true that Fred Moracco had stolen $13,000. Within weeks all the newspapers in northeastern Ohio had carried the story.

After the fourth negotiating session I knew it was time for some new ammunition; the stalling tactic was wearing thin. I got a lucky break. It so happened that Local 47's patience was also wearing thin, and I heard through my network that the union would soon hold a strike vote. Well, nothing makes as sweet music to the ears of anti-union management as the word *strike*—particularly in the fall of 1981. In August of that year the most powerful man in the world, the president of the United States of America, had pulled off the biggest union bust in history. That month President Ronald Reagan fired thirteen thousand striking federal air traffic controllers—who were striking essentially for safer working conditions—and allowed their employers to hire permanent replacements. Reagan also had five union leaders prosecuted under a never-before-used law prohibiting strikes against the government. In firing the strikers, and calling their leaders criminals, the president, himself a former union official as onetime president of the Screen Actors Guild, displayed his contempt for organized labor. The firing annihilated the air controllers union, PATCO, and crippled all labor organizations by destroying their most powerful economic weapon, the strike. What I did not know was that a few months later, Reagan would outlaw PATCO itself. Thus, in ninety days Ronald Reagan recast the crimes of union busting as acts of patriotism. When word came to me of Local 47's strike vote, I grinned. I knew the moves. And I would start making them immediately.

I called an urgent supervisors meeting to get the word out about the union's dastardly plan. This is what I told my audience: "Many of you may have heard that the union is considering calling a strike. It should come as no surprise, that's what we've been saying would happen all along." The supervisors nodded but kept their wide eyes on me. They knew more was coming. "What may come as a surprise is that only the people who signed union authorization cards have been invited to vote." My congregation gasped. "That's right. Now why do you think they would do that?" I asked with a smarmy tone.

The indignation was palpable. Even the LPNs, many of whom had managed to hold on to their ideals and keep their friendships throughout the crusade, looked grief stricken. Could it be true? Could they have been wrong about the union?

It was true—half-true. True, only workers who had signed authorization cards eight months earlier would be allowed to vote. Also true, however, was a very compelling reason, which I did not mention: the law. Only union members are allowed by law to vote on union issues. And until a contract is signed and membership dues collected, only signatories of the authorization cards are considered by law to be members. The fact was, the union had no choice about who got to vote and who didn't; it was only doing what it was legally bound to do. The inference I knew my congregation would draw, however, was that the union was trying to stack the vote in favor of a strike by allowing only pro-union people to cast ballots. The union representatives, who were sixty miles away in Cleveland, had a hard time countering my charges.

That fire ignited, I went about developing a "strike contingency plan." Such a plan purports to set up a system so that vital business operations can continue if workers walk off the job. Sounds reasonable and benign. In truth, strike contingency plans have but one dual aim: to scare the workers and rout the union. My plan would scare the workers all right—scare them into thinking a strike would be dangerous; scare them into believing a strike would be prolonged; scare them into thinking a strike would be futile; scare them into believing strikers would lose their jobs. That was my plan. Once again the workers would be made to feel they could not possibly win.

I hit on all fronts. To show that Copeland was preparing for a long strike, I had Claude run Help Wanted ads in all the local town newspapers. We wanted workers to know that the moment they walked out the door, plenty of eager job seekers would walk right in behind them. I got the word out on the grapevine that Claude already had a backlog of applications and that he had started interviews. The message was not lost on the Copeland work force. Since most of the employees who would be striking held unskilled positions, they knew their jobs would not be hard to fill. They began to worry.

My next move was to tighten security around Copeland, a clear indication that management expected the strike to be violent. At my direction Claude installed bright lamps in the unlit employee parking lot. He told supervisors directly that the lights were being added for the protection of workers, due to the increasing hostility of the union. Claude assured his worried supervisors that a security force would be hired in the event of a strike to protect supervisors and those workers who chose to continue working rather than join the rabble on the pavement. In my most cunning antistrike play, I convinced Claude to buy an old schoolbus, to be used to shuttle loyal employees safely across the picket line. We let supervisors know—and they let their subordinates know—that anyone who wanted to work through the strike would be picked up, taken to work, and driven home in the Copeland bus. That way they would not have to drive alone past angry picketers or leave their cars to be vandalized in the employee parking lot. We even drew up a dozen alternate routes to employees' communities, so that the bus could take a different course each day—sort of like a moving missile plan—and thus evade any enterprising union people who might want to show up at the stops to try to talk the workers out of boarding. The employees worried a little more.

Finally I dispatched maintenance workers to paint a white line at the edge of Copeland property, a line picketers would not be allowed to cross. Companies do not have to allow strikers to picket on their property, and Copeland certainly did not intend to. As it turned out, Copeland property stretched all the way to the end of the long driveway. Since there was no sidewalk, the white line put the picket zone in the street. The strikers would have to share the road with cars and the occasional bus and truck.

With all but one round of my contingency plan fired, I began hearing talk about union supporters trying to enlist friends to carry picket signs for them. They were very worried now. We sat back and waited.

About nine months after bargaining had begun, Local 47 asked its newest membership for authorization to call a strike. The Copeland voters overwhelmingly approved. A month later union reps notified us that the workers planned to walk out. Labor law requires unions to give health care facilities ten days advance notice of a strike so that the institution can arrange for meals and vital care for patients or, if that is impossible on site, transfer patients to other facilities. Ten days was plenty of time for me to unleash the final phase of the strike contingency plan. That's when I called a meeting with the residents committee.

Claude and I made our point of view clear: those nasty union people were planning to abandon the sweet old ladies for the picket line, we said. They wanted more money, and it looked as though they would stop at nothing to get it. Well, we wanted the residents to know that management would do everything it could to protect them from the unpleasantness. But they also needed to be aware of how to protect themselves. Besides keeping their doors locked and their valuables hidden, the residents should not engage in any unnecessary conversation with the union workers. Some of the union people were a little crazy, we confided; we couldn't be sure they wouldn't abuse the elderly folks if it suited their cause. For that reason we would see to it that no resident would ever be left alone and unprotected with a pro-union employee. As that message was being duly disseminated by the residents committee, Claude sent his own letter to all residents, apologizing for any worry the union strife was causing them and assuring them of management's abiding concern for their well-being.

At 7:00 A.M. on strike day, as the morning shift was due to come on, management took its battle stations and braced itself for the assault. Poof! Nothing happened. No one walked out. The day dragged on. No one showed up with picket signs. No one. Strike day came and went; it was the quietest day Copeland Oaks had ever known.

Nine down, three to go.

On the heels of the strike that wasn't there, I got a call from the union. We were nine months into negotiations and nowhere; would I consider meeting with a federal mediator? Hell, it was fine by me. I said sure, I'd go to the damn meeting. I knew the federal mediation system was bullshit, so I wasn't worried. The idea is laudable, I suppose. The mediator is supposed to meet separately with each side, find some common ground, then bring them together and bless the marriage. But the joke is that the mediator can do nothing to compel agreement. He has no authority, no power, no force of law behind him. I spent a day at the federal building in Akron going for cups of coffee with the mediator and my committee. It just used up time and maybe made me look as though I were really trying. Meanwhile the clock went tick, tick, tick.

In November 1981 preparations were begun for the opening of the adjacent Crandall Medical Center, the construction of which was nearly complete. The new medical facility was to bring with it an expansion of Copeland's traditional mission and heighten both the prestige and income of the Sebring retirement community.

Employees were as eager as Dr. Roe to cut the ribbon. What no one but I knew was that Crandall was a booby trap. From the beginning Crandall had been talked about as a company distinct from Copeland and was, in fact, separately incorporated. The point was made early and often in the Copeland campaign that Crandall would not just be an extension of Copeland Oaks. Indeed, the letterhead I had used for Claude's "Dear Staff Member" letters listed the names of both institutions, followed by the written elbow jab, "two separate and independent legal entities." It had been my argument, fully supported by Lou Davies, that should Copeland Oaks somehow go union, Crandall could still be preserved as Claude's union-free rumpus room. It was a different company. Now the time had come to make use of that carefully guarded distinction.

With the opening of the medical center one month away, Copeland management began the task of staffing the facility. The job vacancies were heavily advertised in the area press, and Copeland employees were welcome to apply—along with the rest of northeastern Ohio. Copeland employees were told that since Crandall was a separate corporation they should not expect to be hired there automatically. At my insistence, Copeland employees wishing to work at Crandall were required to fill out job applications like everyone else and join the competition. Even workers whose jobs were being transferred to the medical building next door had to apply for the "new" Crandall positions, which, of course, were non-union jobs.

It was a scam. I designed the Copeland-Crandall shuffle, specifically to get rid of unwanted—read "pro-union"—workers. In fact, almost fifty Copeland jobs were to be transferred to Crandall, including all dietary positions, all laundry, most of the nursing, and some housekeeping. The jobs were moved, but at my direction the executive director of Crandall, who happened to be a certain Claude L. Roe, slyly refused to let the people who held those jobs go with them.

The union cried foul over the transfer game. Officials argued, rightfully so, that Copeland and Crandall were clearly one company, regardless of the legal technicalities. The jobs being transferred to Crandall would remain essentially the same as they were at Copeland, they said, and the bosses would be the same. In protest of the ploy, union officers advised members not to fill out job applications. It was a mistake, but not one that really mattered, since we would have gotten what we wanted either way. As jobs were moved to Crandall, the corresponding positions at Copeland were eliminated. Suddenly a nurse's aide or housekeeper would find herself unemployed. She could fill out an application for Crandall and maybe get hired there—or maybe not. Or she could refuse to fill out an application, as several of the strongest union supporters did, and lose her job for certain.

One nurse's aide, a forty-two-year-old single mother named Winnie Waithman, decided to play the game and fill out an application. She was told there was no job for her at Crandall. All the medical positions had been filled. Funny thing: Winnie just happened to be an inside organizer, election observer, member of the negotiating committee, and designated union spokesperson.

"The ones of us they didn't want over there, the 'undesirables,' were told there was no place for us," Winnie says plainly.

The big day came in December 1981. Crandall opened its doors, and eighteen Copeland employees lost their jobs.

Meanwhile, a hand-picked committee of anti-union workers began circulating a petition calling for a vote to remove Local 47 as their bargaining representative. Thirty percent of the rank-and-file workers signed, and the decertification petition reached Region 8 of the NLRB before Christmas.

Ten down, two to go.

The NLRB regional director had barely begun looking over the decertification petition in the early days of 1982 when he received a package of legal forms from Local 47. In the package were twenty unfair labor practice charges against Copeland Oaks. The union accused the company of bad-faith bargaining, refusal to bargain, and eighteen counts of firing an employee for union-related activities.

The charges worried Claude. He was counting on the decertification election to bury the union once and for all. His hopes faded when he received the notice of the charges and the admonition that the decertification petition would not be considered until all unfair labor practice charges were resolved. He summoned Lou Davies and me, turning first to Lou and pleading with him to defend Copeland.

Lou would not be moved from his Pontius Pilot stance: "Claude, I know Marty's been surface bargaining. How can I go in there and defend Copeland against charges of which I know it's guilty? I can't do it."

Claude next looked at me. No, I couldn't argue law before the NLRB, but I could help. Since I hadn't been needed around Copeland Oaks much lately, I had managed to pick up a couple of other union-busting jobs. Through one of the companies, Cyberex Inc., an electronics manufacturer in Mentor, Ohio, I had met an attorney. He was sharp, he was tough, and he owed me. I told Claude I was sure he'd be glad to take on the work. He was Earl Leiken, the eggheaded lawyer who would ride with me in half a dozen union busts over the next four years, including the bash at Cravat Coal.

The NLRB suspended the decertification petition and set a hearing on the first two of the string of unfair labor practice charges pending against Copeland. It began with the bad-faith bargaining charges. The board sent agents out to Copeland to interview everyone who had been in on the bargaining sessions and a number of people who had not. As the investigation plodded along, I found myself getting uncharacteristically nervous. I was beginning to doubt that we could win this one; my hostility and intransigence at the bargaining table had been pretty transparent. I had rarely even planned a move. It was all off the cuff. Maybe the board would see through it.

Luckily for me, I had President Reagan on my side—again. During his first year in office Reagan had filled the NLRB and its regional agencies with pro-management members. The president had also slashed the board's budget, making it difficult for agents to carry out full, lengthy investigations. All that made it harder than ever for unions to convince the board to issue unfair labor practice complaints.

With those clear advantages, Earl went to bat. In his unspectacular style he won a most spectacular victory. Using the few morsels I gave him—like the fact that I had initialed off on several contract items and the fact that I had agreed to meet with the federal mediator—he concocted a solid defense. The union members reported what they saw and heard, but, amazingly, it wasn't enough to prove that the company had no intention of reaching a contract. The board dismissed the charges.

Eleven down, one to go.

The union's twelve months were up in February 1982. The NLRB was still scratching its way through the unjust firing charges, but I was no longer needed. Negotiations had been suspended. I moved on to work my scam at other companies in northern Ohio, leaving it to Earl Leiken to finish the Copeland bloodletting.

I was a happy man. My nineteen-month part-time stint at Copeland had netted me $160,000.

In March 1983 the eighteen women who lost their jobs in the Copeland-Crandall shuffle won their case. The NLRB issued eighteen complaints against the company, ruling that the employees had been fired in retaliation for their union activities. The board ordered reinstatement and full back pay for all. Only one of the eighteen fired employees, Winnie Waithman, chose to return to her job. The same month as the board ruling she was hired back as a nurse's aide at Crandall Medical Center. The reason for her return: "They said I'd never be back. I wanted to show them."

But it was already too late for Local 47. By that time the union had given up. As the unfair labor practice hearings had dragged on, the union's chances of winning in a decertification election—which would be reactivated with the resolution of the firings—had grown dimmer and dimmer. Its strongest allies had long since been fired or promoted or had quit, and scores of new, carefully screened employees were now cleaning the sheets and changing the bedpans of Copeland and Crandall residents. Hardly anyone was left who believed in the union, and even the believers' faith had been badly shaken. Local 47 had given nearly three years to the Copeland effort, invested thousands of hours of staff time, and spent tens of thousands of dollars, and still a contract between Local 47 and Claude L. Roe seemed as remote as it had in the autumn of 1980.

Joe Murphy decided to pull the plug. On December 6, 1982, Local 47 filed with the NLRB a brief form called a "disclaimer of interest." With that, the union walked away from Copeland Oaks and cut its losses in Sebring, Ohio.

A decade after the union election, Jim Horton, Art Worthy, and Joe Murphy had all retired from Local 47. Claude Roe, Bill Hogg, and Kathleen Taylor had retired from Copeland Oaks. Judy Stanley was married, had a daughter, and was doing PR for the Copeland admittance office. Jean Householder was working as a factory seamstress at a non-union company. Phil Ganni had died. Winnie Waithman was still a nurse's aide at Crandall Medical Center. She was making $5.97 an hour, and she still had no union.

As for Fred Moracco, his life was ruined. Copeland's anti-union campaign not only cost him his job, pension benefits, health coverage, and life insurance, it had also cost him his future. Fred sued Claude Roe and Copeland Oaks for $2.8 million for firing him without just cause and for defaming his character. As the lawsuit ground through the legal system, Fred underwent major surgery, watched his diabetes intensify—he believes due to the stress—and his eyesight deteriorate. For a while he hunted for employment, but it was hopeless. In interview after interview he was asked to explain what had happened at his last job; over and over he told the story. He never worked again.

Anna got a nursing job at Alliance Hospital and for ten years—until her back gave out—was able to support her ailing husband. At the judge's insistence, Fred's lawsuit was eventually settled out of court, for what Fred calls "a pittance." He cannot elaborate because of a nondisclosure rule in the settlement, but he offers that the dollars have brought little comfort to a sick, half-blind old man.

Gates Mills

I couldn't believe how much money I was making. Copeland Oaks was only the beginning. Suddenly everybody seemed to need a union buster. Business came out of nowhere. I would have established a waiting list if I could have, but in my game nobody ever could wait. So I began working campaigns back to back and sometimes juggled two or three at a time. I rarely went to the NLRB office to pick through petitions. I didn't have to. One job inevitably led to another and then another as corporate attorneys or board members pointed me to companies in their charge that faced the threat of a work force able to think and act in unison. I did the hits, and the money flowed. Ten thousand, fifteen thousand, sometimes twenty thousand dollars in a single month, in checks made out personally to Martin Jay Levitt, in gratitude. There was so much money that it confounded me.

I opened a bank account in my own name—for the first time since leaving the honor farm. Then, as Earl Leiken was trying to dig Copeland out from under the unfair firing charges, Alice and I took off on a whirlwind of buying. For once, and for the only time in our lives, we couldn't seem to spend the money as fast as it came in. We bought and bought and bought and never looked back. We bought brand-new bedroom furniture for the boys, and a $300 pedigreed golden retriever puppy as a playmate for our basset hound, and a state-of-the-art color television set. I bought Alice thousands of dollars' worth of jewelry made of precious stones, which she hardly looked at, imported perfumes that she displayed but rarely used, and a $10,000 full-length black mink coat. The coat she liked—that is, after it had undergone $2,500 worth of style alterations. She thought the coat was quite practical, and she donned it whenever she went out to the driveway to shovel snow. She bought a $1,000 compact disc player, I leased yet another Mercedes-Benz, we ate expensive food, we bought the boys all the latest toys, and still our cup was brimming over. Life was glorious.

Alice was beginning to think maybe it hadn't been such a bad idea to join me in Ohio after all. Her husband was the mighty hunter again, slaughtering enough game each day to feed the entire village. She was proud to be his helpmate and eager to pamper him so that he would be able to go on hunting. It was the way she had always dreamed it would be. The ideal American marriage. Alice cooked me elaborate meals; she joined me in my drinking; she made love to me. Her adulations were intoxicating—and addictive. I felt helpless beside her and grateful for her attentions. Our rekindled romance saturated me in a sweet illusion of well-being and transported me back to our early days in Marin County, to the days before the affairs and the cocaine and the drunkenness and the lies and the honor farm. I swore I would do anything to keep it like this.

Alice had tired of the shiftlessness of our lives, as had I. To my beloved, the remedy was for us to buy a house. "We need a home, a real home," she said one day in a velvety whisper. "It's not good for the kids to keep moving all over the place. We have the money now, thanks to you, Marty. It's silly for us to keep on renting."

I agreed. Renting always irritated me, too; it made me feel so unattached. I was excited by the prospect of buying a house—it would mean security, commitment, permanence. With our own home and a steady income, why, we'd be a regular family again. The only reason I was at all reluctant was that it pained me to think of leaving the grand old colonial-style brick house we had been leasing in University Heights for the past year. I loved that house. It was noble and solid and real, with a great big fenced yard, like the homes I grew up in. It felt protected there, secure, happy. The lease-option on the house listed the asking price as $60,000; I told Alice we should make an offer. But Alice had strong ideas about homes and neighborhoods, and University Heights did not interest her. She knew exactly the kind of house she wanted; she could describe it in detail, although she had seen it only in her dreams. She was sure it was out there somewhere. She had only to find it. She got herself a realtor, and while I was off combating the working class, she was off shopping the greater Cleveland housing market.

Weeks went by, then months, and nothing happened. Alice couldn't find her dream house. She was getting discouraged, and I was getting restless. I tried talking her into University Heights once again, then promoted an English Tudor we had seen in the upper-class suburb of Shaker Heights for $160,000. No, she said. Absolutely not. Alice was determined to find Wonderland, and she wouldn't settle for anything less.

Then, one day, one fateful day, I came home to find her over-wrought with excitement. She greeted me at the door jumping up and down like a high school cheerleader. Her eyes sparkled, her face was flushed. When she spoke, her sentences burst forth in a pulsating stream of breathy exclamations: "Today! I found it! It's fabulous! The most fabulous place I've ever seen! It's just perfect! The gal has to sell right away! The owner. She's getting divorced. It's worth two fifty, but she'll sell it for two twenty-five! You have to go look at it, Marty. You have to see it. Come on, let's call my realtor now! I know you're gonna love it!"

How could I resist?

The drive out to the house in question took us through some of the most spectacular countryside in northern Ohio. Once out of Cleveland, the car wound through wooded hills and past glimmering streams on the half-hour trip east from Cleveland. When the car turned onto the scenic Chagrin River Road, I was stunned. When it passed the sign that noted, discreetly, Village of Gates Mills, I couldn't help chuckling to myself. Gates Mills, me? Who would have ever thought?

Gates Mills was a vintage carriage community built for the richest of the Cleveland rich more than a century earlier. The houses were immense and elegant; many had been designated as historical landmarks and were included on sight-seeing tours of old Cleveland. When I was a kid, Jews and blacks couldn't even drive through the village, it was so exclusive. The racial and ethnic barriers had lifted—in regard to the gawkers, at least—but many of the village traditions still held. The Gates Mills telephone directory read like a *Who's Who* of Ohio blue-bloods. The village still sponsored yearly fox hunts, an annual celebration of old money and Anglo-Saxon aristocracy. What was I doing house hunting in such a place?

Our car came to a stop in front of a house that went by the name of Stony Creek. The postal service knew the property as number 699. Alice sighed expectantly. I looked out the window.

There it was: Alice's dream. Peeking out from amid a forest of leafy oaks and abundant fir trees stood a sprawling, split-level country house. The house was made of wood, painted white with crimson shutters and gray trim. It was actually quite a simple structure, if one ignored its almost ludicrous length, low-brow even, compared with the stately mansions we had passed along the way. The same complaint could not be made, however, about the grounds. The house was set way back from the road, beyond a rolling half acre of pale green short-cropped grass, at the top of a sweeping, circular driveway. The immense lawn, which wrapped around three sides of the house, was larger than most of the parks I had played in as a boy, and more lush. Dark green ivy lolled at the base of the old oaks and climbed up their dark gray trunks. Raspberry bushes and pink-and-white peonies bloomed in the narrow beds that lined the driveway and adorned the base of the house. Fat, sturdy green shrubs stood guard before the long windows. It was an incredible garden and would have been a yard for five families anywhere else in Cleveland. I was ready to turn back just at the thought of mowing that thing. But then I would have missed the secret to Stony Creek. For that impossible front yard could not even hint at the stunning beauty and sheer immensity of the estate that lay beyond the house.

Alice's dream house stood on five acres of virgin woods, surrounded by acres and acres more. The property was a paradise of grand oaks and firs, populated by mischievous squirrels, stealthy raccoons, cryptic owls. The Chagrin River itself tumbled through the property, brimming with crawdads and minnows and frogs. An old barn, half refurbished to include a fireplace, stood back from the house, next to it a large chicken coop filled with a dozen cackling, laying hens. The forest beyond was thick and green, a magical kingdom for innocent young boys, a tranquil refuge for troubled adults.

I hated it. Sure, it would be nice to take a drive to a place like that and spend the day, but live there? What for? I could enjoy looking at it, but I didn't need to buy it. I was a city boy. I didn't want land, just a backyard I could mow in twenty minutes. The Gates Mills property intimidated me, and the house left me cold. The house was a design disaster, for one thing. The layout zigzagged all over the place; rooms seemed to have been added on, one after the other, in no particular order until all the building material was used up. The huge children's bedrooms sat over the garage, up a winding staircase at the extreme back of the house, as far from the main living areas as they could be. That would seem fine for teenagers, but our kids were only seven and four years old, and I imagined we'd want to be in touch with them. The kitchen, which of course would be my workstation, was hideous. Small and narrow and dark, it sat at the far north end of the ground floor, railroad car style. The rest of the rooms, all rather small for such a big house, were strung out from there, connected by narrow halls and skinny doorways. The house needed work, too, a lot of work. The walls were dingy, and in some places the plaster had begun to crumble away. The downstairs was too dark, as if the builders had overlooked a window or two. With my native tendency toward depression, darkness was dangerous; I would need to punch out a wall right away and let some sun in. I was not one to roll up my sleeves and replaster a wall myself, so to me what 699 Chagrin River Road forboded was an endless stream of contractors and invoices.

"We don't need this," I pleaded with Alice after our tour. "We have enough money to get a house that's all ready to go. We don't have to buy a fixer-upper."

Alice retorted that since we had the money, we could afford to redo the house the way we liked. She had a point.

When we got home Alice was incorrigibly excited about Gates Mills and determined that we should have it. I whined about the layout, the land, the community, but my objections just seemed to strengthen Alice's resolve. Oddly, I couldn't come up with a cogent argument—I, who could argue anything to anybody if it suited my purpose. I had a bad feeling about that house, but I could never put the feeling into words.

Alice's realtor kept calling and calling; Alice kept asking and asking for my blessing. Finally, in an attempt to put an end to the whole Gates Mills fantasy, I agreed to make an offer. I had a plan: I would make my offer a low one, not so low as to be insulting, yet low enough to guarantee that it would not be accepted. The owner would reject it, I would have made my concession to Alice's dream, and we could move on to find ourselves a suitable home. In less than a week Alice and I were scheduled to leave on a Caribbean cruise. I sure didn't want to be thinking about down payments and escrow accounts on the beaches of St. Thomas. I wanted this thing over with now. I offered $190,000.

The seller's rejection came back in two days. Whew! For a brief moment I thought I could wash my hands of Gates Mills. Not a chance, sucker. Alice was wise to my game, and she wasn't about to let me off so easily. Neither was the seller. Rather than just flat out reject my offer, the owner had dropped her price to $220,000. Alice was ecstatic; I was depressed. All I was doing was trying to get out from under Gates Mills without upsetting Alice, and every move I made seemed to sink me deeper and deeper into the pit.

Alice wouldn't let up. It was three days to cruise time, so I worked the peace-of-mind angle hard: "Alice, honey, this cruise was supposed to be a chance for you and me to get away, forget our troubles. I don't want to go with real estate hanging over my head. There'll be plenty of houses to look at when we get back."

Alice pouted. I was being a stick-in-the-mud. I was being selfish. This was something she really wanted. Unlike the jewelry and the fur coats and all the other expensive gifts that *I* had chosen to shower upon *her* when it suited *me*, this house was something *she* wanted for *herself*. Why couldn't I let her have the one thing she really wanted? Once again, she had a point.

"All right," I said. "I'll make one last offer. But if it's not resolved before we leave on our cruise, we say good-bye to River Road forever. We don't take it up again when we get back. Deal?"

"Deal!" Alice said firmly.

I gave the realtor our final offer, good until July 15, the day before the *Song of Norway* was due to set sail: $209,000, and one year to make the $42,000 down payment that the owner demanded.

For the next three days Alice and I coexisted in virtual silence: hers the silence of anticipation, mine the silence of dread. On Friday we took the boys and dogs over to my parents' house and said good-bye, then went out to dinner. We returned home to finish packing for the trip. By late evening Alice's mood had grown dark and mine perceptibly lighter. Needing to make some noise to express my feeling of relief, but not daring to mention the house, I laughed aloud at the television sitcom we were watching and made idle chatter about our upcoming excursion. I felt utter joy.

Then, at about ten o'clock, the phone rang. It was the realtor. "Great news," announced the perky voice on the other end of the line. "The seller accepted your offer."

My heart sank. This couldn't be. "It's too late," I tried weakly to argue, looking across the room at my wife's face, which was aglow with hope. In desperation I persisted in my stern demeanor, hoping my sharpness would burst the miserable bubble of euphoria that seemed suddenly to have enveloped my living room. "We're leaving at seven in the morning," I snapped. "There's no time to do the paperwork. I'm sorry."

"I'll be right over," was the chipper response.

So there we sat at nearly midnight, Alice giddy as a teenager and I glum as the father of a teenage bride, signing the papers that would drop us in Gates Mills and commence the unraveling of our lives.

We moved into 699 Chagrin River Road before our Caribbean tans had faded. I had just finished squelching an organizing drive at Cyberex Inc., the company that introduced me to Earl Leiken. The chief executive at Cyberex had wanted to keep me on board to do postelection union-evasion work and had agreed to pay me a $15,000 retainer. The retainer went directly into Gates Mills, as the first installment of the down payment.

The boys headed for the backyard forest the moment we arrived at the estate and were instantly ecstatic. The two roamed the Chagrin River acreage for hours and hours during those long August days, wading in the river—a slender creek during the dry summer months—climbing trees, and staging battles with the neighborhood boys they met on their forays. I had never seen my boys happier, more alive, and the sight of the two of them racing through the trees and creek and up the hills assuaged, at least a bit, my abiding disgust for the house I had just bought.

I also had never seen Alice so alive; Gates Mills seemed to fill her with vigor and pride. She was a fine lady now, she had a fine house, and she intended to lead a very fine life. From the moment we got our new address, she talked about the house incessantly. She had decorating schemes for every room, landscaping plans for the grounds. She began haunting Gates Mills yard sales and dragging home antique treasures, from brocade stuffed armchairs to porcelain knickknacks. She bought a $5,000 John Deere tractor mower for cutting the lawns and had a great time riding around on it. She took long walks through the community and met the neighbors—and loved them all. She talked to other Gates Mills mothers and investigated the schools—and was thrilled. The public schools in Gates Mills were better by far—that is, more exclusive—than any of the expensive private schools Alice had looked at in Cleveland and California. To Alice, Gates Mills was lover, friend, and child. She cherished the house, cared for it, dressed it up, made plans for it, boasted about it, dreamed of it. As the house became her world, Alice remade herself in the image of the upper-class WASP housewife and emptied her imagination, energy, and bank account into that coveted new role. She had reached Wonderland at last.

As for me, I was surprised to find that I disliked the Gates Mills house even more after we moved in than I had on that first tour. I hadn't thought that would be possible. Usually it works the other way; as they get to know their new houses, home buyers often discover their hidden charms. But I just kept uncovering absurdities. To me, number 699 was an intolerable house until almost $20,000 of work had been done, and then it was only barely livable. First off, I had to have an intercom system installed throughout the entire house just so that family members could communicate with one another. Without the intercom Alice and I had to go on search missions whenever we needed to find the boys, and I kept missing phone calls because I didn't hear the ring and whoever answered couldn't find me. It did no good in that house to yell; the curves and corners created natural sound barriers. And looking for someone was just impossible, the layout was so baffling. During our early weeks at Gates Mills, in fact, four-year-old Justin got lost several times on his way down to dinner from his remote bedroom. To the intercom system I added a telephone network. I saw no reason to run around the house in pursuit of a telephone. The telephone was my main sales tool, and I should have one handy wherever I went. Seven phones were not one too many, I decided.

The communication system made Gates Mills a little more bearable, but I wouldn't stop grumbling until something was done about my kitchen. I wanted that monstrosity gutted and completely rebuilt, and I would have it no other way. Hardly bothering to ask about the cost, I had contractors break out walls, install the latest in built-in appliances, and, finally, cut a large, bright, cheery bay window into the kitchen wall. It was beautiful. At last I could breathe.

To me, the thousands I spent in those first few months were nothing. I could earn that much in a few weeks. I was working more consistently than I ever had before, more consistently, in fact, than I liked. The PATCO bust of the previous year seemed to have unleashed a pent-up demand for anti-union services, and I was *the* hot property in northern Ohio. Every CEO seemed to know another CEO who had used me to "resolve his union problem," and suddenly I found myself getting more jobs than I ever wanted. I would have liked to spend more time just hanging around, but I was charging $1,000 a day by then, and the money was just too fabulous to turn down. So I took every job, ran campaign after campaign after campaign, and brought home thousands and thousands of dollars for Alice. I was more impressed with myself every time a CEO ordered a check cut for me. The amounts were so huge, and the executives didn't even flinch. They just got me the money. I must really be something, I said to myself.

As Alice involved herself more and more in her giant playhouse, I immersed myself more and more in drink. It used to be that when I was busy I drank less. But no more. The thing that kept me busy, my work, only heightened the alcoholic impulse. I was mightier than ever on the job, more frightened than ever on the inside. With the Copeland campaign and my return to front-line union busting, I had begun to think of my work as absurd and vulgar. I tried to suppress such thoughts; the job was so easy for me, and it brought me ever greater riches and accolades. But it was also such a fraud, I knew, without wanting to know. I was like the Wizard of Oz, a powerful, angry sorcerer to those who beheld me, but knowing all along that inside I was just a weak little man. I lived in fear that at any moment someone might happen along and pull aside the curtain, exposing my fragility and my shame. I was a fraud, my work was a fraud; when would we be discovered? I turned to drink to quiet the cacophony of my internal discord. I didn't want the vulnerable little man in me seeping out and messing things up—as he had after my brother, Harvey, killed himself; as he had when Alice was having her affairs. The drink seemed to help; for quite some time I managed to keep the wizard in charge and the humbug hidden from view.

When I was on a job the drinking was easy to accomplish. I drank with clients at lunch or dinner—they usually preferred martinis—and always managed to find a congenial bar near the company, thus making sure I would never be too far from a bottle. But I also organized my home life to facilitate my drinking. We had lived in Gates Mills only a few months when I had our fancy wet bar in the family room stocked with the best labels of every kind of liquor: tequila, gin, rum, and plenty of my favorites, vodka and Scotch. I poured myself a drink as soon as I got up when I was home and as soon as I got home when I was working. I began with the concoctions I liked most and moved down the line until I was greedily chugging stuff I actually detested. To pass the empty afternoons and evenings, I found a few watering holes around Gates Mills village that I liked. My favorite spot was Tony Roma's Rib House; the bartenders were friendly, and the atmosphere was cozy. I could spend long hours on a bar stool at Tony Roma's, feeling quite at home and getting quite drunk.

By the time we were a rich Gates Mills couple, Alice had learned to drink at my pace. She had pretty much abandoned marijuana and cocaine, having found it so much more convenient simply to join me in my vice. We drank together all day long when we were both home; but each of us also drank on our own. Alice befriended the gay couple who lived in the white-columned mansion across the road. Before long she was scurrying across the street as soon as Jason and Justin were at school, mixing up breakfast screwdrivers with Daniel and Geoff and gabbing with them as if they were a trio of old ladies. Daniel was a high-priced interior decorator who boasted of having decorated Liberace's Las Vegas home. That detail made me laugh, but it only intensified Alice's affection for him. Soon the screwdriver chats began to revolve around fabrics and finishes; before long Alice had handed Daniel carte blanche to rejuvenate and restyle number 699.

Alice brought her fondness for vodka and orange juice home with her. As she cooked or folded laundry or chatted on the phone, she habitually poured herself tall tumblers of the sunny beverage and often left a half-finished drink tucked away in a bathroom cabinet or a kitchen cupboard, to be retrieved later. I was even more cunning. I started keeping a bottle of vodka out in the barn for the inevitable days when Alice would object that my drinking was getting out of hand and insist that I stop. On those days I would leave the house with the pretext of settling my head or getting some air, fish my precious bottle out of its secret spot, and carry it with me on a long evening walk about the Stony Creek grounds. Sometimes, after I was good and drunk, I would mount the John Deere tractor and ride round and round in circles for hours.

Poison

In November 1982, after eight months of solid work, I hit a brief lull. I wouldn't have minded taking some time to loll around Gates Mills, sit by the fire, gaze out the window at the snow, listen to some music, maybe, and just wait for work. But only four months into our new home, Alice and I had done some pretty wild spending, and I could not afford to slow down. It amazed me even then that we could manage to spend every nickel I made no matter how many millions of nickels there were. I needed to keep the cash flowing, so I took a drive to downtown Cleveland and dropped in at Region 8 of the NLRB.

Two days later I was on my way to Earl Leiken's office for a meeting with him and the ownership and management of a manufacturing company called Plastic Molders Supply. Under the corporate name of PMS Consolidated, Inc., the New Jersey–based company made freeze-dried color pellets under contract to plastics manufacturers, from half a dozen factories across the United States. The client companies used the paint concentrates to put color into everything plastic from shampoo bottles to toys to auto parts. The color maker's Ohio district consisted of the original and flagship factory, which was located in the industrial town of Norwalk, fifty-five miles west of Cleveland. There, Plastic Molders Supply was known simply as PMS.

PMS was no union-busting virgin. A year before my meeting with the management, the United Auto Workers local from Toledo had tried to organize the plant's one hundred equipment operators, lab technicians, and production clericals. PMS had responded to the organizing attempt with a nasty anti-union campaign designed and directed by the ubiquitous Jack Hickey, the Columbus-based nemesis of SEIU Local 47. In the course of his PMS campaign, Hickey had pulled lots of tricks, and the UAW had filed unfair labor practice charges with the NLRB Region 8, accusing the company of threatening to close the plant. The UAW also had accused PMS management with allowing eight employees who were not part of the designated voting unit to cast ballots, and they moved to have the votes disqualified. The eight workers in question were administrative secretaries, women who worked closely with management in a sparkling office area separate from the plant floor and rarely saw the gritty production workers who sought to organize. The secretaries, it was supposed, identified more with their bosses than with their blue-collar co-workers, and they were very likely to vote against the union. The UAW challenged their votes and filed "blocking charges" with the NLRB, which sealed the disputed ballots until the issue was resolved.

Ultimately the NLRB ruled that the secretaries' votes were, in fact, legitimate. The UAW withdrew its blocking charges and promptly lost the election—by seven votes. Management hardly got to gloat over its victory, however. Although it found in the company's favor on the ballot issue, the labor board ruled against PMS on five of the union's unfair labor practice charges. The board ruled that management's lawbreaking had tainted the election and invalidated the vote. The NLRB ordered a new election and set the date for December 17, 1982.

I won the Plastic Molders job away from Hickey and Associates in what Earl Leiken later called a "minor miracle" of salesmanship. PMS bosses had liked Hickey fine during the first union drive—his style hadn't bothered *them* a bit—and they were planning to seek him out again for the new election. I talked them out of it.

Pointing out that the first election had been uncomfortably close, I warned that the employees would remember Hickey's tricks well and would be more resistant to bullying this time around. More of the same, and the company would be buying itself a union. PMS needed a new approach, I argued, and management needed a new image. Rather than beating up on the employees, the bosses had to make it look as though they had changed their ways. To win votes they needed to show that they were truly listening to worker complaints and trying to respond.

"I'll work magic with your foremen," I told my incredulous audience. "You'll see. They may just be dirt-dumb factory workers now, but I'll turn them into ambassadors for the company. You'll be amazed at what they'll be able to do in just a few weeks. They'll win this thing for you."

The PMS contingent looked doubtful; when I met their foremen I understood why. But at that first meeting I assumed their skepticism was made of nothing more than usual management resistance to anything that sounded soft.

"Look," I said, "do it Jack Hickey's way and you'll just make the union madder. He's an outlaw, and the union knows it. They'll come after you again and again and again, and they won't leave you alone until they win. On the other hand, I always work with the finest attorneys, like Mr. Leiken here. I know how to win a campaign lawfully. Go with me, and PMS will never face a union drive again."

The man in charge of PMS Norwalk was a rigid and impenetrable district manager named E. Timm Scott. Scott didn't go for the nice-guy approach. It wasn't his style. Scott—Timm to his intimates—showed no compassion for the men and women who labored at the noisy and grimy paint-processing machines, so far removed from his humongous office suite, with its fancy furniture and its escape door to the parking lot where he kept his Cadillac Fleetwood. I figured I knew Scott's type. I had met his kind many times before—in other factories, at nursing homes, in coal mines. They were bosses who didn't know their workers and didn't particularly care to know them. To such men the production crew was part of the machinery; the stupid bastards should just do their jobs and keep their mouths shut. They should be grateful for a paycheck.

But the decision to hire me was not up to Timm. That privilege belonged to the owners of PMS, a family of New Jersey blue-bloods named Bradbury. William Bradbury, Sr., had started his company in the Norwalk plant in the 1940s. The company started out as a machine shop but had been transformed into a color manufacturer when the market savants were predicting that someday everything would be made of plastic. In 1982 Bradbury had nine color-pellet factories from coast to coast. By the time I met him, however, the old man had relegated the day-to-day operation of the plants to hand-picked managers like E. Timm Scott and the corporate details to his preppy son, Bill Jr.

The Bradburys happened to have a trip to Ohio scheduled at the time the second organizing drive was getting under way, and the distinguished family attended the meeting with Earl and me. They liked what I had to say. The older man still liked to think of his employees as family—children, really—even though he rarely saw them, and he seemed genuinely concerned about their well-being. But he could not bear to think of a union intruding on the family business. The younger Bill wasn't interested in the part about management listening and responding and changing. But when I said he would never have to face another union drive, his cherubic face brightened. Bill Jr., blond and dapper, seemed to have contempt for his factory workers and a distaste for his father's business. He preferred to spend as little time as possible down in the plants—he'd rather be playing polo—but with this union thing going on, he seemed to be in Norwalk all too often. The place was taking over his life. Bill Jr. wanted nothing more than to kiss PMS Norwalk good-bye, and I seemed to be his ticket to the farewell. When our discussion turned to details like fees and expenses, I knew I had won the Bradbury blessing.

I lounged with a glass of vodka in my Gates Mills family room on the eve of my first day at PMS Norwalk (I had switched from Scotch to vodka on the improbable theory that clear alcohols produced milder hangovers), puzzling over how I was going to build my fantasyland of cooperation to a bunch of workers who had just watched their bosses lie and cheat their way to victory.

My approach would have to be different this time, I decided, a little more sly than usual, a little splashier maybe, too. The workers would have heard all the usual union-bashing stuff before; they'd probably just laugh at it this time. They would have been saturated with threats and bribes, and they would understand all too well what their bosses were up to. I was going to have to grab their attention, and I would have to grab it fast. The PMS campaign was going to be a quick one, I knew. The NLRB already had determined the voting unit as a result of the union's 1981 vote challenges, so there wasn't much room left for maneuvering a delay. The election date was set. Earl would try to buy me some time, of course, but he wouldn't have much to work with in a rematch that had been ordered by the board. It was going to be a blitzkrieg.

My visit to PMS dashed any hopes for an easy win. The place was begging for a union. As I took my first walk through the bright, airy PMS offices on my way to Timm's office, I judged the company to be a pretty nice place. The office area was clean, cheery, spacious. Light poured in from the ample windows, green houseplants flourished in the little painted pots that adorned secretaries' desks. Telephones jingled, and women chatted freely. The mood was relaxed. Even Timm, when he greeted me, was unexpectedly friendly. There was nothing to prepare me for the dungeon of a factory plant that lay on the other side of the soundproof wall at the far east end of the offices.

After a congenial planning session, Timm offered to take me on a tour of the plant. I agreed enthusiastically. As a man who had never gotten his hands dirty on a job and never intended to, I always enjoyed a voyeuristic peek into industry. In two decades of union busting I had vicariously experienced just about every possible way to earn a wage in the United States. I was always particularly fascinated by manufacturing; the process of taking some mysterious material and making a recognizable product out of it seemed like magic to me. Deep inside I admired the workers who made it all happen. I was looking forward to my tour of Plastic Molders Supply and hoping to learn a great deal about plastics and color.

Timm led me from his suite back through the outer offices to a heavy door. When I stepped through that door into the factory, I had to keep my mouth from dropping open. I felt like a person who one day discovers that the friendly couple next door has been torturing their children for years. I was both astonished and appalled; I had been in factories before, but only once had I seen a plant dirtier than this. The office door opened onto a large storage area stacked high with pallets full of bags and cans and bottles of God knew what. Beyond the warehouse lay a large room that was dark and noisy, separated by dividers and some walls into four departments. In some areas the air and floor were thick with colored dust, greens and browns and blues. Men and women labored over the large machines, lifting and pouring bags of colored powder, scraping multicolored globs out of equipment, adjusting levers and plates. Some of the workers wore coveralls over their street clothes and respirators over their mouths and noses; many did not. A few were covered from head to foot in a soot of many hues.

Near the center of the plant was a laboratory, closed off from the dusty factory floor by a set of heavy double doors. There, technicians in white coats studied samples of colored plastic material that had been sent by client companies and, with the help of computer analysis, set about to duplicate the hue and determine its chemical formula. Once the formula had been identified and tested, the chemical recipe was sent to the dry materials processing area, where the manufacture of color concentrates began.

The dry color department was the dirtiest and noisiest part of the plant and the department in which all new factory hands were supposed to start. There, workers measured large amounts of various colored chemical powders according to the formula and placed them in bags. The bags were then sent next door to the batch-making room, where workers mixed up specified quantities of the powders in giant steel Hobart mixers to create the desired hue. The batch makers then emptied the colorful powdered concoction into bags once again and cleaned out their mixers with dry cloths or paintbrushes in preparation for the next batch. The mixed color batches were sent to equipment at the far east end of the plant to be freeze-dried and, from there, to processing machines on a mezzanine level where the flakes were compressed into concentrate. Finally, the concentrated color was put through a pellet-making machine called an extruder and the pellets packaged for shipment to the client. The process was repeated over and over again all day and all night.

PMS materials-processing workers earned a starting wage of about $4.50 an hour. They breathed air thick with poison—lead- and cadmium-tainted paint dust—and prayed to someday make it into the less oppressive areas of the plant. In 1980 federal health and safety inspectors had levied a $1,800 fine on PMS for the high levels of lead in the air of the dry processing room, batch room, and freeze-dry area, for insufficient monitoring of the toxins, and for the inadequate protection of workers. A year later the same Occupational Safety and Health Administration had fined PMS again, $680 this time, for similar violations. OSHA inspectors had visited PMS again six months before my tour of the plant and had found $1,000 worth of health violations relating to lead contamination. Things apparently had not improved much.

At the time of my visit, every processor seemed to dream of being an extruder operator. The operators worked in cleaner, quieter areas of the factory; they earned a little more money and handled a little less poison than the dry materials processors. Except for the days when they had to open up the machinery and scrub the chemical colors off gears and out of corners, the operators could leave the factory looking as clean as they had at the top of the shift. Yet the job of extruder operator was not without its health risks. Machine cleaning exposed the operators to high levels of lead, for one thing. And there were other hazards. In 1983 OSHA would be called in after workers in the extruder area complained of chest pains and nausea. The inspectors would find that workers using a dangerous chemical called Tinuvin were not wearing respirators and goggles even though the label on the container called for those precautions.

My introduction to chemical processing had left me dumbfounded. The plant seemed so menacing; the work shocked me. I'm not sure why PMS got to me more than any of the other horrid little places where I had fought against the employees. Maybe it was the obscene contrast between the PMS factory and my Gates Mills estate, which was growing more luxurious by the day. Maybe my increasingly heavy drinking made me more vulnerable emotionally to the sufferings of the PMS crew. Or maybe it worked the other way around: maybe I started drinking more and more during the PMS campaign partly to dull the pangs of guilt about the people I had been hired to beat. I don't know. What I do know is that I found myself feeling sorry for the PMS workers. Every time I saw someone from the factory floor—which I made sure was rarely—I felt vaguely sick inside. I had to fight the impulse to tell Timm that it looked to me like the place could use a good union. Yet I never considered throwing the PMS fight; my ego and my lust for money would not allow that. Instead I used my misgivings the way I always used the law, to help me devise a cunning anti-union game plan. It looked as if I were going to have to be especially clever in this one. It seemed to be just a matter of time before the union would be successful.

My meeting with PMS foremen didn't assuage my anxieties. Collectively they were about the most motley bunch I had ever met. There were only a handful of supervisors at PMS: Timm, the plant manager, a few department heads and administrators, and the six plant foremen. As usual, I was counting on the foremen to carry my words of faith, hope, and love to the angry working masses. But when the foremen dragged themselves into the tiny PMS conference room and plunked themselves down before me, I knew they would be of no use. The men were tired and dirty. They looked beaten. Their eyes said, "No more," and I was inclined to take heed. These men, I remembered, had just been put through an exhausting campaign. Under orders, they had carried the letters, they had pressured their crews, they had talked of layoffs and plant closures and strikes and dues, they had lambasted the UAW. They themselves had probably parried more threats from the bosses than their workers. They had won, at long last. Then, suddenly, they had lost. Now, here they were again, starting all over, just as they had begun to patch things up with their workers. Now who the hell was *I*? What did *I* want?

I put on my usual kick-off show but did not get the usual response. Even my most engaging sequences were met with tired moans. It wasn't that the foremen particularly supported their workers' organizing efforts; the union business bugged the hell out of some of them. But so did the bosses, and so did I. These guys didn't want to listen to me any more than they would want to listen to a shop steward. They had been at PMS a long time, and they had been working hard. These were no prima donna supervisors pacing up and down behind the assembly line buffing their nails. These were workers. Their fingernails and hair were dirtied with multihued chemical soot just like those of their crews. They worked long hard days—or nights—just like the processors and operators and batch makers they directed. And they didn't get paid a hell of a lot more than their crew, either. Management never included the foremen in any decisions, never sought their opinions on processes or policies that affected the plant, never bothered to train them to supervise, never invited them into the offices. The only thing they got by way of special treatment was special pressure—to keep productivity high in their departments. Now here I was telling them, "You're the backbone of management," and they weren't buying it.

The way PMS line workers saw it, their management was blind, deaf, and dumb: blind to workers' problems, deaf to their ideas, and just plain dumb. But the foremen had many of the same complaints as their subordinates. Line workers and foremen alike complained that the only policy at PMS was the lack of policy. Pay raises, promotions, and perks were handed out with unapologetic arbitrariness, to friends, allies, sycophants. A pay raise system, instituted by Scott two years before and touted as an innovation of progressive management, had only intensified workers' anger. Under Scott's "merit raise" system, pay raises would be used as rewards for good work rather than applied automatically and equally to the lazy and the industrious as in the past. After the first round of raises, however, it became clear to the men and women on the floor that the "merit raise" had nothing at all to do with merit and was anything but innovative. It was, quite plainly, favoritism institutionalized, an excuse to hand out favors to toadies and punish the truculent. The PMS merit system rewarded but two things: workhorse productivity and the willingness to obey. It did not recognize creativity or intelligence or leadership or integrity. A bigmouth who was also a bright and conscientious worker was a bigmouth first, and he would be penalized for it. As one longtime PMS employee said, years later, "All it [the merit system] amounted to was, whoever was the biggest suck-ass got the biggest raise."

A similar nonpolicy held for job assignments, promotions, and even layoffs. PMS foremen ran their departments with the bluster and capriciousness they saw in their own bosses. Since they seemed to have such little import in the big PMS sea, the foremen wielded what power they could in their own small ponds. Wherever their decisions were not automatically preempted by upper management, the beleaguered foremen were tyrants. *They* decided how things would be done in their departments, and for once they didn't have to listen to anybody. *They* passed out the favors, and they withheld them; *they* said who should get a raise, who should be promoted; *they* decided how to handle tardiness, absence, sloppy work among their crew; *they* said "yes" or "no" as it suited their fancy. These were tyrannized men, and their flurries of supervisory bravado were all they had to keep them proud.

The most powerful weapon in the PMS arsenal of arbitrariness was the company's policy regarding layoffs. PMS was essentially a supplier to manufacturers, and the company's economic health therefore was tied to that of its clients. When client industries fell into an economic downturn and cut production, then orders for supplies dropped off, and PMS had to cut production as well. That usually meant putting workers on temporary layoff. Well, at PMS the feisty employees seemed to be the first to go and the last to be called back. Some workers found that they were never called back from a layoff, even though shorter-term employees had returned to their jobs in weeks. There was no such thing as seniority rights. If the out-of-work employee objected, PMS management referred to its ancient company "rulebook," which stated that any employee could be terminated after being on layoff for sixty days. After sixty days the former employee could be hired back, but only at an entry-level assignment and pay rate. Quite a clever policy. With such a "rule" at their service, PMS managers could get rid of anyone for any reason without worrying about justice or ethics or any other such nonsense.

Against that backdrop my kick-off performance droned on and on. I could see that my message was not finding fertile soil in the minds and hearts of my fatigued listeners. Some of the foremen had just put in eight hours on the floor and badly needed a shower; others were just beginning their day; one weary fellow had to come in during his time off. They were not a happy group. I was coming to the end of the first act, running out of material, and clearly getting nowhere. I could see I would find no spirited crusader, no anti-union evangelical, no smooth-talking seductor in this bunch. If the foremen were to follow my plan at all, they would do so halfheartedly, and then only if they could be sure there was something in it for them. What, for God's sake? Clearly there had been nothing with Jack Hickey.

Still puzzling over what to do with my pitiful cadre of foremen, I launched my usual saturation letter campaign. In honor of the latter-day travails of the United Auto Workers Union, I laid heavy emphasis on the 22 percent unemployment rate among union members, and I harped mercilessly on the UAW's historic wage concessions to Chrysler Corporation in 1979, concessions that, I did not bother to note, had been established by President Jimmy Carter as a condition of the federal bailout of the automaker.

"The UAW wrote the book on concession bargaining," I quipped during my early meetings with foremen. That at least got them to look up. The automotive industry was at its nadir in the early 1980s, and layoffs by the Big Three automakers and their suppliers had devastated the UAW. Automakers, having for more than a decade refused to respond to rising energy costs and the resulting changes in consumers' taste in cars, had found themselves trounced by foreign competitors, especially the Japanese. American auto plants were closing; management was exacting huge pay cuts from workers; strikes were dragging on and on; and auto companies were using the economic avalanche to weasel out of the handsome labor contracts they'd once bragged about. Emboldened by the PATCO firings, management was going about replacing striking autoworkers with impunity and refusing to hire them back. All of this should have filled the captains of U.S. industry with shame, of course. I used it, however, to fill the laborers of industry with dread. The crisis of the UAW was of much less relevance to PMS Norwalk than I made it seem. Although PMS Norwalk at the time did sell its colorant product to automakers, the factory was by no means dependent on the auto industry. Among the plant's largest customers were manufacturers of household products, companies that would not be affected in the slightest by the declining sales of American cars. Nonetheless, my rantings about auto plants and strikes and layoffs guaranteed that the PMS shop floor would sizzle with debates over the effectiveness of the UAW.

Current events seemed to be mounting in my favor, and an anti-union drive in that environment should have been a cinch. Not at PMS, though. Mistrust of management ran so strong at PMS that my anti-union letters and meetings were to become mere background music to the real show. The headline performance at PMS was going to be a magic act—the remake of management. Timm Scott seemed to have contempt for his foremen and no interest at all in the people who answered to those losers. All the workers thought they knew Scott. Well, I would have to change what they knew, and fast. With just eight weeks from petition to election, the management makeover had to begin right away; and I had precious little to work with.

My opening number was as simple as it was bold: I had someone fired. Timm Scott liked to dump the blame for all the factory problems on the plant manager, Richard Woolsey. The way Scott told it, the plant manager was supposed to resolve all problems on the factory floor. If morale was low, Woolsey was to pick it up. If productivity was down, Woolsey was to raise it. If processes didn't seem to be going smoothly, Woolsey was to work the kinks out of the system. If employees were complaining about a supervisor, Woolsey was to intervene. Woolsey dealt with grim-faced OSHA inspectors and unhappy foremen and angry line workers. Then he answered to Timm Scott. In reality, Scott had never given Woolsey the authority to make the kinds of changes the workers were asking for. Woolsey couldn't grant raises or improve medical insurance or rewrite the layoff policy or design a seniority system or fire a bad supervisor. Scott had no intention of discussing business issues with his employees, either in person or by proxy through Woolsey. But that was just reality, and reality didn't matter to me. I was concerned only with perception. All I was looking for were a few cosmetic changes that would enhance the image of management and buy me the election. Woolsey was the management person most visible to the rank and file. He would be the perfect sacrificial lamb.

"Get rid of him," I told Timm plainly. He didn't flinch. "You need to show the employees you're listening to them. To do that in as little time as we have, you're going to have to do something big. You ax the old plant manager, say he wasn't taking care of business, wasn't responding to the workers. We'll play the plant manager as the symbol of the old bad ways that are now going to change. Then you bring in a white knight. A fresh face from the outside, a golden boy with a big smile who will talk to the people and make them feel good. It'll give them hope. They'll see you're serious about making changes, and they won't feel as strongly about the need for a union." The game of musical plant managers was not original to me; lots of union busters did the same thing. But PMS workers had never seen the ploy before, and that was all that mattered.

Timm wasted no time. A few weeks into the second PMS antiunion campaign, Richard Woolsey was gone. In his place, Timm installed an unknown East Coast Italian named George Mitro. On the outside, George was a hail-fellow-well-met. He grinned all the time. He patted guys on the back. He looked the workers in the eye, and he listened to their stories. He did his job well; for that was just what George was told to do. His assignment was bridge building. George was to be the new face of management to the people, and it was to be a kinder, gentler face, to borrow a cynical phrase from a future U.S. president.

The George Mitro I saw behind closed doors was everything he was not out on the shop floor. He was crude and intransigent, an unrefined version of E. Timm Scott himself. In describing the pro-union workers, George made liberal use of the word *asshole;* the workers in general he referred to as "morons." George seemed to really enjoy his dual role of savior and head basher. After a while, his failure to lead would earn him the contempt of his subordinates. But for the first couple of months, at least, I saw that George managed to smile more than he sneered, and his presence gave PMS the illusion of change.

While George was out warming up the shop floor, I went to work on the supervisors. I had little hope of reaching the production workers through their foremen; my chances of manipulating lab workers and secretaries was much better, however. I knew that technicians and secretaries tended to distinguish themselves from factory workers, and I used those distinctions to drive a wedge into the PMS work force. Being skilled workers, lab technicians like to consider themselves professionals; secretaries and clericals think of themselves as part of administration. Both groups often feel more closely aligned with management than with the rank-and-file production laborers. At PMS I capitalized on those divisions and amplified them, presenting the interests of the factory crew as competitive with those of the lab and office employees.

It so happens that the union did not wholly disagree with this assertion. During its 1981 effort, the UAW had tried to remove the twenty-some color technicians, quality-control workers, and front office clericals from the PMS union-voting unit, arguing that those workers did not share the legally required "community of interest" with the production crew and therefore should not be in the same bargaining unit. Such positions are always legal gray areas in regard to bargaining units and are usually fought over. PMS management, knowing that the two departments were likely to vote against organization, had fought just as hard to keep them in. Ultimately the NLRB had sided with management.

I was sure to hammer hard on the idea that the union did not want to represent the lab and office workers at PMS. Through the supervisors I spread the argument that the UAW was an oldtime industrial union—not a professional association—and that it had no interest in technical and clerical employees. Reminding lab and office supervisors that, should the union win, their employees would belong to a unit that was 80 percent factory workers, I warned that the union might trade away the interests of the minority in order to please the majority. The truth is, in most cases workers have more in common with one another than they do with management. Despite vastly different job descriptions, the fundamental interests of employees are strikingly similar. They all worry about pay and medical insurance; they all wish for fairness, consistency, equity, autonomy, a process for redress of grievances, employment security, health, and safety. The white- and pink-collar workers at PMS were subject to the same arbitrary approach to pay and promotions as the factory crew, and their jobs were no more secure. Many of them did not see it that way, however. As long as management's arbitrariness tended to work in their favor, the lab and office workers could be counted on to oppose the collective action of their brothers and sisters on the factory floor.

"The UAW is stuck with your people whether it likes it or not," I told the white-collar supervisors. "I'm sure your people don't want to be stuck with the UAW."

I was right. The office and lab departments remained convinced that they were part of the PMS inner circle, intimate members of the family, and overwhelmingly opposed the organizing effort.

To reinforce the concept of company as family, I dragged in old Bill Bradbury one week, having convinced him to take a rare tour through the factory. His visit was meant as a sign to all employees that the founder and owner of their company still cared deeply for them. To be certain, the senior Bradbury once took a personal interest in the well-being of his workers; when he started his company he had established a generous profit-sharing plan that promised to take good care of the older factory workers in their retirement. However, the elder Bradbury had long since stopped feeling the bond with employees he'd felt when he'd run the shop with his heart and his own two hands; Junior surely did not embrace his father's paternalism. I wanted workers to think otherwise. I wanted them to believe that old man Bradbury still thought of them as family, still cared about them as people, still would take care of them the best he could. The company needed a human face; Bradbury's was best. His face was soft and elderly and honest and intelligent and kind. The workers may have mistrusted E. Timm Scott, but they would never doubt old Mr. Bradbury. As Bradbury paraded through his flagship factory one December afternoon, he stopped to talk to old-timers who long ago called him "boss," openly admired the energy of the younger workers, and thanked them all for their loyalty and dedication. He reassured the supervisors who weren't buying into my program; he got Scott off the hook by blaming the latter-day troubles on the fired plant manager; he promised the workers they would get the health and safety improvements they wanted—once the election was over. Those who met the company's founder that day would not soon forget him.

With the lab and office workers I had ten, maybe fifteen sure votes. I was counting on another thirty or so production workers who seemed to lean strongly against organization and probably voted against the UAW the first time around. George Mitro was doing all he could to tip the scales by keeping things friendly, upbeat, and decidedly "pro-company" on the shop floor. I could see the white knight was having an effect. But it wasn't going to be enough. The UAW campaign was being run by a stocky, gray-haired man named Hugh Smith. Smith, a former auto worker and a fifteen-year veteran of organizing, had just come through the Hickey war, and he knew how to fight. Hugh ran a steady-paced but very understated campaign. He called plenty of union meetings and kept his plant organizers busy answering workers' questions and leading discussions and rebutting management's anti-union charges. But he didn't sling mud, and he didn't bury the workers in handbills, and he didn't make outrageous promises, and he didn't play tit for tat. Hugh's was a quiet campaign, and quiet campaigns always made me nervous. I liked to turn the union's silence against it when I could, wondering aloud what the phantom organizers were up to and suggesting that we weren't hearing from them because they had nothing to say, nothing to offer. But inside I was always a little worried—worried that the organizers weren't making a lot of noise because they didn't have to, because their campaign was going very well, because they knew exactly where they wanted to go and exactly how to get there.

To trip them up, I introduced the anti-union circus. In the final three weeks of the PMS campaign I unleashed the biggest pro-company party the company had ever known. It was nonstop fun and games, anti-union good times sponsored by a chastened and caring management who had but one simple request: Vote No. I wanted the PMS anti-union campaign to look like good clean fun, a challenge to the good sportsmanship of union supporters. Even as I bombarded the workers with reports of strikes and plant clo-sures and layoffs and pay cuts, I wanted to keep their spirits high. It was quite a trick, and I pulled it off. I did it with fun. I did it with buttons and hats and posters and stickers, with contests and displays and lots of laughs. The jocularity brought to the PMS plant was designed to make the union look foolish, unimaginative, dreary even, in comparison with the spirited pro-management forces. From the midpoint of the campaign on, the factory workers saw only the lighter side of their bosses' anti-union drive. Every move I made, hour by hour, day by day, was calculated to create a mood of festivity within the PMS plant that would render the union complaints ridiculous. Union organizers would frown at the fun and games, I knew, for they were dead serious about their issues and their efforts. But I hoped their sour faces would only make them look like whiners, like bad sports, and would lead the fence sitters to conclude that they really did not need the gloomy old union after all.

With three weeks to go, I let the fun begin. It came in many forms. One afternoon, for example, I sent secretaries to the local supermarket with the cash equivalent of one year's union dues, at the time about $200. The secretaries were told to buy as much as they could of common family grocery products: cereals, breads, macaroni, apples, canned peaches, cookies, popcorn, and the like. The shoppers were to avoid expensive items like meat, since I wanted a great big pile of purchases. When the secretaries returned with the goods, I had them stack the cans and bags and boxes high in three grocery carts and put them on display on the factory floor. There the goods sat, for several days, under a big sign that read "Here's what you could buy with just one year of union dues." I wanted every worker on every shift to see the exhibit; foremen were to make sure they did. In fact, the display attracted a great deal of attention. Workers could see, touch, smell what their wages could buy today; they did not know what benefits they might receive through their union dues. People started talking. Before the novelty of the grocery display could wear off, I had the shopping carts removed from the floor. The magnanimous E. Timm Scott let it be known that he had donated the baskets full of goods to a local charity.

The grocery display brought workers' families into the heart of the anti-union campaign, and it seemed to have an effect. I decided to keep it up. A week or so later I had PMS management sponsor a "Vote No" anti-union poster contest for the children of supervisors and foremen. Cash prizes and ribbons were offered to all entrants, with a big $100 award for the winner. Well, I had kids; I knew it would not be difficult to coax them into drawing a big picture to win a prize. On contest day a dozen proud parents showed up to work with their children's anti-union artwork. The posters were laid out in the office area and judged by executive secretaries. The secretaries decorated all the drawings with prize ribbons and marched into the plant, where they hung them on the factory walls. Most of the drawings were simple and very childlike, although the content clearly had been directed by a zealous adult. The winning poster, however, was a masterpiece of propaganda art. Created by an eleventh-grade art student, the drawing was a bleak rendering done in shades of gray. The scene was dominated by a locked chain-link gate topped with barbed wire. A "Closed" sign hung from the links. On the ground in front of the gate lay a pile of trampled picket signs bearing the words *On Strike*. Weeds grew up around the faded placards. A decrepit gray factory stood beyond the gate, smokeless, abandoned. The youngster's painting gave a grim and haunting image of union failure. It was a portrait of hopelessness and futility. It was perfect.

The drawing was, however, legally problematic. By displaying the drawing, PMS management could be accused of threatening plant closure during an organizing campaign, as Jack Hickey so boldly had done. I did not want to repeat the Hickey mistake, yet I desperately wanted to let that poster make its statement. The kid's drawing gave me a way to threaten the employees' livelihood without uttering a word. I did not want to pass up the chance.

I called Earl Leiken. After hearing my description of the poster on the phone, Earl said I had better not put it on display. The company would be risking an unfair labor practice charge, he said; he had to recommend against using it. Well, that wasn't what I wanted to hear.

"Is it *defensible*?" I asked. That's all I wanted to know.

Earl said yes, it was. The questionable poster went up that day, along with the rest of them, and hung on the factory wall for a week.

Ten days before the election I launched the "Vote No" saturation carnival. I had "Vote No" hats, buttons, and T-shirts printed up. Supervisors and foremen were ordered to wear their "Vote No" vestments every day and to give away T-shirts and trinkets to any workers who asked for them. Almost everyone ended up wearing something; whether it was out of conviction or fear didn't matter. What mattered was that the "Vote No" message was everywhere. It hung on the walls, it danced atop people's heads, it rode upon their chests. A jolly atmosphere reigned on the PMS shop floor during the last week and a half. It seemed impossible that anyone would feel free to talk against management in that chummy environment. It seemed impossible that union proponents would have any momentum or any support or any hope left.

Yet when I checked with foremen and supervisors, I found that the vote count hadn't changed much. Some people had moved to management's side, but not many. There were still plenty of unknowns and plenty of stalwart union supporters. From what my informants told me, the only thing that seemed to be swaying people against organization this late in the battle was the latter-day impression that management had lightened up. Suddenly things were a lot nicer around PMS, and that niceness had eroded support for organization. Some workers thought that maybe they had already won. Management had learned its lesson. Now the bosses knew that workers were serious about getting themselves a union; they would be more careful about how they treated the employees. They would never let things get this bad again, no sir.

One big black hole remained in the theory of management's rebirth, however: E. Timm Scott. Although workers seemed to believe that the lower-level supervisors were willing to change a bit, they were not at all sure about E. Timm. He was just the same as he had been before. Maybe the guys a few rungs down were thinking things over, but if E. Timm stayed the same, PMS would stay the same. There would be no more justice on the job after this union thing was over than there was when it started a year and a half before. E. Timm was the boss.

I sat in my little office tapping my pencil, flipping through PMS campaign letters, and thinking about Scott. There were three days left to go, and he was still a big problem.

E. Timm Scott. E. T. Scott. I noticed that was how he signed all my "Dear Fellow Employee" letters. "E. T. Scott." E.T. Huh! I chuckled to myself. Suddenly my client's name struck me as funny. "E.T." How about that? Just like the wrinkled little other-earthly protagonist of the Steven Spielberg blockbuster movie. *E.T., the Extraterrestrial* had just been released in Norwalk the summer before, and the tender little alien being had quickly become the passion of all children and romantics. E.T. the movie hero was innocent and sincere and loving and loyal—and playful. There couldn't have been a character more unlike the E.T. that I represented. Nor, I mused, could there have been a character more true to the image I would have hoped to create for my despotic client. Then it came to me. With the help of the lovable E.T. I could recreate the image of E. Timm Scott in an afternoon.

"What? Are you kidding? Not a chance!" That was how E. Timm Scott reacted when I presented him with the big rubber E.T. mask and the long rubber forefinger with the light-up tip. I wanted E.T. the boss to dress up like E.T. the little alien, go out on the plant floor, and give his employees one good laugh. I wanted him to show the workers that he didn't take himself as seriously as they all knew he did. I wanted Scott to parade around the factory the way Mr. Bradbury had, selling the happy new face of PMS to all the employees who still had their doubts.

Scott was dumbfounded. He couldn't believe what I was asking him to do. "That would be so undignified," he objected sternly. "How are the workers ever going to respect me if I walk around in a silly costume looking like an idiot? I won't do it."

I had only one answer, the same I had given Ed Daly eight years before when I'd asked him to apologize to the employees at World Airways: "Timm, I don't think we can win this thing if you *don't* do it. The vote count's at fifty-fifty now, and there's no time left. If you can't convince those assholes out there that you're one hell of a nice guy, you'll find yourself sitting across the bargaining table from Hugh Smith. You've got to do it, or get ready to shake hands with the UAW."

And that, of course, was that. Scott agreed.

The next day E. Timm Scott swallowed his pride, donned his mask, light-up finger, and Vote No T-shirt, picked up a large placard that read "E.T. SAYS PLEASE VOTE NO," and climbed into a shopping cart. The plant manager, George Mitro, grabbed hold of the cart, strapped on a grin, and pushed his way onto the plant floor.

The whole place busted out laughing. Workers stopped what they were doing to take in the unlikely scene; Scott indulged them by waving and touching an occasional arm with his costume finger. Every time it lit up another burst of laughter rose from the floor.

If the whole caper had ended there, it might have gone down as just another clever idea. But the E.T. ploy mushroomed quite spontaneously into a brilliant piece of PR. As E. T. Scott made his way through the factory, one supervisor, whose young child was particularly fond of E.T., asked Scott if he could call his wife and tell her to bring his son down to the plant to meet his extraterrestrial hero. His kid would be heartbroken if he found out E.T. had been at Daddy's work and Daddy hadn't bothered to tell him. Scott, who was beginning to enjoy the celebrity, said fine.

The idea caught on. Pretty soon everybody with a child was phoning home. I jumped on my stroke of good luck as soon as I found out and had Scott's secretary call the local newspaper. The *Norwalk Reflector* always liked a good photo opportunity, and the paper had a photographer at PMS within the hour. E.T. spent the afternoon touching the noses of awestruck four-year-olds with his magical finger and spreading a final, friendly anti-union message throughout the plant.

A six-by-nine-inch photo of Scott as E.T., seated in the shopping cart pointing at his "Vote No" sign, made the front page of the next day's paper. The lengthy caption that accompanied the photo was headlined "Anti-union E.T." In a last-ditch bit of disinformation, we lied to the paper about the level of union support at PMS. Our lie was printed. One day before the election, workers and the entire community of Norwalk read: " . . . management sources claim only about 20 percent of workers want to unionize."

With a little effort, I convinced Scott to dress up as E.T. one last time. The following day was voting day, and I wanted workers to get one last look at their amiable, fun-loving prankster of a boss in his hilarious getup before they walked into the voting booth. But I had another, more personal motive for insisting on an E.T. replay. I got positively gleeful at the thought of seeing the look on Hugh Smith's face when he stood face to face with the living trivialization of his organizing drive. Scott indulged my fantasy, dressing up as E.T. for the obligatory preelection conference, during which both sides meet with the NLRB agent fifteen minutes before the polls open to go over the rules.

As the moment of confrontation drew near, I stood outside the conference room door waiting for the show. I was not disappointed. When the UAW organizer entered the room and laid eyes on his mocking antagonist, he lost his usually unshakable composure. Doubtless Smith had seen the newspaper the morning before and had come to the conference already seething. But when he saw the E.T. getup, his anger bubbled to the surface. Smith's face reddened, and his jowls shook. His eyes widened. He could barely speak. He gestured erratically, as if he were fighting an invisible assailant. He looked small and impotent and pathetic next to the six-foot-six-inch figure who had just made a big fat joke out of his union.

The workers' second organizing effort ended in defeat. On December 17, 1982, fifty-eight employees at PMS Norwalk voted against the UAW, while forty-seven voted in favor. I had won it by eleven votes, just a pinch more than Jack Hickey's margin a year earlier. I hadn't even managed to capture all the lab techs and clericals, the natural allies of management.

E. T. Scott won, but his victory was hardly decisive. Nearly half his work force was clearly unhappy, and that was not about to change unless he did. He would not. A year later PMS workers would pass out union cards again and in three days would gather enough signatures to file a third petition. In early 1984 I would be back in Norwalk, this time with help from an old employer, Modern Management.

Descent

I was relieved to leave PMS behind me. I had hated the hour-and-a-half drive from Gates Mills to Norwalk; I had detested the plant; I had found the PMS employees unpleasant; and I hadn't even liked E. Timm Scott. In fact, the only thing I really did like about my two months on the PMS trail was a little *hofbräu*-style bar I had discovered just a few minutes' drive from the factory. During my weeks in Norwalk the *hofbräu* became my church and my family; I stopped in almost every afternoon before heading home, to purge my conscience and alter my consciousness with a lot of drink and a little conversation. There were, at my beloved *hofbräu*, two women bartenders so charming and glib that in their company I could easily forget the perverse details of my days. I flirted with the two of them with gusto, in that wonderful, open way that is possible only when everybody involved knows there is not a chance that anything will actually come to pass. The hours spent with my two gals were invigorating and titillating. The young women made me feel charming and attractive and interesting—and important. In their presence I was a big shot, a rich daddy with money and wit always at the ready. After six or seven vodkas and a hundred minutes of delightful banter with the *hofbräu fräuleins*, I found myself ready to make the transition from factory bully to Gates Mills aristocrat.

As I drove back home to the estate, I never knew what expensive surprises awaited me. One day it was a pair of taciturn contractors steam-gluing fancy fabric to my dining room walls. Another day the common living room curtains had been traded in for those elegant draperies that seem to use at least ten times as much fabric as necessary, most of it hidden in gathers and folds.

Every week I seemed to bump into an antique chair or table or credenza or china cabinet or telephone stand that I had never seen before. Large oil paintings in gilded frames appeared on the walls; rooms changed color; the ordinary carpeting that once covered the floors was ripped out and replaced by thick, plush, top-of-the-line wool carpets; new china and silver filled the dining room cupboards; imported Oriental area rugs and hand-painted vases made their expensive little statements in alcoves and hallways. Alice never showed me a receipt for her extravagant buys; indeed, she seemed never to know how much things cost. She just gave Daniel and Geoff the money, and they did the buying for her. Alice did all her buying through Daniel, who had convinced her that he could save her money through his decorator's discount. I never knew if that discount was authentic, but I doubted it, for I never saw an invoice or purchase order or price list for anything. All we had was his word. And all I knew was that the purchases went on and on. The money came and went, came and went.

Although my memory emphasizes the spending excesses of my wife during our Gates Mills era, I have to admit to giving Alice energetic competition. I had no interest in the decoration of the house, but, boy, did I like toys. Toys for me and toys for Jason and Justin. I filled the house with six television sets, including a state-of-the-art big-screen TV in the family room and a little color set in each boy's bedroom. There was also a TV in the kitchen, one in the master bedroom, one in the den, and one out on the patio. By the early 1980s it was accepted dogma within the upper-middle class that every family needed a computer. Well, I wanted my family to have the best, so I bought Jason and Justin the latest model of Apple computer that was used in schools at the time. Such a purchase may not seem extravagant in itself, but I was sure to make it so. Not wanting my precious sons to have to *take turns* on the computer, I bought each his own, just as I had with televisions and phones: two boys, two computers, two printers, and a load of software so the princes would have everything they needed in their separate kingdoms. And little Justin was only five years old. I also bought my sons another of the consumer "musts" of the early 1980s, those dangerously popular motorized three-wheeled dirt bikes called "all terrain vehicles." The kids loved their ATVs, rode them all around the estate and through the surrounding woods. The bikes were great toys. That wasn't good enough for me, though. After the boys had learned to ride competently, I traded in their small models for a bigger version. They had to have the best. At the same time I bought an even larger dirt bike for Alice, one of the few gifts from me she really liked. I never gave up buying her jewelry and other unwanted finery; no matter how many times such gifts were rebuffed, I just kept on buying. I wouldn't hear her, couldn't believe her, when she told me over and over again that she didn't want the stuff.

The toys I bought were not always for the rest of the family, however much I wanted to believe that at the time. The Gates Mills years were a time of conspicuous accumulation, and I brought home lots of expensive novelties just for myself. Our cars, of course, were always the best, the most expensive models of Mercedes-Benzes and BMWs. But there was more. A glimmering $6,000 antique Wurlitzer jukebox stood boastfully in our family room, alongside two antique slot machines. I used the slot machines, which cost $2,000 each, as a sort of icebreaker for our very occasional visitors. I kept an ashtray full of nickels and quarters next to the machines and invited guests to try their luck as soon as they had entered the house. As it happened, however, Alice and my friends were so few that my vintage one-armed bandits got the most action from cocky elementary school kids, the buddies of Jason and Justin.

By early 1983 I was making $15,000 a month and living check to check—literally. I was richer than most people ever dreamed of becoming, and still I had no money. Every job I took meant $50,000, $80,000, sometimes $100,000 at a pop, but by the time I got the check to the bank I was just as broke as when I started. I was a high-priced whore and a junkie, turning tricks and spending the money on my gilded dope. Then I had to turn another trick so I could get another fix. And another and another, on and on. I couldn't stop.

I was at the apex of my career; I was on top. I was making more money than I ever had, more than I ever would again. But as I climbed to the peak of financial success, I was sinking fast into moral decrepitude. My barroom drinking was actually among my most civilized behavior. At a bar, the fear of making a complete ass of myself in public usually kept my drinking under control, so at least I was able to remain conscious, and often I could be quite charming. At home, however, the disease took over. I drank a fifth of Absolut vodka a day, filling a juice glass with my personal poison first thing in the morning and tossing away an empty bottle by evening. Sometimes I didn't even make it to the trash cans, having passed out on the family room sofa or on my bed before dinner. The following morning I was always sick, wretchedly, pathetically, disgustingly sick. I shook, I heaved, I sweated, and I cursed. My head throbbed and my stomach convulsed. Often I was still half-drunk in the morning, woozy and thick-tongued and barely able to walk. I stunk of stale booze, and my mood was as foul as my stench. After a blackout I remembered little of the night before. Often Alice wouldn't speak to me in the morning, and sometimes I could vaguely recall a noisy fight or an unpleasant phone call. But what had I said? What had I done? I had no idea. Jason and Justin just sat at the breakfast table and stared at the frightening stranger who was their father.

Every time it happened, I desperately wanted it to be the last. I felt humiliated before my family. I hated myself, and I hated John Barleycorn. But I knew there was only one thing that would make me feel better—so I reached for the vodka and filled a juice glass.

Alice had begun to intuit that there must be some connection between my drinking and my job. She thought there must be something terribly wrong with what I did for a living if it drove me to drink the way I did. Maybe it was the stress, she told me, the pressure of the elections, the constant unknowns. But she suspected it might be something worse. Many evenings I came home from a job and immediately subjected her to a brag session about my day. I delighted in how I had gotten rid of some son of a bitch or how I had planted a really nasty rumor about some poor slob. Alice would wince.

"Marty, how can you do that?" she would ask, quite moved.

Even though she had been right in the midst of things at Copeland Oaks, she had never understood what her clever husband was doing. Now I was telling her, and it made her uncomfortable. Many times she used my confessions of malfeasance as evidence that I should give up labor relations. "Marty, I don't think this work is right for you," she would say. Then the suggestions would come: "You don't have to do this anymore, you know. You're such a good salesman. Why, you could sell anything, luxury cars, real estate . . . You know, real estate is really hot right now. If you sold two good houses a year, you'd make as much money as you do now. You could do it, Marty, I know you could. You'd be the best."

But Alice never could outargue me, and once I objected, she couldn't persist. After all, she too was trapped, addicted. To reject the way I made money would mean to give up Gates Mills, the acreage, the dream house, the life of luxury she had embraced. So, after a while, she stopped complaining. She buried herself in the house and numbed herself with vodka and orange. I dumped my money into thousand-dollar trinkets and blinded myself with straight vodka. Alice and I had lost our souls, sold them, really. We weren't going to get them back for free.

By the dawn of 1983, I weighed two hundred pounds, about forty pounds more than I should and twenty-five more than the day I was married, all because of alcohol. I hated the way I looked, and I hated the way I felt. Yet when spring rolled around I was still drinking. Summer came, and I was drunk every day. I was also working almost every day, which really was much more than I could handle in my degenerated condition. Not that anyone noticed. Union busting was the perfect gig for an alcoholic. For years I had occasionally gone to jobs with a hangover. In the beginning I had thought it was sort of funny. In fact, one of the reasons I had established the custom of never signing out from a company when I left was so that I would be able to take care of myself following a night of alcoholic excess. I could easily disappear for an early lunch, report to a nearby saloon for some "hair of the dog," and not go back that day. By mid-1983, however, I had hangovers almost every morning; I was leaving jobs more often and earlier. If my clients had been less willing to hand over their businesses to me, I might not have gotten away with it. But their greed was such that they would overlook anything as long as I did the job. You don't get into discussions with hit men about their methods, and my clients rarely asked questions, even about my disappearances. I kept on winning, so really, nothing else mattered.

It mattered, however, to Alice. And it mattered to me. Although I could hide from the truth all day long, the morning after I always knew it. I was sick. I had enjoyed occasional periods of sobriety in the past, and I decided I wanted to feel that way again. It was early summer, and my sons were home all day: they were watching as I drank; they were listening as I growled at Alice; they were there when I passed out. I knew I had to stop.

I called an alcohol treatment center called Glenbeigh Hospital in rural eastern Ohio and scheduled myself into another twenty-eight-day program, my fourth. I had long known it was time for me to try again to get sober, but I had a ready-made excuse for not doing it—my work. I was self-employed, a soloist. There was no one to take over for me in my absence, no one who would keep his foot in the door for me. Leaving town meant leaving business behind, which meant leaving money behind, and the money was way too good for me to consider that. I had no colleagues, only competitors, and the competitors were hungry. How could I walk away? That conundrum kept me immobile for many, many months, but once I decided definitively to check into Glenbeigh, I hit on a plan. It was high time, I decided, to rekindle my association with Tom Crosbie and the boys at Three M. We hadn't parted on such terrible terms as with Sheridan, and as successful as I had become on my own, I missed the camaraderie of the early 1970s. I picked up the phone and dialed Chicago.

Tom Crosbie sounded genuinely happy to hear from me. "Hey, Marty, we hear you've been doing great," he said with an unusual tone of enthusiasm. "They've been keeping you busy, huh?"

Well, life wasn't bad, I had to admit, and I indulged myself in a little braggadocio about the Copeland Oaks bust and my Gates Mills estate and other such trophies. "But it's almost too good," I admitted, getting around to my point in calling. "I'm getting so much work now, I can't handle it alone. I was thinking it might be beneficial to both of us if we worked together." Then I leveled with him: "Look, Tom, I'm going into the hospital in a few days, and I just landed a counterorganizing job at a limousine company in Cleveland. If you'd like the work, you can have it. Just pay me 20 percent of whatever fee you charge."

Tom had to decline, since he was going out of town on another campaign, but he didn't let me go. He said he was sure one of the associates would be glad to take on my limousine company for me. We made the deal.

I called Three M back as soon as I was released from Glenbeigh. It was August 1983. I had been sober for a month and thought for a moment that I would be sober forever. I felt healthy, energetic, fierce, and totally unrepentant. With head flushed clean and my body well rested, all I wanted was to get back out there and make some serious money. My treatment had saved my liver and my kidneys, perhaps, but it had not altered my heart or my mind. I had not embraced the lessons of humility or remorse, and until I did, my search for recovery would be futile. I arrived home with my vanity as bloated as ever and phoned Crosbie to see how things had gone with the limousine company.

Crosbie was glad to hear from me. He told me he had handed over the job to an associate named Kevin Smyth, and that Smyth had won handily. Crosbie and I both alluded to the lucrative potential inherent in a long-term relationship between our two companies, and with that in mind, my old friend talked me into paying a visit to Modern Management.

I was excited; as much as I loved the independence of solo work, I yearned for the good old days of barroom banter and bravado with the boys. Possibly I had hit on the perfect combination. In association with Three M, I could have the best of both worlds. Besides, I had never seen Three M's latest digs, but I had heard they were fabulous. The next day, filled with anticipation, I took a first-class flight to O'Hare Airport. I drank on the plane.

Since the company's golden years in the mid-1970s, Three M had run its anti-union operation from a glistening new office tower in the Chicago suburb of Bannockburn, a half-hour drive from the airport. I knew to expect only the most ostentatious from Three M, but even I was dumbfounded by the immensity and elegance of its offices. Modern Management occupied almost an entire floor of the building. The floor was set up like that of a major law firm, with an expansive conference room in the center and the associates' offices around the perimeter. The last I had heard, Three M had nearly one hundred consultants. I didn't wonder why the place looked so deserted on the day of my visit; if the company was doing well, the associates *shouldn't* be there, they should all be out working. I assumed they were.

Herb Melnick did happen to be in the office that day, and he greeted me warmly. By then Herb had told his partners and associates that he soon would be getting out of the consulting business. He was too old for the day-to-day work, he said, too tired. Herb said he had lost interest in counterorganizing campaigns; he planned to start a company that would produce management training films. Naturally his new firm would not compete with Three M.

Crosbie, Melnick, and I sat down to discuss the business of joining forces. In a matter of minutes we laid out the terms of the arrangement: For every job I brought to Three M, whether I worked the campaign or not, I would be paid 20 percent of the billings. The 20 percent would apply only to the daily pay rate, not to the consultants' expenses, but it would include any post-election work at the company, since it was understood that without my brokerage Three M never would have been invited in.

Tom and Herb were very agreeable throughout our meeting. They nodded and seconded everything I said. I was tickled. It was the fastest, easiest deal I had ever made. There was no haggling, no tussling, no wounded egos. Everything was very friendly. My vanity being what it was, I understood Tom and Herb's acquiescence as a demonstration of their high regard for me. Gee, they must really like me, I concluded; they must be thrilled to have me back.

Well, they were thrilled all right, but not for the reasons I supposed. What I did not know then was that Three M was in retrenchment. I learned from Crosbie later that over the previous few years Three M had shrunk by nine-tenths. Only ten consultants remained at Three M—not the hundred that I had presumed—and even the few remaining couldn't find enough work to keep busy. Most of the company's former associates had abandoned ship in the early 1980s and gone into direct competition with their mother firm, their signed noncompete pledges notwithstanding. Only weeks after my tour of the Bannockburn suites, Herb himself would leave, but not to start a film company. He would open HGM Enterprises in Chicago, a full-service labor relations, union-busting firm.

When I met with Crosbie and Melnick one hot August day in Chicago, I already had found the Cravat Coal petition and had made my first phone call to Mike Puskarich. I told Crosbie I was hoping we could start our joint venture right away; I suspected I would really need help out at the coal mines. I estimated how many consultants I would need out at the mining company, and Crosbie pretended to ruminate over whom to send. I was grateful that there were some experienced consultants readily available for what I anticipated would be a difficult campaign. I could not know, of course, that when Crosbie showed up in Cadiz, Ohio, with Kevin Smyth, Dennis Fisher, and Ed Juodenas, he had half the firm at his side. It turns out I had called Three M just in time. Had I not started funneling jobs to my old employer just when I did, Modern Management might have gone out of business. Instead the firm was revived, and, although weaker, it endured, even into the 1990s.

*   *   *

An optimist I cannot claim to be, certainly not with respect to the human character. Yet I have seen that the most horrible calamity can sometimes bring on a rebirth. My reacquaintance with Modern Management was just such a calamity, and it bore the seeds of my awakening and repentance. Only through my reaffiliation with Three M did I begin to see myself as I really was. Tragically, my epiphany was to be prolonged and laborious, for my resolve was weak, my powers of denial quite strong. Over the next four years hundreds upon hundreds of men and women—and their children— would suffer because of my weakness, for it would take that long before I would gain the courage to reject the money and power and glory that were mine. But eventually it would come to pass.

My trip through hell began the day I resumed work in the company of Modern Management. For four long, torturous years, beginning at Cravat Coal, I was forced to look at myself through the mirror of my companions. For a time I did not see my true reflection; I refused to acknowledge that I was one of them. When Ed Juodenas papered the wall of the Cravat interview room with oversize charts that reduced all employees to arithmetic symbols, I was impressed. But I was also uneasy. His treatment seemed so cold, so crude. It was different from what I did on my legal pads, I told myself. Sure, I designated employees' loyalties with pluses and minuses, too, but I did so very much more. What about all those notes I took, all the anecdotal information I gathered on the workers? Why, I really knew those people, didn't I? They weren't just a bunch of marks on a paper, a "yes" vote or a "no" vote. They were stories, personalities, puzzles of anxieties and tribulations. Wasn't my way more human? I kept telling myself it was. Because my words were more stylish, my act more entertaining, I was able to distinguish myself intellectually from my collaborators. I clung to the desperate conviction that the silly diversions I added to my campaigns somehow absolved what I was doing, made me different, morally superior. I called myself an artiste, convinced myself that I was a superior breed of animal. As time went on, however, I found it harder and harder to substantiate any differences between me and my co-conspirators. The distinctions blurred, and the only thing that remained clear was the common truth—we were all animals indeed. I began to understand that what Crosbie and the others were showing me was my own soul stripped bare.

*   *   *

Shortly after New Year 1984, the paralegal student I had hired to do my runs to the NLRB—and whom I paid an incredible dollar a day for her trouble—phoned me with the list of newly filed petitions. Among the companies was one called Plastic Molders Supply, PMS; the union, the UAW. I was stunned, not that the workers were going for it again—that was inevitable—but that E. Timm Scott hadn't called me as soon as it happened. I wondered why, and I put in a call to him.

Scott was embarrassed, and rightfully so. I had warned him when I left in 1982 that he was going to have to make certain changes if he hoped to discourage another organizing effort. Now, just over a year later, he had to admit that he had ignored my recommendations. He hadn't believed the workers had it in them to go through it all again. Clearly he had been wrong. But Scott had a concern other than personal embarrassment in hesitating to call me as he faced his third straight counterorganizing effort—money. Earl Leiken and I had cost him more than $60,000, and he didn't want to spend that much again. Scott was tempted to look for someone cheaper, yet as determined as he was not to accept union representation for his employees, he preferred to go with a sure thing, and that was me. So he made me a proposal: I could have the job if I were willing to put a cap on my price. Well, I was hardly thrilled about the prospect of meeting the tattered PMS crew again, and a price cap made the job even less appealing. Yet I didn't want to let go of the work altogether. Money was money. I decided I would try to hand off the job to Three M. Under our agreement I would collect 20 percent of the PMS billings without doing the work, so really there was no reason for me to go to the trouble. Without mentioning my plan, I set up a meeting with Scott for the next day.

By the time I shook hands with Scott I had my lines memorized. I told my old E.T., "I want to do the job for you, Timm, but I have so much work right now it's going to be hard for me to find the time. Besides, I think your supervisors need to see a fresh face. I so saturated them last time around, if I walk in there alone again, they're going to take one look at me and moan, 'Oh no, here we go again.' The campaign will be a lot more effective if there's a new personality involved." I told Scott about my relationship with Modern Management—he thought he had heard of the outfit— and proposed bringing in a Three M consultant to work the campaign with me.

Scott protested. He didn't want someone else; he wanted *me*. But, gently, I sold him on the idea. I assured Scott that I knew just the right person, a consultant as experienced and professional as myself who would do a great job for PMS. I told him he was going to love this guy. Besides, I lied, the second man would only be my backup, nothing more; I would still be in charge. Scott consented.

As soon as the meeting ended, I ducked into my old office and phoned Crosbie. I needed somebody to help me—fast. I told Crosbie the fancy footwork I had done with Scott and said I needed somebody who could meet me out at PMS the next day. By then Three M was down to about six people, four associates having left the company following the Cravat Coal campaign. I didn't know any of them. I was counting on Crosbie to dig someone up.

Crosbie said he thought he had just the man, an associate with the unusual name of Bristol Maginnes. I found out later that Bristol had a substantial background, having formerly worked as the personnel director at Duke University. But that's not the résumé Crosbie felt compelled to offer. The detail everybody found most interesting and most marketable about Bristol Maginnes was the fact that his sister Nancy was married to Henry Kissinger. Before I had a chance to ask a question about my future partner, Crosbie crowed, "He's Henry Kissinger's brother-in-law." If that was enough for him, it was enough for me. I said fine, send him.

A short while later I got a call from a thick-voiced man with a folksy southern accent. It was Bristol. He would meet me at the PMS-Norwalk plant the next morning. We swapped descriptions of ourselves so that we could pretend to be old pals when he appeared in the PMS offices, then I skipped over to Scott's office to report the good news that my colleague and dear friend Bristol Maginnes would be able to back me up in the campaign. I was surprised to find myself adding, "He's got a famous brother-in-law, you know. Does the name Henry Kissinger mean anything to you?"

Bristol was a big, round, bald-headed good ol' boy, slow and easygoing. He loved to travel, he loved to sit and chew the fat, and he loved to drink. As it turned out, Bristol's down-home charm was perfect for PMS and very appealing to Scott. Scott was happy with my second man and in fact ended up liking him better than he had me. With Scott's enthusiastic blessing, Bristol took the lead in the four-month campaign almost immediately, which left me free to come and go as I pleased. I stopped by PMS once a week in between other campaigns to help with interviews or write a letter or put some hot idea into play, but mainly to go drinking with my buddy Bristol.

In Bristol I found a drinking companion like no other. I was amazed by his rate of consumption. Bristol started drinking earlier in the morning than I did, drank more, drank faster, and continued drinking long after I had passed out. The next morning, sick and wretched, he often was at it again. My fortuitous introduction to Bristol through PMS led to a three-year drinking conspiracy between us. Since my union-busting skills were still in great demand at that time, I had my pick of campaigns as well as my pick of Three M assistants, and I made sure to work with Bristol whenever he was available. When I drank with Bristol I felt like an adolescent student trying to keep up with an admired teacher, and I was able to convince myself *I* didn't have much of a problem. Generally I liked to work jobs close to home so that I could enjoy the comforts of family life while I practiced my dark art. But whenever Bristol was to be with me I arranged for us to stay at a hotel. It made drinking so much easier. When I was on a job with him we made a second home for ourselves in the hotel lounge and drank the afternoons away, and the evenings, into the night.

Each time we met in the hotel restaurant the morning after a night of abuse, Bristol and I would stare at each other's gray-green faces and bloodshot eyes as if into a mirror; perhaps we would have laughed, had it not been that the nausea and splitting headaches made us feel like crying. My companion, after wincing and grunting to settle himself onto our restaurant booth, would speedily order his Bloody Mary, sigh in anticipation of the relief, and begin in vain to try to mop the sweat from his naked head. It was the one thing that got me to chuckle through the pain: the sight of Bristol's shiny bald pate spurting beads of sweat like a hundred little geysers and the big man's clumsy attempts to sop up the profusion. Bristol's head-top effervescence led me to dub him "Old Faithful" in honor of the famous, reliable geyser. The image made him smile.

Although it sounded dreadful at the time, I usually ordered eggs on my morning afters, thinking I would be better off if I ate. More than once I was forced by the entry of the eggs into my abused stomach to dash back to my room, where I vomited my breakfast and vowed never, ever, to let myself get that bad again. Then it was off to the anti-union campaign of the day.

Apocalypse

On one particularly horrid midwestern winter day Tom Crosbie and I sat at a small dark table in the lounge of some dreadfully cheery Holiday Inn somewhere in Ohio. We were downing martinis, mine with vodka, his with gin. The two of us had been there a very long while, killing time at some client's expense, when I began to feel vaguely apprehensive; I sensed our conversation was building to something, but I could hardly imagine what.

Tom and I were boasting about our work, as usual, but not in the typical tomcat way. Rather than simply crowing about how we sure had fucked Supervisor So-and-so, we started talking about reason and purpose, the meaning of it all, if you will. Thousands of drunken words were spilled that afternoon, many of which have been washed away, perhaps forever, from my consciousness. Yet the essence of our shameful philosophizing remains clear: that gray afternoon Tom made me recognize that every act we performed every day was motivated by but one base desire—a lust to dominate.

When our conclusion left me uncharacteristically silent, Tom looked me coolly in the eye. I saw him smirk. My face must have revealed the disgust I felt at having heard the raw truth. He chuckled. Why did I seem so vexed? he teased. Who was I kidding? Domination, power, control—wasn't that what both of us had always aspired to in our work?

I returned to Gates Mills on the weekend emotionally tattered. I tried not to think of my conversation with Tom, yet I couldn't stop thinking about it. I reached for the vodka. The more I thought, the more I poured, until finally a thick blackness fell over me and snuffed out all thoughts.

*　　*　　*

It was the autumn of 1985. I felt that I was decomposing from the inside out. On the job I drank to not think about my work. At home I drank to not think about my life. Alice was after me all the time, it seemed, wanting more and more. Every change she made in the house compelled another, more expensive alteration; nothing was ever finished, and nothing was ever good enough. I felt like that poor fairy-tale fisherman, the one who catches a magic fish that offers to grant his wishes. At first the fisherman says he wants for nothing, but his wife has different designs. It turns out she is impossible to satisfy, and she sends her hapless husband back to the sea over and over again to demand of the fish ever greater riches. He is too weak to refuse her. For a while the fish obliges the woman's every wish. In an expressionistic foreboding that is lost on the wretched fisherman, the sky grows darker and the sea stormier each time he returns to shore to call upon the fish. Eventually the couple are punished, he for his impotence and denial, she for her greed. They are left with nothing.

I didn't see it coming, but the time of retribution was upon us. It began the day Alice told me she wanted a Jaguar. The classy British sports cars cost more than $35,000 at the time, and I was disinclined to spend that much on another set of wheels. After all, we already had a Lincoln and a 1957 convertible Mercedes 220S, which we drove each year in the Gates Mills Fourth of July parade. By that time Alice and I were $50,000 in debt to various contractors and furnishing stores for our home improvements. I told my wife we simply did not have the money.

Alice didn't believe it. She was angry and perplexed. The fisherman had always come through before. Sure, he had grumbled and objected, but in the end he had always said yes. Why this sudden attack of circumspection? She wondered: Why would I buy her thousands of dollars of jewelry that she rarely wore, then refuse to buy the one thing she really wanted? Now that we had the money, why wouldn't I make her happy?

I fired back, my aim helped along by vodka. "If it hadn't been for this goddamn house you got us into, maybe we *would* have the money. You spend every morning with those two across the street, drinking yourself silly, then write them out blank checks. How stupid can you be? They have been ripping us off since the day we moved in here, thanks to you. *That's* why we don't have money for your precious Jaguar, Alice. That's why."

Aha! said Alice. So that's it. The fisherman was jealous.

I knew how much Alice loved Jaguars; I believed she was attracted as much by their social statement as by their beauty. There was, however, a reasonable side to her wish. She found our vintage convertible impractical for many domestic errands and totally useless in the winter, during which we kept the automotive showpiece shrouded in canvas and locked in the garage. All right, Alice, I said. You can buy yourself your Jaguar—just as soon as we sell the Mercedes.

I called the dealer who had sold us the Mercedes and asked if he would place it in his indoor showroom. He convinced me to wait until spring; since it was a convertible, I'd get a better price then. Alice said that was fine. She could wait. I thought I had won. The fisherman had said no. But it was too late.

One afternoon, a few days after the silence had set in, Alice called me at a job with some distressing news: Both our cars had been stolen. Naturally we were both very upset. But Alice kept her wits about her. After sharing the obligatory exclamations of anger and bewilderment, my level-headed wife assured me: "The insurance is bound to cover it."

That same day she reported the theft to the Gates Mills police and filed a claim with our insurance company. Alice saved the punch line until I arrived home that evening. That is when my wife told me that she had made a deal with an auto mechanic, one of the drinking buddies she had met through Daniel and Geoff. The plan had been for the mechanic to steal both the Mercedes and the Lincoln. Alice would collect the insurance money and use her little windfall to buy the coveted Jaguar. It was a stupid plan, totally irrational, and obviously concocted under the distorted haze of alcohol. But now it had been done.

My knowledge of Alice's deed threw me into a panic. I drank even more than usual to deaden my nerves. I hardly slept, and what sleep I did manage was tormented by nightmares about the public ridicule I would suffer should my wife's criminal antics ever be made known. Someone—I always suspected someone from Three M—had sent documentation of my Marin County convictions to the AFL-CIO a few years before, and the labor federation had gleefully published the information in its *RUB Sheet*. That nationwide publicity had caused me to be removed from a union-busting job in 1984. I feared it could happen again. I was determined not to lose the business advantage I had built over the past five years and vowed that Alice's deeds should forever remain a secret. So I lived in fear. Whenever I was at home I imagined I heard cops knocking at the door. On a job, I held my breath every time my current client's executive secretary announced a call for me.

The police found the Lincoln two weeks after the theft—in possession of a local professional who apparently moonlighted as an auto thief—then they paid a visit to Gates Mills to talk to Alice. When I came home that night I learned that Alice had broken down in tears under police questioning and confessed the whole scheme.

Both Alice and I were indicted for insurance fraud. The embarrassing details of my wife's insurance scam came out during the ensuing legal tangle. Thanks to the intervention of Earl Leiken, we found a criminal lawyer willing to represent us—for $20,000. During one of our humiliating meetings with the attorney, Alice turned to me in a fit of anger and yelled, "One of the reasons I did it was to punish you!"

Alice pleaded guilty to three felonies. I pleaded guilty to a misdemeanor charge of not reporting the crime. Funny, it had never occurred to me that my wife was an alcoholic or that her drinking could have had anything to do with this regrettable episode of her life. It was sure clear to the judge, however. He sentenced Alice to three years' probation and ordered her to attend weekly Alcoholics Anonymous meetings.

Alice and I escaped to the Caribbean. Drinking and dancing and tanning on the deck of the elegant cruise ship *Vistafjord* for two weeks, we could pretend that the ragged pages of our storybook lives had been pasted back together again. Upon our return to Ohio, however, we were hurled back into the pit. Once in Cleveland, we found that a very cheeky story on Alice's escapade had been published in the *Cleveland Plain Dealer*. The article devastated me even more than I had imagined, for its writer was clearly delighted to have unearthed such a story and had a wonderful time revealing the details of rich people's secret, sordid lives. The article ridiculed Alice—and by extrapolation all the privileged women of Gates Mills—as a grown-up spoiled brat. Worse, for me, was that the writer identified Alice as "Mrs. Martin J. Levitt, the wife of a labor relations consultant from Gates Mills." Early in 1986 a glib report on the car theft scam and a recap of my 1979 crimes appeared in the *RUB Sheet*.

*　　*　　*

Our public shame was perhaps more painful for my wife than for me. Gates Mills was everything to Alice. With an address in Gates Mills she could believe she was somebody, an important somebody, even. Through her house, her property, and her cars, she had fashioned for herself a cloak of prominence and had managed to repress her self-loathing. Following the *Plain Dealer* article, however, she could no longer believe in herself, for the character she had created had been destroyed. She imagined that she was shunned by our Gates Mills neighbors. Our maid quit in a huff of disapproval. Alice was miserable. She rarely left our property for fear of running into someone who would give her a nasty look— or worse, scurry away, refusing to look at her at all. Soon she began to talk of leaving Gates Mills. She could bear to live there no longer.

The emotional havoc wrought by Alice's humiliation impelled me on my own agonizing epiphany; I set out to uncover all instances of treachery in my life. I began by unearthing the offenses of others; I did not know then that my moral pilgrimage would not end until it had led me back to myself. Unhappily, I found enough malfeasance among my associates to postpone my personal judgment day for many months. Among my comrades at Three M I discovered a cornucopia of inequities, the variety and plentitude of which surprised even me. I discovered that my brethren were routinely overcharging clients even more audaciously than was traditional in my business. Not that I was surprised by the routine: for one thing, Tom Crosbie already had told me how he appropriated business from his own firm, taking the most lucrative jobs for himself and working them as an independent consultant rather than through Three M. But this squeezing of *my* clients angered me. Since I had found the clients, I should have been the one to determine just how far bill padding would be allowed to go. Three M's extremes were putting my good name—such as it was—and thus my future in jeopardy.

I scolded Tom for his presumption and carelessness. He didn't flinch. Perhaps, I thought later, he even laughed. Because in reprimanding my old colleague for his shameless thievery, I had revealed my ignorance of his greater crimes. It was not until a few months later that, quite by accident, I discovered his secret: Tom Crosbie was also taking from me. Practically from the beginning of our reaffiliation three years earlier, I learned, Crosbie and his firm had been quietly cheating me out of my percentage. After working a campaign with me, Three M was pretending to take leave of the client company, then returning on its own to do post-election work, letting the client believe that I was party to the arrangement. Only Three M wasn't telling me about the work, and it wasn't paying me my 20 percent. What is amazing is not that it was happening, but that it took me so long to catch on. After all, I had seen members of the union-busters club do that kind of thing to one another time and time again for twenty years. Yet I never imagined it happening to me. I uncovered Three M's game accidentally, when I made a random phone call to a client to see how things had been going in the aftermath of the election. The client, interpreting the question as a checkup on my associates, assured me that Three M was doing a fine job with postelection training. What? I called another client. Yep. Three M had been there, too. And another, and another, and another.

The discovery of Tom Crosbie's betrayal threw me into a rage. I began calling every client I had worked for over the preceding three years, fishing for more evidence not only of Crosbie's treachery toward me, but of any other misdeeds as well. I knew there would be more. Usually I made the calls drunk. Every tidbit I gleaned from the conversations led me to another drink—and to another phone call. I was wounded and angered by what I saw as Tom's betrayal of our friendship. But more than angry I was scared, scared for myself. My discovery of Tom's apparent double cross opened a wound in me into which another revelation began inevitably to seep: I, too, must be a fraud.

With all my power I resisted admitting that possibility. I was very different from Tom, I told myself. He was bad; I was good. I stole from my clients, sure, but that was petty theft. I squeezed my eyes shut, tried to picture myself as the dedicated father, the caring husband. Instead I saw the dumbstruck faces of my young sons, staring at me in silence the way they had so many times as I fell onto the sofa and passed out. I saw the slender form of my wife, curled up in a ball on the bed, trembling. And I heard her sobs. Slowly the images of my two selves, which I had kept so clearly separate for so many years, began to blur. I fought hard to picture myself in an executive suite barking orders to some lowly syco-phant, but another image superimposed itself on the first: that of a fat, middle-aged man puking up eggs in a motel bathroom.

*   *   *

Alice agreed to sell the house. I agreed to go in for alcohol treatment. In May 1987 I packed my bags, took a jet to Minneapolis, and checked into the Hazelden Foundation, one of the premier residential treatment facilities in the nation. Before I left, Alice and I had accepted an offer of $325,000 for the house. I knew our marriage was probably over, and I was sad. But en route to Hazelden I felt secure in the knowledge that at least the family soon would have money again. Soon we would all be out of Gates Mills, and soon I would be sober. Whether together or apart, we would have left the nightmare behind us.

Hazelden didn't have much luck with Elvis Presley. But the treatment program was renowned throughout the world for having liberated many other rich and famous people from the despair of addiction. I had high hopes, and in my eagerness I drank myself into a nice fine drunk on the plane trip north.

A Hazelden alumnus met me at the airport and in a Hazelden van drove me to the three-hundred-acre wooded estate that would be my home and my church for the next twenty-eight days. I was delighted when I saw the grounds, and almost immediately I felt the old, cocky Marty Levitt come to life. Gone were the remorse and the fear that had brought me to this place. Gone were the shame and the regret. I felt safe and happy. I took a look around and said, sighing, "This is going to be okay. It'll be a nice vacation."

I was assigned to a very interesting unit. The thirty-man group, which was to become my family during my treatment, boasted alcoholics from every walk of life, including a television newscaster, a billionaire oil man, an artist, a physician, a gay Catholic priest, a dentist, and an auto worker. For the first week, at least, I felt as if I were at summer camp. I went to the daily lectures, yakked and yakked during group therapy, performed my little chores, but otherwise did as little as I could get away with. I barely skimmed over the daily reading assignments and never thought about them. While others were busy writing volumes on their lives, I grudgingly jotted down a few notes on mine.

During the second week my turn came to tell my story to the group. Every drunk gets his chance, and I was really looking forward to mine. I had been feeling dejected for so long, I relished the chance to mesmerize an audience once again. I couldn't wait.

When the time came, I puffed out my chest and launched into a monologue that dragged my listeners practically back to the cradle, through my teenage exploits to my early ball-busting days with Sheridan to the poor-me episodes of the 1970s and my heartless wife's despicable affairs, to my latter-day triumphs as the biggest, baddest name in labor relations. I subjected my group to the whole union-busting ruse, combining every sales pitch and kick-off meeting I had ever done into one ego-intensive routine. Before I finished I was generous enough to share some of my finest union-busting tricks. Then I sat back, waiting for my audience to express its awe and its gratitude.

For a moment no one said a thing. They're overwhelmed, I thought, poor things. Then it began. It started slowly, one word at a time, then built to a full-blown barrage. They tore me apart. For more than two hours two counselors and twenty-nine fellow drunks stripped my soul naked. They called me pompous and self-important. They accused me of showing off. They called me a bore. They said I was lazy. They called me a liar and a fake. They told me I was cruel and cold and heartless. They rebuked me for blaming everyone else; whatever misery I suffered, it seemed to them, I had brought on myself.

Later that day two men from my unit came up to talk to me. They were factory workers, union men. They looked at me with an expression that was more hurt than angry and said they just wanted to know what made me do it. They had listened to me that morning, and what I had said had sickened them. They wanted to know just how I justified the suffering I had caused all those thousands of people. I couldn't answer. Then the men told me about themselves, about their wives and their children and their hometowns and their troubles and their hopes for the future. They told me how grateful they were for their jobs and wondered if I ever thought about all those people who, because of me, would never have the same chance. Did I know the names of my victims? they wanted to know. Could I see their faces? No, I said. I did not. I could not. I was sorry. It was nothing personal.

I slept fitfully that night. For hours I lay awake, sweating, tossing, turning, moaning. I wanted to see some faces. I couldn't. My semiconscious mind brought me bodies—arms and legs and torsos of people, some dressed in dirty factory clothes, others in starched white uniforms, some in ill-fitted dresses. But no faces. I saw the back of somebody, I wasn't sure who, leaning over a large machine.

I saw two women link arms as they walked down a hallway, away from me. Still no faces.

I buried my head in my pillow and looked deep into my past. From the darkness an image emerged; the blurred outline of a huge, human crowd. The mass moved slowly toward me. I strained through closed eyes to see who my memory had brought forth to ease my torment. A hundred gray men walked together, slowly, coming closer and closer. I began to relax. When they get near enough, I thought, I will see a face I recognize. Then I can make my peace.

I saw the men's heads, their necks, their shirts, their hair, and the place where the faces should have been. But no faces. Not one. Just a fuzzy, fleshy spot. God, no! Please! Just one face. Twenty years. Twenty years' worth of victims, and not one I could remember.

I started to pant. I was panicking. Names. That's it. Calm down. I'll try names instead. But it was no use. I could recall lots of Marys and Joses and Jacks and Anns, but without the family names and the faces, they meant nothing. No faces, no names.

The eighth rite of passage in the Twelve Step recovery program calls for the addict to make a list of all the people he has harmed through his disease. Later he must confess his wrongdoings and attempt to make amends to those who have suffered because of him. But my victims were invisible. They were everyone everywhere, yet I could not see them. I could not name them. Of whom, then, would I ask forgiveness? To whom would I make amends?

The staff at Hazelden was convinced I needed long-term treatment. I agreed. And I was ready. I transferred over to the center's Jellenek facility for hard-core alcoholics and resigned myself to staying there at least six months. At last, at long last, I thought, I would be free.

But as so many times before, my resolve crumbled in the face of conflict. One week into my stay at Jellenek I received a phone call from Alice. She was leaving me, she said—right away. She had called to say good-bye. She was taking the boys and moving back to California. The phone call hit me like a kick in the stomach, and I found myself unprepared for the jolt. I felt suddenly abandoned, alone. The sense of purpose and hope I had gained in Hazelden evaporated. In my desperate insecurity I imagined that Alice would take all the money from the sale of the house and leave me with nothing. I would be alone, jobless, friendless, penniless, with no home and no family.

I threw all my belongings in a suitcase and told the Jellenek counselors I was leaving. They strenuously and very earnestly objected. One of the prerequisites of entry into Jellenek was a promise to remain until the staff decided I was sober enough and strong enough to leave; to breach that promise would mean that I could never again return. Perhaps, then, I would never recover. I could win the battle, my guardians told me, but not yet. It would be a huge and horrible mistake to leave now.

Still, I fled. The next morning I caught the earliest flight back to Cleveland. I got drunk on the plane.

Alice received my sudden reappearance coolly. Not long after my arrival, the sale of our house fell through, and she and the boys ended up staying the summer and fall in Gates Mills as originally planned. It seems I had left Jellenek for nothing. I was as sick as ever, and as miserable.

I rattled around the house for a couple of weeks, drinking, hating myself, and trying to figure out what to do. The July heat was stifling; I was uneasy, irritable. Then, one hot, still morning, an immutable calm came over me. I knew what I had to do. Hazelden had not helped me beat my addiction, perhaps, but it had opened my heart and ignited my conscience. I would see to it that my stay there ended in victory after all.

Back at Gates Mills, I dialed the telephone company and told the operator to disconnect my business number. Then I took a drive to the post office and canceled the post office box assigned to Marty Levitt and Human Resources Institute. When I returned home I placed a call to the AFL-CIO office in Washington, D.C., and spoke to the editor of the *RUB Sheet*. I told her I was renouncing my field. I would be a union buster no more.

There remained but one demon to exorcise—Tom Crosbie. A greater man might have been able to walk away from a past such as mine with no need for revenge. Not me. I wanted Crosbie punished for what I believed he had done to me, to the others, to everyone—for what he was, for what we all were.

I called Tony McKeown at Three M offices in Bannockburn and brusquely demanded all the money his firm owed me. Unruffled, Tony purred that he happened to be passing through Cleveland in a couple of days on a visit to a Three M client, the renowned Cleveland Clinic; couldn't we arrange a meeting? I agreed to pick him up at his hotel at the end of his stay and drive him to the airport. We'd talk then.

I looked forward to my reunion with one of the most charming and most terrible human beings I had ever met. The moment I saw the older, yet still roguish-looking redheaded chap, a wave of nostalgia washed over me. I suppose it's a little like that when old mobsters get together. Ohhhh, what we'd been through. Ohhhh, what we knew.

Tony and I climbed into my brand-new gray Corvette and drove to the airport, where he was to catch a plane back to his adopted home in Boston. We talked easily, reminiscing about the old days and the old names, exchanging boasts, lamenting about how things had changed. Eventually I brought up Crosbie. I revealed everything I suspected—how I thought Tom was cheating his clients; how I believed he had cheated me; and finally, how he seemed to be bamboozling his own partners.

Tony listened in silence. Seemingly unperturbed, he thanked me and said he would look into it as soon as he got back to the office. I hadn't expected more.

As we sat in the Corvette outside the Cleveland Airport, I disclosed that I was getting out of the business. To my surprise, Tony confessed that he, too, had tired of union busting. He was looking for something a bit more glamorous, a bit easier, perhaps. He shook his head and clicked his tongue. A look of revelation washed over his face, and a wry smile appeared on his lips.

"You know, Marty," he said in the brogue that wouldn't go away, "when I think of everything, all the shit we've done over the years—damn, it's a dirty business."

Epilogue

Of all the regrets I must carry through life, perhaps the most painful springs from a decision I made not long after publicly condemning union busting: I worked one last campaign. Two months had passed since that ride with Tony McKeown, and I hadn't worked a minute or made a dime. I had lost the Gates Mills house; not having the money to cover the $150,000 balance due on my mortgage, I had asked my father-in-law to pay it off. He had and in the process had become legal owner of the property. Alice and the boys were preparing to move back to California—without me. Once again I had no family, no home, no bank account, no credit. I had money-making ideas, sure. But to build a new career was going to take a while. What would I do in the meantime?

I was sitting alone in my family room as I had for so many hours over the previous four years, drinking and brooding, when the phone rang. I had disconnected my business phone weeks before, and the family phone number was unlisted, so I was unprepared for what I heard when I picked up the receiver.

The frantic voice on the other end belonged to Dom Strollo, president of an Ohio manufacturing company and an enthusiastic fan of mine. I had met Dom a few years back when I'd busted a union at his Ohio plant. At the time, I remembered, I had given him my private phone number, as I often did with friendly executives. Now, it seemed, Dom was having union troubles in California; he had tracked me down to ask for help. Dom told me the Teamsters were making noise at the company's southern California division, a manufacturing plant in Pomona called SCI, for Structural Composite Industries. My former client feared the union might have a chance at SCI; he heard that the people out there were really unhappy.

I cut Dom short. There's something you should know, I told him. I've quit the business. I've had it. I chuckled as I confessed that I had even called the AFL-CIO to put my renunciation on the record.

Dom chuckled, too, but he didn't relent. He needed me, he said, this union could ruin his company. I tried to be helpful. Why didn't he call Three M or some other consulting firm? I suggested. These days there were plenty of hungry union busters to choose from. But Dom Strollo was a powerful man, and he knew what he wanted. As far as he was concerned, there was only one man who could take care of business for him, and that man was Marty Levitt. He begged, he pleaded; my ego swelled. He talked of money; my heart turned to stone. SCI meant $40,000 and a ticket to California. I needed money. It was that simple, that ugly. I took the job.

I am deeply ashamed of having worked SCI. At the time, of course, I told myself all kinds of lies to justify the decision. It was just one more; I had no choice; this time it would be different; I would run a model campaign, really force the company to change; and on and on—so much crap. If there were a way to hide the fact that I lost the resolve to quit my life of terrorism after just a few weeks, perhaps I would. That final campaign is a source of embarrassment every time it comes up. Each time, a look of disappointment comes over the face of my listener that no words can drive away. How can I explain why I did it? I cannot. So I have to live with that look. Worse, those last two hundred victims of mine haunt me more relentlessly than all the rest. I can see their faces, and I even know some of their names. I wish to God I had said no. But I did not. I said yes, and I confess it for one very personal and one very pragmatic reason.

The personal side is that as part of my recovery from alcohol addiction, I must confront all my misdeeds and stop the cycle of deception that kept me on the bottle for twenty years. I need to come clean.

But the pragmatic reason is actually more important: There are thousands of people out there, consultants, attorneys, and businessmen, who would like to shut me up. Since my first public talk on union busting—the speech at the Carpenters convention in March 1988 with which I open this book—I have spoken to hundreds of thousands of union workers, university students, and members of the general public about the viciousness and insidiousness of the war on unions. The word is getting out about what management consultants and business executives and labor attorneys have been doing to employees all these years under the benign label of "union avoidance," and the folks who make money off that system are getting nervous. Since what I say is true—my enemies cannot defend themselves—their only hope is that people simply will not believe me. To that end they seek to discredit me, so they endeavor to portray me as a drunk, a maniac, a crook, a lunatic, or simply an opportunist. Unhappily, I have made it easy on them. To a certain extent I have been all those things, and in the course of my life I have provided a lot of great material for my adversaries' character assassination campaign. Those who wish to silence me have dug up my every transgression and vice—and invented some of their own—in order to cast doubt on my character and, by extrapolation, on all that I say. "People won't listen to him," they snicker, "if they know what he's done." So they trot out my criminal record, whisper about my bankruptcy, click their tongues about my drinking, and are sure to mention that I "hopped the fence before," referring to my abortive stint with the culinary union in the 1970s. Thus, to be pragmatic, I am telling it all myself, though so much of it is unpleasant. Here you have it, in this book; everything I have done. And you know what? It doesn't change a thing. Did my co-conspirators think that by my being more guilty they would become more innocent? It doesn't work like that.

My union-busting days ended finally with SCI. Before the campaign was over, the *RUB Sheet* carried an article announcing my renunciation of union busting and quoting me calling the field "a dirty business." The word was out. No sooner had I beaten the Teamsters in Pomona than I was on my way to Washington, D.C., to meet with top officers of the AFL-CIO. The labor federation wanted me to write a "bust the union buster" handbook and make a training film for union organizers. It was not to be. The deal was blocked by executives of the culinary union, who remembered my treason of a decade earlier. I understood. But now I was determined to be heard. Fortunately for me—and for labor—there were many people willing to listen. A few months later I was on a plane to San Diego, where I bared my soul to the Brotherhood of Carpenters. That public confession was to become the first of dozens of speeches I would present to union members and university students over the next few years. To the unions I generally spoke for free or for a small honorarium.

Occasionally a union local has hired me on a longer-term basis to run workshops or to help it combat a union buster in an organizing campaign or negotiations.

If anything is clear by now, it is that I am no saint. I do not hold myself up before the world in order to win admiration. There is something I do hope to win, however, and that is the destruction of a mentality that condemns millions of American workers to a life of futility and humiliation.

God, grant me the serenity to accept the things I cannot change; courage to change the things I can; and wisdom to know the difference.

Index

Acid rain, 15
Advanced Management Research,
  Inc., 150
AFL-CIO, 5, 27, 75–76, 137, 150,
  163, 277, 284, 288, 289
Airline industry:
  counterorganizing campaign in,
    81–113
  and air traffic controllers' strike,
    217
Airline Pilots Association, 98
Alcoholics Anonymous, 157, 158,
  278
Alcoholism, 4, 140, 235–37, 272–73
  guilt and, 245
  hospitalization for, 140–41, 154,
    158, 265–66, 281–84
  and illusion of self-control, 119
  and job-related social drinking, 61
  money problems and, 114, 130
  recovery from, 5, 267, 288
  and stress of job, 263–65, 276
Alinsky, Saul, 60–61
Allen, Jeannette, 3, 5
Allstate Insurance Company, 36, 43
Alpine Designs, 54
American Airlines, 76, 77, 82, 114
American Automobile Association,
  154
American Hospital Association, 73
Ameritrust, 62
Angeli brothers, 56, 57, 59
Anthony, Mark, 47

Application for union membership,
  18–19
Apprenticeship programs, 146
Arbitration of grievances, 90
Arma Lee Barber College, 164
Associated Builders and Contractors,
  146
AT&T, 144
Attitude surveys, 137–38, 141
Attorney-client privilege, 42
Authorization cards, 11, 18–19, 126,
  165, 166, 170, 172–73, 177
  strike votes and signers of, 218
Automatic Electric, 61
Automobile industry, 248–49

B. F. Goodrich, 144
Background checks, 52
Bank of America, 88
Banking industry, 60, 62, 63, 73,
  135
Bankruptcy, 130
Bannon, Jim, 49, 50, 61–62, 70, 74–
  75, 95, 96, 99–100, 106, 111,
  152
Bargaining unit, designation of, 173–
  75, 251
Beck, Dave, 34, 37, 38, 40
Benefits:
  cuts in, 145
  gains in, for union workers, 142
  inadequate, 49, 98, 104
Berkeley Barb (California), 133–34

Index

Betting pools, 29
Billing rates, 2, 5, 11, 50, 53–54
Black Nationalists, 165
Blacks:
  as health care workers, 70, 72, 164
  as union activists, 3
Blocking charges, 240
Blue Grass Mining, 13
B–1 bomber, 151
B&O Railroad, 164
Bradbury, William, Sr., 241–42, 252, 257
Bradbury, William, Jr., 241–42, 252
Brotherhood of Carpenters, xi, 289
Brown, Jerry, 122
Building trades, 143–44, 146, 153
Bumbico, Tony, 22, 31, 32
Burney, Jack, 131–35
Business agents, 99, 125
Byrne, Jerry, 91–93

Caen, Herb, 78–79, 83, 86
Cahners Publishing, 134
California, University of, at Davis, 86
California Canadian Bank, 155
Californians for the Freedom to Work, 146
Cambodia, 82
Campouris, Alice. See Levitt, Alice
Campouris, Stephanie, 126
Card checks, 172
Carter, Jimmy, 145, 147, 248
Celaya, Louis A., 79, 99, 172
Center for Values Research, 150
Central Ohio Coal, 32
Charge nurses, 174
Chase Manhattan Bank, 63
Chemical Bank, 63
Christopher, W. I., & Associates, 138
Chrysler Corporation, 144, 145, 248
Cleveland City Council, 166
Cleveland Plain Dealer, 278, 279
Cleveland Trust Bank, 62
Closed shop, ban on, 36
Coal industry, 4, 7–32, 268, 269
Collective bargaining, 13, 18, 178–79
  bad-faith, 202–24
  concessions in, 248

for employees of nonprofit hospitals, 71, 73
  establishment of right of, 33
  failure of unions at, 151
  federal policy on, 152
  potency of, 142
Communist party, 36, 37, 165
Community relations, 188, 189
Company unions, 40
Concession bargaining, 248
Confidentiality of roundtables, 213
Congress, U.S., 35–36, 38, 41, 71, 143, 144, 151
  investigation of anti-union activity by, 151, 152
Construction industry, 143–44, 146, 153
Construction Users Anti-Inflation Roundtable, 144, 145
Construction Laborers Union, 103, 183
Contract negotiations, 2, 104, 170, 194
  first, after union election victory, 204
  legal complexity of, 4
  See also Collective bargaining
Cooke, Brian, 89, 92, 93, 97
Copeland Oaks, Inc., 163–225, 227, 264, 266
Corruption, union, 37, 38
Council on a Union Free Environment, 147
Counterorganizing campaigns, 2–5, 150
  in airline industry, 86–113
  in banking industry, 62, 63
  billing clients for, 53, 55
  in coal industry, 4, 7–32, 268, 269
  in health-care industry, 70–76, 148, 167–200
  high cost of, 4
  in manufacturing, 287–89
  perks to consultants during, 54
  in plastics industry, 239–59, 261, 270–72
  restaurant, 119–20, 137
  supermarket, 56–59

threats against supervisors during, 52

Crandall Medical Center, 169, 220–22, 224

Cravat Coal Company, 7–32, 172, 223, 268, 269, 271

Crosbie, Ellen, 66

Crosbie, Tom, 12, 20, 51, 66–67, 70, 76, 92, 93, 95, 96, 99–100, 106–7, 109–11, 114, 266–69, 271, 275, 279–80, 285

Culinary union, 119–29, 131–37, 142, 289

Cummins, James, 88–89

Cyberex, Inc., 223, 233

Daly, Edward J., 79, 81–91, 93–99, 101, 102–11, 113, 115–17, 172, 257

Daly, Violet June, 88

Davies, Lou, 168, 169, 171, 172, 174–75, 178–79, 189, 192, 202, 212, 221, 222

Davis, Leon, 71

Davis-Bacon Act (1931), 144, 145

Decertification campaigns, 136, 150, 222–24

Defense Department, U.S., 83, 151

Delay tactics, 58–59
during contract negotiations, 208

DeMaria, Albert, 150

Detroit Athletic Club, 74

Diamond, Virginia, 5

Diamond Shamrock, 45

Disclaimers of interest, 150

Doublespeak, 39, 48

Dues, union, 16, 24, 26
mandatory, prohibition of, 36

Duke University, 271

Eastwood, Clint, 137

Education/Research, Inc., 139

Elections:
betting pools on, 29
coercion and bribery to influence, 38
competing unions in, 76
disclaimer of interest after, 150–51
disqualification of votes in, 240

for health-care workers, 166
lopsided, 55
management and, 11
NLRB oversight of, 31, 258
procedure for, 198–200
under Railway Labor Act, 92, 108, 111
recognition without, 170–72
results of, 31–32
rigged, 37
setting date for, 198
time line for, 25
union victories in, 200–203

Eisenhower, Dwight D., 40

Elizabeth II, Queen of England, 116

Employee attitude surveys, 137–38, 141

Employee relations, language of, 39

Employee roundtables, 39–40, 213

Employees' Bill of Rights, 147

Employee Synthesis Program, 4, 134

Employee Unity Institute, 137

Employment policies, 206

Energy crisis, 143

Engineering union, 151–52

Equal employment opportunity, 211

Estes, Howell, 89, 95

Excelsior lists, 25, 168, 175, 198

Executive Enterprises, 150

Executive recruitment, 2, 45, 48

Executives, humanizing image of, 26–27

Exxon, 144

Favoritism, 247

Fear-mongering, 192–94, 218, 249

Federal Bureau of Investigation (FBI), 47

Federal contracts and grants, 151

Federal Express, 139

Film industry, 131–32

Financial disclosure requirements, 41–42

Fines levied by unions, 16, 26

First Western Bank & Trust, 84

Fisher, Dennis, 12, 20, 268

Food and lodging industry, 119–29, 131–42, 153, 159

Index

Ford, Gerald, 81, 82
Ford Motor Company, 65, 70
Foreign competition, 143
Foremen. *See* Supervisors
Fortune magazine, 104
Fraser Paper Company, 55
Friedman, Harold, 47

Garment industry, 54
Ganni, Phil, 182–84, 224
General Motors, 144
General Dynamics, 139
Geno's food company, 52
GI Bill, 164
Gibran, Kahlil, 133
Gibson, Dunn and Crutcher, 91
Glenbeigh Hospital (Ohio), 265–66
Goodyear Aerospace, 45
Grievances, 90, 98
GTE, 61

Hanley, Edward T., 121–24, 134,
    136
Hansen, Ted, 124, 125, 142
Harassment:
    during contract negotiations, 214
    sexual, 121
    of union officers, 2
    of workers, 38
Harper Grace Hospital (Detroit), 70,
    71, 74–75
Harrah's hotel and casino (Reno),
    128
Harvard Business Review, 150
Hazelden Foundation, 281–84
Health-care industry, 70–76, 135,
    138, 148, 151, 164–200
    contract negotiations in, 201–17,
        220–24
    strikes in, 70–72, 165, 166, 193,
        205, 217–20
Health violations, factory, 244, 245
Henry Ford Hospital (Detroit), 70,
    75–76
HGM Enterprises, 268
Hickey, Jack, 184, 240–42, 248,
    253, 255, 258
Hoffa, Jimmy, 37

Hogg, Bill, 188–89, 193, 224
Hog's Breath Inn (Carmel), 137
Hope, Bob, 47
Hornkohl, Alex, 64
Horton, Jim, 163–66, 170–72, 174,
    181, 183–85, 209, 210, 224
Hospitality industry. *See* Food and
    lodging industry
Hospitals, 70–76, 135, 148, 151,
    164–66, 183
Hotel Employees, Restaurant
    Employees, and Bartenders
    International Union, 120–31,
    133, 142
Hotels. *See* Food and lodging
    industry
Householder, Jean, 213–15, 224
House Subcommittee on Labor-
    Management Relations, 151
Hughes, Charles, 150
Hughes, Tony, 47
Human resources departments, 100–
    101
Human Resources Institute, 4, 9
Huron Road Hospital (East
    Cleveland), 183
Hussein, King of Jordan, 83, 102

IBM, 144
Industrial surveys, 139
Inflation, 143–45
In-service training, 151
Institute of Scrap Iron and Steel, 154
Institutions/Volume Feeding (trade
    journal), 134–35, 141
Insurance industry, 43, 60, 73, 135
Interline Pass, 104
Internal Revenue Service (IRS), 42,
    198
International Brotherhood of
    Electrical Workers (IBEW), 48,
    98
International Laborers Union, 215
International Ladies' Garment
    Workers Union, 60
Interrogations of employees, 17–18
Iran hostage crisis, 84
Irvine, Chuck, 120

Jackson, Lewis, Schnitzler and
  Krupman, 150
Japanese automobile industry, 248
Jews:
  discrimination against, 74
  pro-union, 46
Job security, lack of, 103–4
Johnson, Lyndon Baines, 143
Jordan, 85
Journal of Industrial Relations, 150
Juodenas, Ed, 12, 20, 30, 268, 269
Jurisdictional respect, 76

Kenneally, Jack, 122–23, 125–27
Kennedy, John F., 27, 143
Kennedy, Robert F., 37
Kissinger, Henry, 81, 82, 271
Knoll, Clinton, 129
Krasny, Leslie, 69
Krasny, Michael, 69, 106

Labor Department, U.S., 42, 137
Laborers International Union, 62
Labor force, growth in, 142, 143
Labor law, 1, 35, 177, 205, 206, 219
  anti-union activities sanctioned by,
    17–19
  on authorization cards, 11
  broadening of union voting unit
    under, 24
  on contract negotiations, 204–6
  circumventing, 29
  complexity of, 4–5, 36, 92
  on decertification, 136
  definition of supervisor in, 174
  loopholes in, 41–42, 147, 179
  on recognition without election,
    172–73
  repeal of, 144–45
  restrictive, 36
  on strike votes, 218, 219
  union access to employees under, 25
  on union finances, 16
  See also specific legislation
Labor Law Study Group, 144
Labor-Management Reporting and
  Disclosure Act. *See* Landrum-
  Griffin Act

Labor Relations Associates of
  Chicago, Inc., 33–35, 37, 38, 42,
  43, 48
Landrum-Griffin Act (1959), 40–43,
  181
Lane, Ray, 120–21
Lawsuits, 93
Layoffs, 90, 247–49
Lederer, Charles, 34
Lederer, Fox & Grove, 43, 153
Lederer, Livingston, Kahn & Adsit,
  34
Lederer, Philip, 34–36, 43, 58, 59,
  65, 153
Lederer, Reich, Sheldon and
  Connolly, 154
Legal Defense Fund, 146
Leiken, Earl, 9, 12, 13, 24, 223, 224,
  227, 233, 240–42, 255, 270,
  278
Letters to employees, 58, 96, 109–11,
  119, 177–79, 188, 189, 193–95,
  248
  announcing elections, 198
  cleared with attorneys, 92
Levitt, Alice Campouris, 76–78, 87,
  101–2, 106, 114, 115, 117, 119,
  123, 126, 130, 132, 140, 153–
  60, 179–81, 196–97, 201, 202,
  227–36, 239, 262–65, 276–79,
  281, 283, 284, 287
Levitt, Harvey, 127, 128, 157, 235
Levitt, Jason Edward, 115, 130, 236,
  262–64
Levitt, Justin, 140, 234, 236, 262–64
Levitt, Manny, 47
Lewis, John L., 163
Licensed practical nurses (LPNs),
  173–78, 190, 217–18
Like a Beautiful Child (film), 71–72
Local 1199, 71–73, 75
Lockett, Hal, 7–8, 29
Loyalty report cards, 30

McClellan, John, 37, 38
McKeown, Ann, 66
McKeown, Tony, 51, 65–66, 114,
  152, 284–85, 287

Mafia, 46, 183
Maginnes, Bristol, 271–72
Mali, 85, 90
Man in the Middle, The
   (Shefferman), 38–40
Management Board, 61, 70
Manufacturing, 287–89
Marin County District Attorney's
   Office, 156
Marin County Honor Farm, 158
Marin County Jail, 157
Marin Independent Journal
   (California), 69
Marketing, 131–33
Marriott Hotels, 124, 142
Marshall, Ray, 145
Marvin Window Company, 55
MDM Investment Company, 47, 48
Mediation, 220, 223
Medicaid, 151
Medicare, 169
Melnick, Herbert, 38, 42–43, 50, 54,
   64–67, 73, 87, 95, 152, 267–68
Melnick, McKeown and Mickus, 51,
   64–66, 147, 148
Mendelsohn, David, 84, 85, 87–89,
   91–94, 97, 102, 113, 117
MENSA, 168
Merit shop, 146
Meuhlenkamp, Robert, 72, 73, 75
Micatrotto, Al, 47
Mickus, Ray, 51, 152
Miller, Betty, 176, 187
Miller, Steve, 135
Mining industry. *See* Coal industry
Misappropriation of union funds, 37
Mitro, George, 250, 252, 257
Modern Management Methods
   (Three M), 4, 78, 113, 114, 116,
   129, 139, 142, 147–48, 266–68,
   277, 279–80, 284–85, 288
and congressional hearings, 151,
   152
at Cravat Coal, 12, 21, 268, 269,
   271
and health care industry, 70–76,
   135, 138
at PMS, 259, 270–72

at World Airways, 87, 92, 95, 98,
   99
Moracco, Anna, 189, 215, 216, 225
Moracco, Fred, 215–17, 224–25
Moslems, 85
Murphy, Joe, 165, 209–12, 224

National Association of
   Manufacturers, 146
National Bank of Washington, 63
National Labor Relations Act
   (NLRA; 1935), 1, 13, 17, 33–35,
   71, 73, 92, 93, 103, 147, 152,
   174
National Labor Relations Board
   (NLRB), 8, 34, 55, 58, 59, 92,
   119, 131, 137, 160–61, 227,
   239, 270
and Copeland Oaks, 170, 172,
   175, 177, 198, 203, 208, 222–
   24
and Cravat Coal, 11, 13, 24, 25,
   31
creation of, 35
elections held by, 11, 108, 170
and Excelsior lists, 168, 198
and PMS, 239, 242, 251, 258, 270
under Reagan, 160
unfair labor practices complaints
   issued by, 148
National Mediation Board, 92, 108
National Restaurant Association,
   135, 137, 159
National Right to Work Committee,
   146, 147
National Union of Hospital and
   Health Care Workers, 71
Nations Restaurant News, 141
Negotiations. *See* Contract
   negotiations
New York Stock Exchange, 83
Nixon, Richard M., 73
Norwalk Reflector, 257
Nursing homes, 70, 73, 135, 166–
   225

Oakland, Port of, 83
Oakland Tribune (California), 82

Occupational Safety and Health
  Administration (OSHA), 244,
  245, 249
Office and Professional Employees
  Union Local 29, 79, 102, 108,
  111, 112
Ohio Conference of Teamsters, 46, 47
Ohio School of Broadcasting, 164
Ohio University, 52
Oil crisis, 84
O'Mara, Bill, 128–30
Opinion surveys. *See* Attitude surveys
Organized crime, union ties to, 37,
  46–47
Organizing committees, 23, 170, 174
Owens Corning, 154

Pacific Stock Exchange, 83
Palucci, Geno, 52
Parker Pen Company, 54
Parmenter, Dave, 148
PATCO, 217, 235, 248
Paternalism, 86, 252
Patterson, Charles, 88, 106
Peretto, Gary, 56
Personality assessments, 139
Personnel (journal), 150
Personnel departments, 100–101
Personnel files, information on
  workers from, 21
Personnel theory, anti–union, 35
Plant closures, 143
Plant managers, replacing, 249–50
Plastic Molders Supply (PMS), 239–
  59, 261, 270–72
Plus-and-minus charts, 30
Presley, Elvis, 281
Presser, Bill, 47
Presser, Jackie, 47
Prevailing-wage laws, 144–45
Preventive labor relations, 33, 35
Prince Gardner Company, 54
Profit-sharing plans, 252
Promises to employees, 18
Propaganda:
  anti-union, 35, 96, 193, 205, 254–
    55
  union, 71, 192

See also Letters to employees
Psychological tests, 138
Public employees, 143
Puskarich, Mike, 9–11, 14, 16, 20,
  27–29, 31, 172, 268
Puskarich, Mike, Jr., 27–28
Puskarich family, 9, 21, 22, 24, 26–
  27, 32

Question box, 179
Quirk, Mary, 154

Rabkin, Marty, 139, 141
Racism, exploitation of, 72
Racketeering, 37
Railway Labor Act (1926), 91, 92,
  103, 108
Railroads, 91–93
Rank and file workers:
  ban on supervisors socializing with,
    189–91, 206
  as saboteurs of union drives, 181
  targeting of, 2
Reader's Digest, 120
Reagan, Ronald, 91, 122, 160, 217,
  223
Recession, 143
Recognition of unions, 170–72, 211
Red baiting, 36
Red Lion Inn (Sacramento), 124–26,
  129
Registered nurses (RNs), 173–74
Reno Employers Council, 128, 129
Representation petitions, 11, 160–61
  definition of bargaining unit in,
    173
  filing of, 8, 126, 194
Republican party, 160
Restaurants. *See* Food and lodging
  industry
Retail, Wholesale and Department
  Store Employees Union, 71
R&F Coal Company, 12
Ridgecliffe Hospital (Cleveland),
  45
"Right to Work" laws, 36, 146
Ripa, Tom, 107, 111–12
Rockwell International, 151–52

Roe, Claude L., 163, 167–73, 175, 178–79, 181, 184, 187–89, 191–95, 197, 198, 199, 201–3, 205–8, 214–16, 218–25
Roe, Gladys, 181, 201
Rogers, John, 62
Rogin, Bill, 139
Roosevelt, Franklin Delano, 35
Ross Medical Center (Marin County), 140–41
Rotating employee committees, 40, 213
Roundtables, 39–40, 213
Rousselin, Michel, 89, 91, 93, 96–98
Rubenstein, Iris, 47–48, 56, 64
RUB Sheet, 5, 277, 278, 284, 289
Rumors, 22, 181
    during contract negotiations, 212
Rusky, Betty, 214–15
Rusty Scupper restaurant (Oakland), 119–20

St. Elizabeth's Hospital (Boston), 148
St. Helena Hospital (California), 154
St. Joseph's Infirmary (Louisville), 55
St. Luke's Hospital (Cleveland), 164, 183
Sales calls, 118, 119, 137, 161
Salinger, Pierre, 37
Samoa, 85
San Francisco Chronicle, 78, 99
Sangalis, Nick, 51, 53, 56–58, 61, 66, 67, 87
Santa Clara, University of, 86
Schwartz, David, 74
Scott, E. Timm, 241, 243, 245, 246, 249, 250, 252, 254, 256–58, 261, 270–72
Screen Actors Guild, 217
Sears, Roebuck & Company, 34–36, 40
Senate Anti-Racketeering Committee, 37–38, 41
Seniority rights, 247
Service, Hospital, Nursing Home & Public Employees Union, 163–225
Service Employees International Union (SEIU), 163, 240

Sexual harassment, 121
Shefferman, Nathan, 34, 35, 37–40, 42, 48, 152
Shell Oil Company, 12
Sheridan, John, 2, 3, 36, 42–43, 48–55, 59–67, 70, 72, 73, 87, 98, 135, 138, 139, 148, 179, 184, 266
Skilled-care facilities, 169
Smith, Hugh, 253, 257, 258
Smyth, Kevin, 12, 21, 267, 268
Social Security, 169, 198
South Korea, 85
Sposato, Gerry, 189, 194–95
Spying, 18, 33, 38, 177
    loopholes in laws on, 42
    by rank-and-file workers, 181
    at union meetings, 103
    with wire taps, 57–58
Stanley, Judy, 197, 200, 213, 224
Stant Company, 3, 5
Statistics, anti-union, 95, 137
Steffen, Curt, 90, 91, 98–101, 104, 106, 107
Stewart, Anna, 144, 148
Stipulations, 59
Stokes, Carl B., 166
Straw votes, 29
Strikes:
    in automobile industry, 248, 249
    cost of, 95
    forcing, 2
    of health care workers, 70–72, 165, 166, 193, 205, 217–20
    of hotel-casino workers, 121, 132
    of Teamsters, 47, 90
    warnings on effects of, 26
Strollo, Dom, 287–88
Structural Composite Industries (SCI), 287–89
Sturman, Rube, 46
Super Value grocery store, 56–59
Supervisors:
    attorneys and, 91
    ban on socializing with rank and file by, 189–91, 206
    bargaining units and, 173

during contract negotiations, 205–12

and election results, 200, 203–6

emergency meeting of, 112

employees' attitudes toward, 185–87, 189, 196, 256

"fact sheets" distributed to, 14, 19

firings of, 20

individual interviews with, 12, 21–22, 28, 56, 74, 106–7, 113, 115, 191, 196–97

isolation and vulnerability of, 22

kick–off meetings with, 13–20, 99–100, 175, 177, 245–46, 248

and letters to employees, 111, 193–95

mandatory meetings of, 26, 29, 74–75

manipulation of, 94, 96

nursing, 173–78

oppression of, 93, 96–97

rank-and-file saboteurs recruited by, 181

roundtables moderated by, 213

during strikes, 219

sympathetic to unions, 23–24, 27, 36–37, 196, 215–17

targeting of, 2, 10–11, 104–5, 240–41

threats to, 52, 57, 105

training of, 40, 113, 115, 139, 202, 203, 212–13

at union meetings, 103

and Vote No paraphernalia, 30

of white-collar workers, 251–52

Supreme Court, U.S., 25, 33

Surface bargaining, 202–3, 222

Swartzall, Mel, 209, 211

SWAT teams, 27–28

Synthesis, 132–34

Taft-Hartley Act (1947), 36

Tallent, Steve, 91

Taylor, Kathleen, 185–87, 189, 190, 197, 200, 209, 213, 224

Teamsters Union, 34, 37, 46, 47, 52, 90, 98, 287

Threats:

against employees, 17–18, 195

against supervisors, 52, 57, 105

Three M. *See* Modern Management Methods

Tinuvin, 245

Tourist trade, 119, 121, 126

Travel benefits, 104

Triscaro, Louis "Babe," 47

Truman, Harry S., 36

Trunka, Richard, 31

Trusteeship, 124

TWA, 82, 115–17

TWIG (The Word Is God), 158

UAW, 270

Unemployment, 143–44

rate of, among union members, 248

Unfair labor practices, 33, 92, 93, 148, 177, 240, 255

charged against unions, 36

during contract negotiations, 222–24, 227

in defense industry, 151–52

Union activists:

co-optation of, 137

during contract negotiations, 207–8, 213–15

covert war on, 2–3

intimidation of, 33

Union officers:

in contract negotiations, 208

harassment of, 2

in health care organizing drives, 181–84

salaries of, 95

termed "bosses," 26

work hours of, 125

Union Carbide, 144

United Auto Workers (UAW), 3, 5, 145, 239, 240, 246, 248–49, 251–58,

United Mine Workers of America (UMWA), 4, 7–32, 163

United Airlines, 82

Universal Airlines, 98

Victoria Station restaurant chain, 139
Vietnam War, 81–82, 84–86, 143
Violence:
  during strikes, 71, 165, 218
  union, 36, 37
Vollworth Sausage Company, 55
Vote No committees, 28

Wages:
  and competition for jobs, 143
  concessions on, 248
  and contract negotiations, 207,
    208
  cuts in, 143–45
  gains in, for union workers, 142
  of health-care workers, 164, 171
  "merit" system for raises in, 246–
    47
  noncompetitive, 49, 98, 104
  prevailing, 144–45
  in restaurant industry, 136

Wagner Act. *See* National Labor
  Relations Act
Waithman, Winnie, 222, 224
Wall Street Journal, The, 1, 45, 48, 51
Way, The, 158
Wells Fargo Bank, 155
Wheeling Intelligencer (West
  Virginia), 32
White, Harlow, 139–41
White, Jim, 22, 31, 172
Wire taps, 57
Withington, Edie, 102–4
Woolsey, Richard, 249–50
Working conditions, substandard, 49
World Airways, 79, 81–117, 119,
  121, 139, 188, 257
World War II, 35, 83
World Savings & Loan, 155
Worthy, Art, 183–85, 209, 224

Yemen, 83, 85, 90